Copywriter's Handbook

Copywriter's Handbook

A Practical Guide for Advertising and Promotion of Specialized and Scholarly Books and Journals

Nat G. Bodian

iSi PRESS®

Philadelphia

Published by

iSi PRESS® A Subsidiary of the
Institute for Scientific Information®
3501 Market St., University City Science Center, Philadelphia, PA 19104 U.S.A.

Library of Congress Cataloging in Publication Data

Bodian, Nat G., 1921-
  Copywriter's handbook.

  (The Professional editing and publishing series)
  Bibliography: p.
  Includes index.
  1. Scholarly publishing—Handbooks, manuals, etc.
2. Books—Marketing—Handbooks, manuals, etc.   3. Advertising copy—Handbooks, manuals, etc.   4. Scholarly
periodicals—Marketing—Handbooks, manuals, etc.
5. Periodicals—Marketing—Handbooks, manuals, etc.
6. Publishers and publishing—Handbooks, manuals, etc.
I. Title.   II. Series.
Z286.S37B63   1984   659.1'9686   84-15781

ISBN 0-89495-040-1
ISBN 0-89495-039-8 (pbk.)

Printed in the United States of America
90 89 88 87 86 85 84   8 7 6 5 4 3 2 1

Short Contents

Contents

Chapter 2   Copywriting for Space Advertising

Chapter 3   Copy for Direct-Mail Promotion: Principles and Practices

Chapter 4   Copy Approaches Used in Promotions by Various Presses

Chapter 5   Working with Words: How to Improve the Quality and Readability of Your Copy

Chapter 11 Copy Approaches for Book Promotions to the Various Library Markets

Chapter 12 Copy Approaches for Books in Business, Law, and Economics

Chapter 13 Copy Approaches Used by Scholarly Presses

Chapter 14 Copywriting Techniques for Journals Promotion

Chapter 15   Telemarketing Copy: Approaches and Examples

Chapter 16   Publicity Writing for Specialized and Scholarly Books

Preface

This work represents the culmination of a longtime effort to create, for those who labor in the vineyards of publishing, a practical reference and guide for the writing of promotional materials for specialized and scholarly books and journals. Its aims are to fulfill a fourfold purpose:

1. To provide the working copywriter with tested ideas and approaches in current use by various presses throughout the industry.

2. To serve as a learning vehicle for those with little or no experience in the preparation of promotion copy or those who have limited experience and aspire to professionalism.

3. To make available a compendium of information on the craft of copywriting—generally regarded as a difficult-to-comprehend aspect of book and journal publishing—in a tested and proven format.

4. To supply those not presently active in this aspect of publishing with insights into the special characteristics and requirements involved in the preparation of promotional copy for specialized and scholarly audiences..

Why a publishing industry handbook devoted just to copywriting? The answer lies in the way many publishers view the craft of writing copy— usually as *low-level,* in some cases as *entry level.* Because so many of those engaged in publishing copywriting view such jobs mainly as a vehicle for breaking into publishing, relatively few retain these jobs long enough to acquire all the techniques and skills essential for becoming accomplished copywriters. And, usually, those who do demonstrate unusual copy skills move up to better-paying higher-level positions, positions where copywriting skills play a secondary role, if any, to other types of publishing responsibilities.

As a consequence, in many publishing establishments, there is a dearth of seasoned copy "pros" who can provide guidance, training, and inspiration to the less experienced, and to newcomers just entering the field.

This handbook is a sincere effort to meet that need. It is a pioneering effort in a single area of book and journal publishing promotion. Virtually all of the contents of this volume have been written specifically for the copywriter, rather than for his or her manager or supervisor.

Selected entries in this volume have been extracted from the chapters on copywriting in the two-volume book industry reference, *Book Marketing Handbook,* which I wrote earlier (published by R. R. Bowker: Vol. 1, 1980; Vol. 2, 1983). Further, the format of this handbook follows the widely acclaimed format of *Book Marketing Handbook,* described by Gordon Graham, chief executive of The Butterworth Co., in *The Bookseller* (15 October 1983) as ". . . a data-base [book] of which you can ask questions, using the keyboard [contents, glossary, and indexes] to find the relevant passage on the terminal [page]."

The contents of this work, for the most part, reflect my own views and experience as a writer of promotional materials for specialized and scholarly books and journals over the past 25 years, and prior experience as a copy and publicity professional. It also draws from the experience of numerous other industry professionals whose contributions are acknowledged in the text.

In the course of writing this handbook, I have consulted with countless publishing professionals who are now copywriters, or were earlier in their publishing careers. Their counsel, encouragement, and suggestions have been the inspiration for many of the 273 entries that follow.

The writing of this bellwether work has been stimulating, challenging, and gratifying. At the same time, I have tried to make the content interesting, enlightening, and easy to absorb. I hope I have succeeded.

                                                            Nat Bodian

June 1984

1

Copywriting: An Overview

1:01   The Magical Power of Writing

In 3000 B.C. people believed that writing was magical. Thoth, the Egyptian god of learning, was said to have invented written language, and the ancient Egyptians thought that words possessed supernatural power over the objects they symbolized.

Marie Jean Lederman (CUNY) in
Chronicle of Higher Education,
9 February 1983.

Words can possess magical power. When you write copy, especially as it relates to professional and scholarly works, this power is not in the words, but in you, the writer.

If you choose your words wisely, you have the power to inform, educate, and motivate the readers of what you write to whatever action you wish them to take. And, you can, by your words, make them respond in a way that is above and beyond what might be considered ordinary.

On the other hand, you also have the power to inject mediocrity into your writing. If your copy is badly organized, badly worded, incomplete, or lacks information the reader considers essential for whatever action is desired, it will be ignored or viewed unfavorably. Badly presented, your words can put your press in a bad light. They can also reflect unfavorably on the works being offered.

Writing, as the opening quotation says, is indeed magical if you recognize and respect its magical qualities and apply them to your copywriting efforts. When you write to an identifiable audience, mentally visualize one individual within that group and write directly to that individual as you would speak to him or her. Be sincere. Be forthright. Be honest. Be factual. Be persuasive if circumstances call for it. If it would embarrass you to say it, don't write it. Choose your words wisely and they will indeed have magical power, and serve you well.

1:02   Way to Use the Good Ideas Of Others to Stimulate Your Own Creativity

Don't hesitate to copy other people's ideas. Just be sure to copy successful *ideas.*

John Caples in *How to Make Your Advertising
Make Money,* Prentice-Hall, 1983.

"Creativity" is the realignment of established concepts in new relationships. You can be truly creative. You need only to start with the established concepts. One way for you to have them is to assemble, early on, your personal "swipe" file. As you go through your mail, through magazines, periodicals, journals, be sensitive to unusual copy concepts, to unusual headlines, to unusual ways in which ideas are stated. Copy the ones you find impressive, or cut them out and file them in your "swipe" file.* Your swipe file can bail you out when you've run bone dry on ideas, and especially when you are under pressure to turn out something great in a hurry. A short review of your swipe file and presto! In seconds your creative juices are flowing again, and your creative thinking process has shifted into high gear!

It takes only a few minutes to browse through such a refresher file. Then you're ready to lick the world—to be inspired and determined that you're going to improve on anything in your file.

Start your swipe file soon. Keep adding to it as the promotional efforts of others pass through your hands. Save the ones that strike you as new, different, unusual.

I've had one such file at home on my desk for years. I have others, by subject, in my desk at work. I put the terse ideas on 3″ × 5″ cards. Complete pages, ad layouts, and brochures are filed in folders by subject.

You may not want to go to that extreme, but at least try the 3″ × 5″ card file as a starter, either by subject or alphabetically. Chances are, you'll be filing by subject before long. If you're into creative copy, don't be without your own personal "swipe" file.

---

*Headlines are maintained in a separate 3″ × 5″ card file. The entries in the chapter on headline writing are from my "headline swipe file."

1:03   **Eight Sources of Fresh Ideas**
to Keep You From Going Stale

1. Develop an interest in and general awareness of *all* advertising.
2. Watch for different ways in which ad elements are assembled, and for provocative copy approaches.
3. Save ads you consider new, unusual, innovative.
4. Notice ads or copy themes frequently repeated; repetition implies effectiveness.
5. Know what your competition is doing.
6. Study promotional efforts from branches of publishing other than your own.
7. See what approaches other mailers are using; there are often good ideas you can adapt.
8. Maintain an idea file, classified by types of ideas.

1:04   **You Can Write Effective Book Ad Copy:**
Basic Skills and Guidelines

There are three prerequisites you must meet if you want to become expert at writing advertising copy for specialized and scholarly books:

1. A reasonable command of English grammar and language.
2. Imagination.
3. A desire to learn.

If you have these prerequisites, here are four steps you can take to become a skilled practitioner:

1. STUDY AND PRACTICE

Study the specialized and scholarly advertising that other publishers in your field use in periodicals and in their mail advertising. Be alert to how others are writing their copy.

Examine the competition's sentence structure, word arrangements, length of copy. Bear in mind that the copy approaches being used reflect not only the experience of the copywriter, but often also the best efforts of supervisors who may be seasoned copy pros.

2. RECOGNIZE PRESENTATION FORMATS

After study, you will notice that the various presentations of the competition generally fall into fairly standardized formats. When you have learned to recognize formats for types of copy presentations in your publishing or interest area, you will find that those same formats can be applied to virtually any copy assignment you may have within the same subject area or discipline.

3. RECOGNIZE AND LEARN FROM GOOD COPY

You will find before long that, having developed a copy sensitivity, you will readily recognize good copy. Essentially, good copy is copy that will

- catch and hold your attention and interest
- appeal to the self-interests of its intended readers
- get a message across that is sufficiently compelling to make the reader want to order, or at least want to take a look at, the book

By studying examples of good and bad copy, you will quickly recognize that good copy informs, describes, and provides features and, in direct mail, usually also benefits to the reader.

4. COLLECT AND SAVE EXAMPLES

When you find examples you consider particularly appealing, clip and save them for future reference, preferably filed by subject. Then, when you face a copy assignment in the same subject area, you can review your copy file for ideas, inspiration, and stimulation. When you have repeated this exercise many times, you will find that you have developed a mental inventory of what good copy should be. Your copywriting skills, with repeated practice, will gradually improve, and ultimately, you will know almost instinctively what good copy should look like with less and less need to refer to your idea files, except in special cases.

1:05   Another Good Source of Ideas for Professional and Specialized Book Ad Copy

Here's another good source of ideas for writing specialized book ad copy: Study the reviews that the book has already received. Reviewers of scholarly books, often peers of the author, frequently include phrases and copy approaches in reviews that even the most skilled of copy pros would never dream of.

If the book is fairly current, or the periodical prestigious, some of the material can be used as direct quotes. However, often the reviews may appear in little-known journals or when the book is well settled into the backlist and merits little or no advertising.

Still, the review may contain copy, phrases, ideas that are too good to file and forget. Extract the words, phrases, and ideas you deem worthwhile and save them in your idea file, or set up a separate "copy idea file." Then, at some future date when you're in need of a good phrase, combination of words, or apt description for a similar title, your copy idea file can fire your imagination and possibly provide just the right combination of words to make your copy seem just right.

Remember that reviewers often see the book in a different light than the author, or recognize different strengths in a book that perhaps the author or you as copywriter overlooked. And the reviewer's observations may provide selling ideas for the book that are better than the author's. Heed the wording in reviews carefully; there are nuggets to be found in them for the copywriter.

1:06   The Starting Point in Copywriting:
A Checklist for Professional and Scholarly Audiences

Copy is the published message. Not narrowly the words. The impression intended—the logic advanced—the idea exploited."

George P. Metzger in *Copy,*
Doubleday, 1926.

If you understand your audience before you start writing your copy, and if you present your copy in a way your audience is likely to understand, finds interesting, needs to know, or will enjoy, *then,* irrespective of format, provided it is delivered to that audience, its chances for success will be very high.

The following checklist is a useful starting point for the copywriter, especially the beginner or non-professional, in preparing copy for a professional or specialized audience.

1. Who is audience for whom the copy is about to be written—academic, professional, researcher, librarian, student?
2. What need or special interest can your copy appeal to? What benefit can it offer?
3. Is the audience already familiar with the subject?
4. What is the audience's attitude toward the subject, and can you prepare copy that will have a positive effect on that attitude?
5. Can you provide sufficient information to hold or satisfy their interest?
6. If the purpose of your copy is to get a reaction from that audience, does it spell out the desired reaction in a clear, understandable way?

1:07   The Copywriting Process:
A Copy Pro's Point of View

The primary concern of the copywriter is whom to please. Should it be the marketing manager, the copy chief, or the artist?

According to Peter Robinson, a freelance copy professional whose background includes copy stints with Wiley and Praeger, the copywriter should please the person who (theoretically) pays his salary—the one who controls whether or not he will continue to write copy.

In the writing of copy for professional and scholarly audiences, beyond that first point, the copywriter must write to please the reader. What does a reader want?

According to Robinson, the reader wants clear, accurate information—lots of it.

Before starting to write, the copywriter should first attempt to find out what is the role of the job at hand in the overall campaign.

Robinson enumerates these points, which should be made clear to the copywriter before he or she starts to write:

- What is the audience for the job?
- What is the main sales message?
- What is the copy slant or tone?

What does the copywriter want before he or she actually starts writing? "Basically," says Robinson, "he wants to write the job just once.

"He wants clear directions from the beginning to achieve this end. All copywriters want to write the best possible copy. Give the copywriter time, information and involve him in the project and you'll wind up selling more books."

**1:08   Before You Start Writing Copy:
Tips from Neil Gray**

"The effective copywriter starts by thinking." So says Neil Gray, marketing manager for the Health Professions Division at McGraw-Hill and a former copywriter.

"He or she organizes his or her thoughts and then organizes pertinent research. If insufficient time is spent on thinking and planning, ineffective selling occurs."

Gray says these aspects are important for effective copywriting:

Researching the titles. How much time do you spend getting a handle on the titles you will be writing about?

You start with the Author Questionnaire, the front matter, and Table of Contents. But intelligent questioning and planning should take you a step beyond learning from the author.

The planning process. If the planning process is to have any benefits, the copywriter needs to be fully cognizant of the book's goals. Why was it written? Some probing with the author and in-house personnel responsible for the book's success may be helpful. You need a full and complete answer of why the book was written.

After you have obtained these goals . . . keep them next to you when you write. Write down everything relative to these goals. A *unique selling proposition* goes back to the goals of the book; it must be kept in mind when writing.

Know your audience. Very frequently, time constraints preclude the copywriter finding where an advertisement is going to run. This is because in some establishments, copywriting is viewed as merely a staff function. Unless there is full appreciation of who will be responding you cannot be effective as a copywriter.

I occasionally use *SRDS Business Publication Rates and Data* for the overall approach of a journal. I also like to take a look at an issue of the journal. I look at the book review section. What are the qualities of the books listed? Why have they appealed to the book's reviewers? These aspects have often helped me.

The editor and marketing or product manager as information sources. These persons are tremendous sources of information. The copywriter should meet with both (preferably together) before starting to write. Often, the editor and the marketing manager may have differing points of view on the same product; getting the total picture on the work at hand can be extremely helpful when you write.

The credit and customer service departments as information sources. Other possible information contacts for the copywriter are the departments handling credit and collections, and customer service. Often these departments can supply feedback on why books are being returned. This information can help the copywriter tighten the copy approach to eliminate misinterpretations, and downplay perceived (albeit inaccurate) weaknesses in a book.

Exhibits and conventions. Another valuable resource for in-house copywriters is attendance at exhibits and conventions. In-house copywriters should be sent to meetings where the publisher's books are being exhibited. It helps them to understand their audience and provides valuable insights about the books and audiences with whom they must deal.

In the long run, copywriters who are knowledgeable about how marketing works will probably write the best copy: These copywriters will also prove to be stronger candidates for advancement within publishing.

1:09   Hard Sell and Soft Sell in Book Promotion Copy: Some Basic Rules

Should your professional and specialized book promotion copy be "hard sell" or "soft sell"? This is a frequently discussed topic in many houses and among book promotion people.

When you are doing copy for books involving business, investment, and finance, hard sell copy may not only be in order, but essential. Look at the advertising for investment newsletters and you'll readily grasp what is meant. And this type of copy seems to work because it is what sells this type of information.

However, when your copy is directed to scientists and engineers and your offerings are in subjects related to their profession, hard sell copy is likely to be counterproductive. Likewise, when you do copy for the library professional, this same axiom holds. The rule is stick to facts, features, and benefits, and avoid hard sell.

1:10   How to Succeed as a Copywriter at a University Press

In this entry, Julie Zuckman offers many valuable insights on the job of copywriter at a large university press, based on her long experience with The MIT Press. She is presently Circulation Manager of *Technology Review,* published at MIT.

Whether your first glimpse of a copy project is a scribble on a cocktail napkin handed to you by your boss, or a folder which comes down to you through the channels of the Advertising Department, you will never have all of the information you need at the start to write the best copy possible. Sometimes you will be expected to work with almost no information at all, not even a firm title. Or, you will have plenty of background information but nothing that gives you that special selling point around which you can frame the copy. Where do you start?

You are writing the copy to please two very distinct groups:

- Your boss and the people to whom the boss reports
- The target audience

It may seem impossible to please both groups. In theory, you should be able to sell your copy in-house on the grounds that it does the best job of selling the book or journal to the potential purchaser. In practice, there may be a "hidden agenda" which takes precedence over your perspective on what the copy should say. You will have to learn to reconcile a pragmatic understanding of office politics with your personal opinions about how to sell something.

One of the copywriter's most important skills is learning how to persuade colleagues that what you have written is good. A proven track record in selling books or journals is about the only guaranteed way to make this happen. So you are back at the beginning again:

- What is this book about?
- Why should someone buy it?
- How can I present this book in the most enticing yet accurate manner?
- Have I included every shred of information that is persuasive or significant without making the copy verbose?

When you are satisfied that you can answer all of these questions, then you are ready to present and defend your copy. To do this, you must begin at the beginning.

START WITH EDITORIAL . . .

Get into the files. Browse through as much as you are allowed to see. In my opinion, the copywriter should be permitted to read everything in the files except the contract negotiations and the proprietary financial information.

The correspondence between the author and editor, the readers' reports, and anyone else who was in on the acquisition is your richest resource. From this raw material you will find out:

- The author's goals in writing the book.
- His opinions about the sales and market potential.
- His sense of what the book is about and why it is special.

The readers' reports contain valuable quotes which you may be able to use, and honest opinions. Other correspondence will reveal the editor's motivations and goals. Even if you are given some of this material before you start the project, try to get a look in the files. If nothing else, reading the editorial files will help to make the publishing process come alive and give you a sense of your role in a complex system.

The editor and the editorial assistant are also good resources for the copywriter. A brief chat with them can be very informative. In most companies, the editor is expected to participate in some way in the copywriting process, either formally or informally.

MOVE ON TO MARKETING . . .

Although the marketing and promotion functions are closely tied, the Marketing staff can be the weakest link in the information-gathering process, because they may not yet have defined their goals. You should find out these important facts from Marketing:

1. The book's price.
2. The book's market position (competition).
3. Its audience.
4. An approximate idea of its sales potential.

If this information is not on paper, schedule a fact-finding appointment with the marketing or sales manager to find out. These expectations play an important role in shaping the copy.

The marketing questionnaire filled out by the author is essential as well. Study it closely. In most companies, the marketing/product/sales manager expects to work directly with the copywriter. The marketing manager has veto power over the copy and will often make extensive changes, revisions, and criticisms. The more you find out from him before you write the copy, the more satisfied both of you will be with your first draft.

It's a fact of life though that some marketing managers don't know what they want until they start red-pencilling your first draft. The information that you need to write good copy may not come through the marketing department, but they will expect you to find it.

YOUR NEXT STOP IS PRODUCTION . . .

After reviewing the editorial and marketing materials provided, you need to look at the book itself. Since it may not yet exist in book form, you can turn to the production or managing editor for assistance. He or she will have, at worst, scraps of the manuscript on hand; at best, a complete manuscript with all of the artwork.

Borrow the front matter, the table of contents, the introduction and/or preface, the first and last chapters, and a few examples of any special features, such as problem sets, charts, sidebars, or chapter questions. Make a good photocopy for later reference.

ABOUT THE AUTHOR...

If there is no information on the book in-house, get permission to call the author. Most authors are pleasant, helpful, happy to hear that the publisher is at work selling his book, and quick to grasp what it is that you need to know. Before calling, write down a list of concise questions.

FINALLY...

Gather all of this information in a folder on your desk and let it ripen for a few hours or days. You should now have everything you need to write copy that sells in-house and out.

1:11   Ad Agency Copywriting: Guidelines for Professional and Scholarly Books

Many professional and scholarly publishing establishments rely on ad agency copywriters for preparation of ad copy on their works. Such agency operations may be "in house" or outside agencies serving a varied clientele.

In such agency-type operations, a frequent agency complaint is the problems caused by client changes in copy already written, and the "damage" such changes wreak on ongoing ad campaigns.

Where professional and scholarly book advertising is involved, I take an opposing view. What some agencies view as "client interference," I view as a very positive and constructive function.

Leaving campaign control totally in the hands of an ad agency may be fine for toothpaste or razor blades. It does make sense that you can be more likeable if your breath is inoffensive, or your health better if you have fewer dental cavities. And when the toothpaste campaign copywriter clues in on such known human appeals, it is likely to be done in a creditable manner.

However, the professional and scholarly publishing client is *unlike* clients in most other types of businesses. Human-interest appeals that might be perfectly appropriate for a toothpaste client will not work for the professional and scholarly book product. Even appeals that have been known to work for popular "trade" books will not work for the professional and scholarly book.

Every P&S book is unique. It is totally different from every other book. The one-of-a-kind compilation may represent the lifetime professional experience of its author. Often, it may address itself to a professional peer audience. Routine or assembly-line approaches are usually inappropriate.

Despite an agency copywriter's claim to "professionalism," there are three client-related individuals who usually know more about the copy approach for a particular P&S book than the copywriter. Yet, copy suggestions from any of these three are viewed by some as "interference with a professional's work." These three individuals are:

1. *The Author.* He or she has, after all, written the book and is in the

best position to know its content and to describe it. Yet, often, the ad copywriter tries to "reinvent the wheel" by juggling the author's words or selecting segments of the author's copy which taken out of context do not reflect the meaning of the book, but which the copywriter deems appropriate (or finds convenient) to describe the book in ad copy.

2. *The Sponsoring Editor.* The editor has already evaluated the author's manuscript, has worked closely with the author, has obtained and read outside evaluations (and criticisms) of each book, and knows its strengths and weaknesses.

3. *The Marketer.* Finally, after author and editor, the marketer is the most logical individual to know and provide guidance on the correct copy approach. It is likely the marketer has studied what the author has had to say about the book (usually in the Author or Marketing Questionnaire), as well as the comments and recommendations of the sponsoring editor. With this knowledge, the marketer presumably has already assessed the market(s) for the book and the appropriate approaches to its core audience(s).

Many agency copywriters fail to comprehend that the P&S book is a highly unique product and that copy must be finely tuned to the highly specialized interests of the professional audience for which it was written.

With such demanding copy requirements, the intelligent copywriter should accept and welcome all the help offered by client-affiliated individuals qualified and willing to provide it. Yet, some agency writers of professional and scholarly book copy do not. They fall into the trap of believing themselves "copy professionals." Such types sometimes resent any corrective criticism of their written efforts, convinced of their invincibility in putting words on paper conforming to the requirements of the ad or promotion at hand.

Such types resent any corrective criticism of their written efforts. They are quick to cry "interference" when alterations are proposed for their precious wording.

Most editors or marketers who endeavor to correct or revise copy have no wish to upstage an agency copywriter through unnecessary changes. Many who do change copy are among the busiest and can ill afford to take the time necessary for making those copy changes. They usually make such changes only when considered necessary.

Most copywriters who strive for true professionalism accept this fact. They realize that, where professional and scholarly book advertising copy is involved, the shortest line to professionalism is to work in harmonious concert with those intimately familiar with the unique product and its specialized markets. When copy help is offered by editors or book marketers, it is almost always rendered because of their desire that the copywriter's message describe the book to its

proper audience in a correct manner, and that it will be read, understood, and accepted as credible.

**1:12   Storing and Recycling Written Copy:
         Procedures**

Copywriting in large multi-divisional publishing establishments is
often done by a central agency or department. Consequently, different
copywriters may wind up writing copy for the same book. A useful
preventative solution is the establishment of a central copy file or
"bank" where all copy written can be filed for future reference or use.
Then, when a copywriter faces an assignment, he or she retrieves
available pertinent material from the central file before beginning the
assignment.

It is useful to identify copy as to the medium or audience for which
it was written. A piece of copy for a particular title may have been
slanted to a particular market or audience. By identifying copy as to
market or audience, there is little likelihood that copy touting the
textbook potential of a title to academics will be used in an advertisement being prepared for *Library Journal*.

Reviews suitable for excerpting should be stored in the same file
so that an appropriate quote can be added from a particular journal
for an ad to that same audience. Ofttimes, a review in the copy bank
may say it better than the written copy.

**1:13   When Title Has "Sell"
         There's Less for Copy to Tell**

In many small publishing operations, marketing, promotion, and copywriting may be the responsibility of a single individual. The copy-
preparer in such cases often has an opportunity to influence book
titling and should make every effort to seize this opportunity. Here
is why.

If the book's title provides an accurate description of the book and
its content, it can be extremely helpful in the sale of a professional
or scholarly book. Many professionals order or recommend a book
after seeing the title-and-author listing in the "Books Received" section
of a business periodical or professional journal. The more precisely
the title portrays the book, the more likely it is to be retained when
ordered on the basis of such listings.

In many areas of scholarly and scientific publishing, authors are
already aware of this and submit books with lengthy compound titles
separated by a colon, semicolon, or comma.

"Pick a scholarly work," says Mary-Clare van Leunen,* "any scholarly work; what's its title? Something-something, *colon,* something-

*Mary-Clare van Leunen, *A Handbook for Scholars,* New York: Knopf, 1979.

something-something.... The use of title and subtitle is justified by the desire to be both catchy and precise."

A study completed in 1981* found that fully two-thirds of all book titles reviewed in *Contemporary Psychology,* a journal of book reviews in psychology, contained a colon.

If the purpose of promotional copy is to inform and aid the sale of your books, you must consider the book's title as one of the most important aids to effective copy. If your input can help reflect the book's content and level accurately, the sales burden on the supporting copy is greatly reduced.

1:14   Ways to Put "Sell" into a Book's Title

As publishers of business and investment books are well aware, a book's title can serve as a mini-advertisement for the book even in the absence of other supporting ad copy. It is therefore important that the book's title be as meaningful as possible. Often, the individual preparing the copy may be working in advance of publication from a working title submitted by the author with his manuscript. On such occasions, you may be asked to or wish to suggest a more meaningful title that will make the book come alive for its intended audience.

Following are a dozen thought-starters (with examples) to help you in your search for a more meaningful book title:

- Title describing content:
  Fundamentals of Computer Programming
- Title identifying book's audience:
  Physicians' Desk Reference
- Title stressing completeness:
  Encyclopedia of Astronomy
- Title providing an industry standard:
  IEEE Standard for High Voltage Testing
- Title that promises a benefit:
  How to Score High on the Scholastic Aptitude Test
- Title that shows level of content:
  Introduction to Chemistry
- Title that stresses a specific location:
  Landfills in Texas
- Title that deals with a specific time period:
  Nursing Yearbook, 1985
- Title that covers a broad field:
  Encyclopedia of Science and Technology

*J. T. Dillon, "The Emergence of the Colon: An Empirical Correlate of Scholarship," *American Psychologist,* August 1981.

- Title that deals with a narrow topic:
  The Large Intestine: Its Role in Nutrition
- Title that stresses credibility:
  U.S. Government Testing Standards
- Title that demonstrates continuity:
  Encyclopedia of Associations, 19th Edition

**1:15   Length of Copy:
Rule for Major Reference Works**

When you're doing copy for a major work, such as an encyclopedia or reference, and it represents a major or one-time purchase, a general rule of thumb is that your copy should include complete information, including contents in whole or part. Where it is not possible to include complete information, the copy should be designed to prompt a request for a prospectus or the additional information that will aid the reader in making a purchase decision.

**1:16   Author Assistance and Alternatives
When Copy Preparation is Difficult**

In most houses, the *Author Questionnaire* or *Marketing Questionnaire* will generally provide the answers to most questions the copywriter needs to prepare copy for the job at hand. However, in many instances there is no such information available. What then?

A simple solution is to go to the source. Telephone the author and ask the questions you feel will produce the answers you need to complete your copy assignment. Prepare an outline of questions in advance of your call. If the questions are right, you'll get far more information than you require. If the topic is highly technical and you're not sure that you will be able to interpret the material correctly, arrange for the author to review and approve the copy after it is prepared. Most authors are anxious for the views expressed in the book to be properly presented in advertising and promotion copy and will welcome the opportunity to assist you in any necessary promotion copy preparation.

If your source material is highly technical and beyond your understanding, as in an advanced mathematical treatise, rather than attempt to extract and risk error or distortion of the book's importance, instead contact the author and ask him or her to write the book description for the ad or the flap to your specifications. This ensures that it will be accurately presented, and the audience to whom this book is directed will understand what the author is talking about even if no one else does.

If it is not possible to get the author to provide the copy you require, the next best thing is to list the complete contents, or if space does not permit that, a partial contents. For many scientists and scholars a title together with contents provides all the information they require for a purchase or purchase recommendation.

1:17 **When a Book Requires Different Copy Appeals for Different Audiences**

Occasionally, you will be asked to write copy for a book that has multi-audience appeal. However, the appeal to various audiences or disciplines will be for *different* reasons.

If your plans, therefore, call for individualized copy approaches for the different audiences, you might consider telling the author of your plans and asking him or her to advise you of the special copy appeal the book may have for each audience.

Obviously, if only certain features of a book will appeal to biologists, while certain other features offer special benefits only to social scientists, it will be useful for you to know in advance what those features are before you start to write. Make the author your partner on the multi-audience books; in some cases, the author may even volunteer to write the special copy for each audience. Copy targeted to the special interest of the reader will always be more successful than a general-interest block of untargeted copy.

1:18 **Simple Way to Obtain Testimonials for Your New Titles**

The reader finds it easier to believe the endorsement of a fellow consumer than the puffery of an anonymous copywriter.

> David Ogilvy, *Confessions of an Advertising Man*, Atheneum, 1963.

... every type of advertiser has the same problem; namely to be believed. ... nothing [is] so potent for this purpose as the testimonial.

> David Ogilvy, quoting Jim Young, *in Confessions of an Advertising Man*, Atheneum, 1963.

Testimonials from individuals prominent in the field of the book help build believability for the copy claims for the book. Such testimonials are from respected individuals, as a rule, and, consequently, their opinions are highly regarded by fellow professionals in the field.

There are the two simple steps necessary to obtain testimonials:

1. Include in the Author Questionnaire (or Marketing Questionnaire) a request that the author include the names of distinguished, authoritative individuals in the book's field who might recommend the book to their students or colleagues, and from whom endorsements should be solicited.

2. Such individuals should be contacted and asked if they will provide an endorsement if sent proofs of the book. The note should specifically request the endorsement and ask permission to use it in advertising.

1:19   Does Ad Copy Travel Well to Overseas Markets?

Science knows no national borders, and English has become the international language of science. Your ad copy, factually and honestly presented for a scientific or scholarly book or list of books, will deliver its message just as clearly to overseas audiences as it does to domestic markets.

When you take note of the great international mix viewing the various publisher exhibits at the large scientific meetings—at ACS, at FASEB, at the Pittsburgh Conference, and the like—you can readily see that the interest in such works is universal and that the message in your ad copy is also. A further example may be seen in the couponed orders that scientific and scholarly publishers regularly receive from book advertising in domestic scientific periodicals that have international circulations. Such orders often bear postmarks from virtually every corner of the globe.

Your copy for scientific or scholarly works will be read and understood if your copy provides these basic details: title and subtitle, name of author (and preferably his affiliation or credentials), page count (or approximate), price, and ordering information. If you are actively soliciting overseas orders, include additional shipping charge for such shipments and stipulate how payment is desired.

1:20   Tips for Copy Directed to International Audience

This valuable copy advice comes from conversations with a number of marketers with long experience in marketing specialized and scholarly books to international audiences.

- Keep your copy simple and clear. Avoid excess verbiage.
- Stay away from specialized language or jargon; it varies from country to country.
- Where possible, have someone with a non-American background review copy for language or expressions which may not be understood overseas.
- Use American rather than British spelling in copy.
- Quotes or review excerpts should be by internationally known or internationally recognized sources or authorities, for maximum credibility.
- If the book is in English, the copy for the promotion should be in English.

1:21   Tips on Good Writing from Robert Gunning*

1. Writing is an art. But when it is writing to inform it comes close to being a science as well.
2. Good writing goes beyond the mere recording of facts. To have effect, writing must communicate facts to readers.
3. To write well and simply you must train your mind to cut through surface details and get at the bones of your thought.
4. The preferred writing is that which delivers the intended thought most clearly in the fewest words possible. Don't write down. Don't write up. Write *to.*
5. If your subject is deep, you should make all the more effort to keep your language simple.

1:22   Copywriting Gems from Ogilvy and Caples

For reliable information and guidance on copywriting, seek out any of the excellent books written by David Ogilvy and John Caples, both members of the Copywriters Hall of Fame. Here are brief samples of their expertise—the first from Ogilvy's *Confessions of an Advertising Man* (New York: Atheneum, 1963), and the second from a Caples interview as part of an advertisement for *The Wall Street Journal* in the 31 March 1978 *New York Times.*

Ogilvy:

1. Don't beat about the bush—go straight to the point.
2. Avoid superlatives, generalizations, and platitudes. Be specific and factual.
3. Include testimonials; the reader finds it easier to believe the endorsement of a fellow consumer than the puffery of an anonymous copywriter.
4. Give the reader helpful [information].
5. Stick to the facts: "fine" writing and unique literary style take attention away from the subject.
6. Write copy in the language your customers use in everyday conversation.

Caples:

1. Headlines make ads work. With a good headline, you're almost sure to have a good ad.
2. Simple words are powerful words. Even the best educated people don't resent simple words.

---

* Excerpted from his book *The Technique of Clear Writing, Revised Edition,* McGraw-Hill, 1968.

3. If you need a thousand words, write two thousand. Trim vigorously. Fact-packed messages carry a wallop.
4. Don't be afraid of long copy. If the ad is interesting, people will be hungry for all the copy you can give them.
5. Get to the point. Don't save the best benefit until last. Start with it.

2

Copywriting for Space Advertising

2:01   **Tips and Techniques for the
        Writing of Space Ad Copy**

The preceding chapter discussed the writing of copy as *copy*. It addressed itself to some of the ways the copywriter should think about the process of writing, the approaches to the task, the different copy appeals for the audiences to whom the copy should be directed, the ingredients that can lead to success as a copywriter.

In this chapter we look at the ways one should approach the writing of copy for advertising in journals and specialized business publications. What are some of the things you can do to make your advertising more effective? What should you put into an ad? What constitutes good ad copy? What pitfalls should you avoid in your copy? What are some "laws" you can use to make good copy even more effective? What shortcuts can you take when you have too much copy and too little space? How should your copy be different for high-ticket books? For new or revised editions? For a space ad as contrasted with copy for a direct mail promotion? What are some practices professionals use to make ad copy more effective. All of these questions are answered in the entries following. The tips and techniques in this chapter should greatly enhance your skills and outlook toward the preparation of book advertising copy for the print media.

2.02   The Nature and Focus of Professional and Scholarly Book Advertising

Highly-targeted promotions for high-level professionals have to speak in their professional language. Failing that, the copywriter is better to stick with content and features.

—Peter Hodges

Professional and scholarly book advertising has one purpose—to sell packaged information, or to influence its ultimate purchase either directly or indirectly by the reader.

Your advertising copy should therefore focus on at least these basic elements if it is to be seriously considered and influence the reader:

1. Source and reliability of the information (book).
2. Credentials and authority of the author.
3. Size and form in which the work is offered (pages, binding).
4. Nature of the information (what the book is about).
5. Highlights (features) of the information.
6. Benefits of the work (may be implied rather than stated).
7. Cost (enables a judgment of the value of the work in relation to what it offers).
8. Availability (where and how to obtain it).

Most professional and scholarly works are serious in nature and involve professional consideration by serious-minded individuals. Attempts at humor or frivolity should not be tried in such advertising, and, as a rule, not in any kind of advertising.

A headline that merely identifies the source may be adequate to establish the authority of the advertiser with no further claims. The words "New from The MIT Press" says it all for a new engineering work to an engineer. Similarly "New from Harvard University Press" would say as much in a headline for a new business book to a manager.

A small or less-prominent press can establish strong credentials for its works by specializing in a particular field and establishing a position as the leading publisher or one of the several leading publishers in that field. Its imprint atop an advertisement would then be readily recognizable to those active in the field and would lend authority to the books being advertised.

When your press lacks either a position in the field or a prestigious imprint, you can gain strength for your advertising by reliance on the credibility or reputation or the author in the field or discipline to which the ad is directed. The author's affiliation is also helpful.

A book by an author affiliated with a world-famous research facility may gain strength. A book by an acknowledged leader in the field will require little more than the author's name, irrespective of the publisher's imprint. A book by an award winner can gain strength from the importance of the award to those in the field: "A New Work by Nobel Laureate John Doe." A new edition can rely on the credibility of the previous editions: "Sixth Edition of an Acknowledged Classic."

Ad copy should avoid literary creativity. When selling an information package, stick to the information. Facts about a book are the best way to sell a book. To a specialist in the field, often the most convincing copy is the table of contents. The specialist often can get the feel of the book just by examination of the contents.

If the subject matter is similar or identical to other works in the field, such as a book titled "Organic Chemistry," then the copy should explain how this book on organic chemistry differs from others with the same title, as well as the level of its presentation—introductory work, undergraduate text, graduate text, professional reference, etc. For a new edition with the same title, copy should explain how it differs from the previous edition.

Facts are indisputable. Give the facts about a book and you are safe. Give the benefits only as space permits, and only if you are sure they are truly benefits and recognizable as such by the reader.

When describing a technical work, stick to the author's own words as closely as possible, especially in areas where you are not professionally qualified to make judgments on copy. If you are uncertain of whether you have selected the most important aspects of the book, or possibly may have taken material out of context, check it out with the author, or at least with someone in your establishment or in the field who is qualified to tell you whether the copy makes sense.

If your copy offers the book for free examination, it may not be necessary to tell too much about the book—only enough to capture the interest of the reader to a sufficient degree so that he or she will want to send for a copy to examine. In such cases, features rather than content are most helpful. This is particularly true in a limited space small ad, or on a card-deck card where you can list 8 or 10 features in the space occupied by a single paragraph.

Follow these precepts and you will find that successful advertising copy for professional and scholarly books is not difficult to write. In fact, it's easy as 1–2–3:

1. Make your message clear and understandable.

2. Stick to the facts.

3. Make it easy to order.

2:03   Ways to Make Professional and Scholarly Book Advertising More Effective

1. A list-type advertisement offering a variety of titles will give you more "mileage" for your advertising dollar.

2. Make your advertisement a mix of new books and active backlist titles.

3. If you have to cut copy in a multi-title ad, reduce the size of the headline or omit the coupon if necessary to preserve what you consider essential copy.

4. Include a key or special code number or name of an individual in your ad signature or coupon so response can be tracked.

5. Avoid cute, clever, or tricky headlines for professional and scholarly book ads; you are dealing with a serious professional audience.

6. If your ad does not include a coupon, inclusion of a toll-free 800 number with an identifying code number will not only help you track ad responses, but also speed them up, since such numbers encourage impulse orders.

7. Readers are interested in the newness of books. Be sure that the publication date for each book is set in boldface or italics so that it stands out in your ad copy.

2:04   What Constitutes Good Advertising Copy?

Advertising sages of the past have never been able to agree on what constitutes good advertising copy. Some have stated it should be *news;* the copy in your offering must present newsworthy information.

Others have been equally strong in the argument that advertising copy should be somewhat similar to a sales presentation; the copy in your offering should be *salesmanship in print.*

Actually, good advertising copy should be a mixture of both. And when directing ads to general audiences, one should heed the words of Ed Nash, head of direct marketing at Batten, Barton, Dustine & Osborn and a longtime writer of award-winning advertising: "One common denominator of really fine copy is that it is 'meaty'—filled with details, choice examples, and clever anecdotes, all of which makes points with examples rather than with broad and empty claims."

When you write advertising copy for scientific and technical professionals, you should avoid hype and present information that will be new, and presumably offer useful information to the reader.

As the same time, your advertising copy should always end with the one basic precept that marks the end of any good sales presentation: ask for the order.

2:05   Pitfalls to Avoid in Ad Copy
for Professional and Scholarly Books

1. Avoid hard sell.

2. Avoid "We're the greatest" type of statements.

3. Avoid any mention of your competition.

4. Avoid overstating the qualities of the book.

5. Avoid writing copy that talks *up* or *down* to the reader.

6. Avoid use of superlatives.

7. Avoid long, wordy headlines; they tend to be overlooked.

8. Avoid clever, cute, or smart-alecky phrases which might be misunderstood or misinterpreted.

2:06 Some "Laws" of Scientific and Scholarly Book Advertising

- An offering by a prestige-name press will produce better results than an identical offering from a lesser-known or unknown press.

- A special offer displayed in a prominent position in an advertisement, such as the headline, will produce better response than an identical offer buried elsewhere in the advertisement (or mail offering).

- A toll-free 800 number in large bold display type, in a book advertisement, will produce considerably more calls than an identical number set in regular weight, in a smaller size type.

- A list-type advertisement in a professional or scholarly journal will attract as high a readership as a solo ad featuring only one title.

- There is no direct relationship between high ad-noted scores for book advertising and ultimate actual purchases of the books advertised. One study indicated that, among numerous book advertisements over a one-year period in a scientific periodical, the five top scorers in ad recollection had these conversion rates of actual purchase to recollection: (1) 11.1%; (2) 6.2%; (3) 22.6%; (4) 8.7%; (5) 12.2%. Ad-noted scores for all five were relatively close.

2:07 Writing Ad Copy for the Multi-Title Sci-Tech Book Advertisement: Guidelines

- Space in such ads is generally limited. Learn from the classified ad writers to make every word count. If you're advertising in *Chemical Engineering,* there is no need to say, "This book is for chemical engineers." Instead mention its level, as for a text, or its special approach.

- Where given only a few lines and a choice of either descriptive copy or a lengthy series name, opt for the descriptive copy and omit the series name.

- Omission of author affiliation can often provide an extra line for descriptive copy.

- Scientists and engineers are very concerned with keeping current in their profession. Always give publication date. Year is sufficient for titles not of the current or forthcoming season.

- Highly technical works that are difficult to describe can be effectively presented by listing full or partial contents.

- Along with publication date, other important ingredients of any sci-tech ad copy should be price, page count (or approximate count), ISBN (especially if it is also your order number), and type of binding if other than cloth.

- Forget about formal openings such as "This book presents" and start with "Presents." You've saved two words you can apply to descriptive copy about the book.

2:08   Useful Copy Ingredients in High-Ticket Book Advertising

Multi-volume references or expensive encyclopedic works are rarely sold solely on the basis of a space advertisement. As a rule, it is necessary to include in the advertising copy an offer to mail complete details or a prospectus that will provide the detailed information needed to make the buying decision.

It is also a useful practice for advertising of high-ticket reference works to include the name and direct-dial number of a responsible, well-informed contact within the publishing establishment who is qualified and will respond to telephone inquiries and/or provide precise ordering information.

One publisher of a line of high-priced professional software does not include a telephone number, but mentions in its advertising that it has a telephone reference service. Customers may call during business hours for answers to any questions or problems arising from their purchase of any software package.

2:09   Guidelines for Use of Coupons in Specialized Publications

1. Most space advertising is intended to make the book's availability known to its audience. When you advertise a specialized book to its intended audience in a specialized publication aimed at that audience, the coupon, as a rule, is unnecessary.

2. Most buyers of professional and scholarly books often buy as a result of many factors, of which advertising is only one. Lack of a coupon will not deter buyers who might otherwise buy anyway.

3. Librarians, as a rule, will not use coupons since they generally order through jobbers or library suppliers. An exception might be when there is a special prepublication offer.

4. Libraries and other subscribers to professional and scholarly jour-

nals of archival value are reluctant to deface their publication by cutting out a coupon.

5. A toll-free 800 telephone number often will satisfactorily replace a coupon. It not only invites ordering, but also appeals to the impulse buyer who might not be inclined to fill out and mail a coupon. Businesses who order in bulk quantities, are more likely to telephone an 800 number and give a purchase order number to the operator than to complete and return an advertisement coupon.

6. A bind-in order card with a list-type advertisement will generate about one-fifth of the total response, both direct and indirect.

2:10 Helpful Copy Ingredients for Advertising a Revised Edition

- Specific changes in structure and content of the revised edition.
- Key features of the new edition.
- Distinguishing features of earlier edition that have been retained. If a textbook, for what course titles is it suited, and at what levels?
- Appropriateness for nonacademic use such as secondary schools, technical institutes, and government, industrial, and union training programs.

2:11 Benefits and Guidelines for Use of Publication-Set Advertising

You've done your copy and a rough layout, but you can't afford the high production costs. Consider having the complete ad set by the periodical in which it is being inserted. Many do not charge for this service, and those who do often charge only a modest fee.

Even if your budget can stand the high composition and production costs, you may want to rely on pubset advertisements for small, limited-circulation but important scholarly journals where the cost of space may be nominal—and the expense involved in composition and preparation of the ad may not be justified.

If your budget cannot stand the high composition and production costs, the pubset advertisement is an inexpensive means of meeting a late deadline, or stretching a tight or overspent budget.

YOUR PUBSET AD

A "shlocky" pubset ad will cost you as much as a highly attractive one. The more precise your instructions, the more attractive your advertisement will be in print. Ask for a copy of the publication's type-specimen book, or if they lack one, ask what typefaces and sizes are available and specify from the same faces and sizes in a book you have on hand or from another publication.

FIGURE 1 Gale Research Company advertisement in the Sunday *New York Times* business section aims a classic library reference at a general business audience. A well-written hard-hitting ad has all the ingredients of a good mail-order advertisement. Copy was written by Roy Hubbard of Gale in collaboration with Gale Art Director Charles Hunt. Note that the advertisement does not carry the Gale toll-free 800 number, which the company does use in advertising to its primary market, libraries. The advertisement was repeated several days later in *The Wall Street Journal*.

Try to provide a good layout showing where your ad elements are to be positioned, as well as clear copy and precise instructions. If you do this, there will be no surprises when you see your advertisement in print.

If you submit your copy and layout sufficiently in advance of the publication deadline, you should ask for a proof. This will enable you to check on how closely your requirements were met and also give you an opportunity to make late adjustments, such as adding a final price, page count, or corrected publication date.

2:12 **Three Major Differences Between Space Ad Copy and Direct-Mail Letter Copy**

1. *Size and Content.* Copy for a space ad is written to fit a precise size in the ad layout. Copy for a direct-mail letter is written for content. There are usually no limitations on copy length; it can run as long as is necessary to tell the complete story.

2. *Copy Appeal.* Copy for a space ad must appeal to the total audience of the publication in which it appears. It is impersonal, terse, factual. Copy for a direct-mail letter is written to a pre-selected prospect list. Because it is targeted to a specific individual, copy can be more meaningful and, consequently, more effective.

3. *Response Convenience.* With a space ad, copy usually must ask the reader to clip and mail a coupon or write a letter—either alternative requiring an envelope which has to be addressed and stamped. With a direct-mail letter, usually, the copy is reinforced on the order form enclosure, either a business reply card or an envelope. This response device usually repeats the offer, is pre-addressed, and is usually postage-paid. In some instances the addressed label of the customer is affixed, and the copy need only ask that the recipient mail the order.

2:13 **Time-Saving Practice When Ad Copy Must Be Approved by Author or Author's Company**

Time is short and your copy assignment involves a book which, for some reason, requires prior approval by either the author, or the public relations or legal department of his employer-company. Such copy constraints occasionally crop up in scientific and technical book contracts and tend to hamper book promotion efforts. They are a likely cause of missed deadlines.

Here is a useful practice which will save much time and aggravation: Prepare the jacket and several ad copy variations at the earliest date possible, while the book is in production, and obtain early approval for any such copy written. The "approved copy" should then be placed in the author's data file or copy bank and used whenever any promotion effort involves the particular book.

2:14 **Remember the Book's Title When Writing Copy: A Case Study**

It was an attractive-looking advertisement for a new edition of a business directory in the official publication of the professional association serving the field.

The two-column × 10″ advertisement had a strong headline, an equally appealing subhead, and then an illustration of the cover of the new directory, followed by support copy and a large order coupon occupying 20% of the advertisement.

But the advertisement had a serious flaw—the name of the directory did not appear anywhere in the advertisement or on the order coupon! The designer/copywriter had designed the ad around the directory illustration, relying on the title in the book illustration to carry the ad. However, the cover illustration had been greatly reduced. What apparently was an 8½″ × 11″ book had been reduced to a cover 1¼ inches high. Whatever the type size of the directory title on the actual cover, in the illustration, the typesize was the equivalent of 3 point type. Only a reader with unusually keen eyesight or using a magnifying glass could make out the name of the advertised book.

The headline asked: "Looking for current . . . information?"

The subhead stated: "Announcing the new Fourth edition of . . ."

The miniature book illustration followed.

The body copy of the ad referred to "The Directory" several times

The coupon said "send me ____ copies of the DIRECTORY"

But nowhere in the entire advertisement was "The Directory" identified.

The lesson here for copywriters is that, irrespective of whatever support illustrations your advertising may carry, always repeat the title of the book in an advertisement. And repeat it again in the order coupon, if one is provided. If you don't, you're advertising nothing, and that's the kind of response you can expect.*

2:15   Should Competitive Works Be Mentioned in Your Advertising Copy?

It has become a fairly common practice among writers of consumer advertising to build credibility for the advertised product by comparing it with its competition. I have never agreed to this practice in principle, and I think it totally wrong when it involves advertising of specialized and scholarly books.

In specialized and scholarly book publishing, each book is a unique effort. It should stand on its own merits and strengths. If the strengths, features, or benefits are those lacking in competitive works, these should be emphasized—but without naming the works in which they are lacking.

If you're expending promotional funds to advertise one of your

* See also 2:17.

publications, it makes little sense to also make the readers aware of available similar publications in the same field, subject, or discipline. Readers who are well versed in the field will know about the competitive books; if they do not know about them, why should you be the informant?

Professionals and academics tend to take publisher advertising claims with a degree of skepticism. Efforts to knock the competition coupled with this inherent skepticism can raise sufficient curiosity for the reader to want to examine the competition as well, and the competitive work may offer advantages that your book lacks.

My advice: Don't knock the competition.

2:16 Identifying Spin-Off Volumes of Larger Works: Copy Practices Used

If encyclopedias and handbooks are part of your establishment's publishing program, your assignment may require that you write advertising copy for spin-off volumes of selected material taken from a larger work.

Examples are given here of the advertising treatment of such volumes from larger encyclopedia works by two major publishers, McGraw-Hill and Wiley.

How do they describe the spin-off volumes in advertising copy? Note from the examples that both lean heavily on the reputation and prominence of the larger work and its contributors.

McGRAW-HILL'S TREATMENT

A half-page display advertisement in *Chemical and Engineering News* features two encyclopedias, *Encyclopedia of Engineering* and *Encyclopedia of Chemistry* (Figure 2). No mention is made in the copy for either volume that it is a spin-off volume. However, at the bottom of the advertisement, two 4 point black horizontal rules encompass this copy:

> Both encyclopedias draw on the unmatched international authority of the up-to-date McGraw-Hill Encyclopedia of Science and Technology, Fifth Edition, "the modern standard against which all other scientific encyclopedias must be judged" (D. Allan Bromley, president of AAAS). Both are oversized (8½" × 11"), lavishly illustrated, use SI units, and contain extensive cross-references and bibliographies for further reading.

The spin-off volumes in the *C&E News* advertisement are but two of the four spin-off volumes from the larger encyclopedia. In another half-page advertisement—this one in *Physics Today*—the other two spin-offs are offered jointly (Figure 2). They are *McGraw-Hill's Encyclopedia of Physics* and *Encyclopedia of Astronomy*.

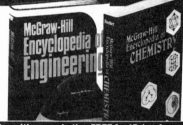
FIGURE 2 Advertisements in *Physics Today* (top) and *C&E News* (bottom) each offer spin-off encyclopedias from the *McGraw-Hill Encyclopedia of Science and Technology,* Fifth Edition. The advertisement for the physics and astronomy encyclopedias cites the parent encyclopedia as its source directly under the headline. The *C&E News* offering of encyclopedias of engineering and chemistry provides the same information at the bottom of the advertisement. Both approaches were equally effective.

In the copy for the latter two spin-offs, copy directly under the headline states:

Announcing—two new one-volume encyclopedias drawn from the recent Fifth Edition *McGraw-Hill Encyclopedia of Science and Technology,* the 15-volume masterwork that "provides the modern standard against which all other scientific encyclopedias must be judged" (D. Allan Bromley, president of the American Association for the Advancement of Science).

WILEY'S TREATMENT

A full page display ad, also in *Chemical and Engineering News,* features the parent work under the heading "the 'bible' of Chemical Technology." The spin-offs are in a boxed-off portion of the advertisement midway down the page under a heading: "Encyclopedia Reprint Series." Lead-off copy in the box, introducing the reprints, reads:

ENCYCLOPEDIA REPRINT SERIES
Selected volumes of reprint articles grouped by subject from the Third Edition of the Kirk-Othmer Encyclopedia of Chemical Technology.

Individual copy descriptions for each spin-off volume (three are listed) also refer to the careful selection of the articles from the parent work.

Both McGraw-Hill and Wiley copy refer to the authority of the contributors. The McGraw-Hill copy includes the line "Contributors include such Nobel Prize-winners as . . ." and it gives names. Wiley copy states "Entries are by acknowledged authorities in their fields."

**2:17   When Illustration Says It All,
Copy Need Say Very Little**

When a work is very well known or the jacket tells it all, let the jacket do the talking, and keep copy to a minimum. A good example is the full-page ad in *Choice* (November 1983) for Columbia University Press's *The Concise Columbia Encyclopedia* (Figure 3).

Under the brief, but catchy, headline (Concisely what you need) is an illustration of the book, standing up, face out. Virtually all the features of the book are on the jacket which stands 7 inches high and 5 inches wide.

In the 1½ inches remaining under the illustration, in three columns, is a paragraph of copy, five bulleted features not mentioned on the jacket, and price and signature. Essentially, the illustration is the

Concisely what you need.

THE CONCISE COLUMBIA ENCYCLOPEDIA

THE MOST COMPLETE AND AUTHORITATIVE DESK ENCYCLOPEDIA YOU CAN OWN

- Over 15,000 entries (one million words)
- Comprehensive and accurate
- Absolutely up-to-date
- Easy to read, easy to use
- Tables, charts, and illustrations— including 16 pages of full-color maps

It's the best, most convenient desk encyclopedia ever published for everyday use—more colorful, more up-to-date, more authoritative than any comparable volume. The editorial savvy and experience that have made *The Columbia Encyclopedia* the most purchased, most respected, most widely used general reference of its kind make this new encyclopedia **indispensable** for home, school, office, and library. Among its special features:

- More than 3,000 articles on scientific and technical subjects
- More than 5,000 biographical articles
- More than 50,000 cross-references
- 16 pages of maps **in full color**
- And much, much more.

See for yourself how much useful information fits in just one handy volume. Handsomely bound and printed on durable acid-free paper. It's concisely what you need.

THE CONCISE COLUMBIA ENCYCLOPEDIA $29.95

COLUMBIA UNIVERSITY PRESS
Address for orders: 136 South Broadway Irvington, N.Y. 10533

entire advertisement and the copywriter, wisely, has chosen to say little more.*

2:18   **Tips from a Pro on What Works in Copy
and What Doesn't**

In advertising, some copy formats work better than others. John O'Toole, head of Foote, Cone & Belding, one of the world's largest advertising agencies, made these observations about effective copy presentation in his *The Trouble with Advertising,* published by Chelsea House, New York, in 1981.

1. Always use a serif typeface. Serifs make reading easier. Why make it harder for a prospect to absorb information?
2. Never make the column width of type more than 55 characters.
3. Don't surprint text on pictorial matter unless the latter has been airbrushed or treated to form a light single-tone background.
4. Do not reverse text (white letters on black or full-color backgrounds).

These observations, says O'Toole, are the result of "poring over hundreds of readership studies and watching, for a long time, what works and what doesn't."

* See also 2:14.

3

Copy for Direct-Mail Promotion: Principles and Practices

3:01   **Direct-Response Book Advertising Copy: An Historical Perspective**

Peter Hodges, a longtime book marketing professional, has written copy for hundreds of successful promotions over the past 20 years in large publishing establishments, and before that for an advertising agency serving a leading publisher. His thoughts on advertising copy, prepared for this volume, provide an historical perspective on book advertising. At the same time, they carry the weight of his long experience and many successes. Hodges' words offer valuable insights to all who aspire to success in the writing of professional and reference book advertising copy.

Copywriters have been plugging away at their craft, in a formal sense for about 100 years. Most of what we do is still closer to witchcraft than science. We are a bit like the barber surgeons of an earlier age who frequently achieved amazing cures. Yet, they were treating the symptoms, rather than the disease.

Advertising copy today, for the most part, still follows the principles developed by the personal sales rep; it uses techniques designed to deal with the prospect face to face. Recent trends in consumer advertising (especially television commercials) draw their effectiveness from motivational research, and produce advertising better suited to the medium used by the advertiser. It is about time that we who are involved in professional book and journal advertising reevaluate our cherished traditions.

The Prentice-Hall Copy Formula

The early advertising direct mail and mail order pioneers at Prentice-Hall developed an approach for print advertising media which still dominates the industry today. Translating the personal sales pitch into words, they created formulas that were consistently successful.

Their copy focused on key sales points that stressed benefits and frequently resorted to extravagant promises. As any of the hundreds of copywriters who worked for Prentice-Hall, either in house or through their advertising agencies, can attest, they wrote to a formula. Often sales points were created first. Once these seemed to have the proper "bite," headlines, body copy, and feature boxes, including endorsements, were added.

A typical Prentice-Hall mail-order ad would begin with a strong benefit headline, continue with a short introductory paragraph amplifying the headline. Then would come the title, an introduction to the sales points, and finally a closing "send in your order" sales pitch.

Around this basic copy there would frequently be short outlines of contents, endorsements, and any other element the copywriter could think of to strengthen the prospect's interest in the offer.

Woe to the copywriter that wanted to take a different approach. The P-H marketing brass knew their formula worked. "Don't mess with success" was the watchword. While this thinking was justified by results, it tended to limit worthwhile experimentation.

How the Prospect Thinks

Most advertising copy is created as if the human mind worked like a digital computer. More and more information is fed into the databank until sufficient evidence is present to reach a buying decision.

This is not necessarily the case for most people. A potential customer comes to an advertisement with a set of pre-programmed data, or needs. From something as small as the outside of the envelope or the appearance of the ad on the page, a decision is triggered either to pursue the advertising message or not. If this almost instantaneous decision is positive, the prospect will make a high-speed scan of the product or service.

He or she takes in the overall message as a single complete pattern. From that point, the basic buying decision is made and it is up to the copywriter to provide the prospect with the supporting rationalizations to confirm that the decision that has already been made is the correct one. At this early stage, the sale has been made. It is now up to the advertiser not to lose it. This, of course, depends on whether the price is perceived to be appropriate, the content sufficiently complete, the writing authoritative, etc.

If we accept the idea that a buying decision is basically due to a Gestalt reaction, then we have to review many of our cherished opinions about copywriting in a new light. Let's take another look at the Prentice-Hall formula, accepting the Gestalt principle. From this point of view, the sales points are not as important as the headline. It is the headline that catches the prospect and achieves the desired buying decision. Further promises of benefit, sales points, and a free examination offer simply confirm the initial positive decision, or, in cases where the prospect does not buy, reverse it.

Promise and Credibility

If the right promise of benefit is the key to a positive sales reaction, credibility is the prime clincher. An ad headline promising "The first tested plan for living forever in good health" would attract strong interest and probably have good sales. If it was accompanied by the fact that this plan was developed at the world-famous Mayo Clinic, the offer would be the success of the century.

Another case is the book *Zero-Based Budgeting,* published in the mid-1970s. It was a moderate success until Jimmy Carter was elected president and said he would make Zero-Based Budgeting a key strategy in the management of his administration. In four months, sales increased 400% over those achieved in the first four years after publication.

This was not just credibility, but the fact that the prospects brought to the advertisements for the book a strong interest in the subject that had not been satisfied previously. When they saw the book's title, the Gestalt reaction was "That's it! How do I get it?" Only the smallest amount of supporting evidence was needed to clinch a direct mail sale, or send the prospect to his local bookstore.

Beyond Reasonable Doubt

Even if your headline has presold your offer, we who write direct mail copy have the same problem as the attorney. We have to show beyond reasonable doubt that the proposition we are making is one that the prospect wants to accept. Here's where the Prentice-Hall type of sales point comes to the fore. It is *very* specific. It points out the things that the book can and supposedly will do for the reader. A Prentice-Hall sales letter to this day is a string of sales points separated by just enough copy to keep the letter from looking like a checklist.

RIA (Research Institute of America) has taken this approach and developed it further. They use an attractive "report" format that essentially does have a "checklist" on the front under a strong headline. Then, they basically follow the Prentice-Hall approach.

To my mind, the RIA and Prentice-Hall approaches work best when the promotion vehicle delivers a series of "tips" that the prospect can clearly identify as desirable and perceive how they apply. The promotional vehicle is highly trageted.

And Don't Forget to Ask for the Order

One thing I learned from my own experience as a writer of advertising copy for Prentice-Hall (through their ad agency) was to ask for the order. Most ads and mailings did it at least three times. I've always tried to remember that over the long years since my Prentice-Hall experience. Restate the entire deal at least twice in the mailing package and be sure the prospect knows that something special is expected.

3:02   Difference Between Direct Mail and Direct Response

The terms *Direct Mail* and *Direct Response* are frequently mixed and used interchangeably. Actually they are very different and serve entirely different purposes.

Direct-response mailings have a single purpose—to generate direct responses from those to whom they are mailed. Many types of professional and reference books lend themselves to direct response (also referred to as direct orders or mail orders) and produce profitable returns when such offerings are properly targeted.

Direct mail, on the other hand, is really a shortened form of the term *direct-mail advertising.* Its function, in professional and scholarly book publishing, is essentially the same as publisher space advertising: to place advertising about the publisher's offerings in the hands of a targeted audience, with measurable response a secondary consideration.

3:03   Copy Guidelines for Book Mail Advertising

1. Include name of series with book description. If series name and volume number are not integral parts of the book title, include them as the last sentence in the descriptive matter. Put the series title in italics. If contents are also in the advertisement, the series title goes with the copy, not at the end of the contents.

2. Include book's contents if possible—at least with the first announcement of the book. Potential buyers are more interested in content than in the publisher's claims for the book.

3. If space does not permit full contents, list partial contents and cite the most important chapters.

4. If book is a symposium or a volume of contributions by noted authors, list names of chapter authors after each chapter. (Names will stand out better if in italics and parentheses.)

5. Because the mailing piece may go to many different lists, include in the description, as the case warrants, the primary audience for which the book is intended.

6. After the author's name, include his or her affiliation.

7. Stick to Arabic numbers for part numbers and volume numbers. Avoid Roman numerals.

8. Quote liberally from favorable reviews. If a single review describes the book more appropriately than your own description, use the review quote as the copy. Be sure to attribute the review to its source.

9. A moderate review from a widely respected journal in the field will carry more weight than a rave review from a little-known journal. Favor the reviews in prestigious or core journals whenever possible.

10. Avoid superlatives in your copy—unless they are part of a review and can be attributed to others.

11. Your audience is intelligent, educated, and sophisticated. Keep all copy factual, objective.

12. Rely on facts obtained from the author questionnaire or other information supplied by the author. Do not use your own opinions.

13. Combine action verbs with tight, fact-packed copy. For example, say "Demonstrates methods," "Describes results," "Presents techniques," instead of "Methods are demonstrated," "Results are included," and "Techniques are presented."

14. In direct-mail pieces, a featured title should have a headline— preferably one that points up one or more important benefits of the book.

15. When copy must be short, such as four or five lines for description, open all sentences with action verbs. "Covers entire field of lasers. Gives current treatment of applications. Omits developments prior to 1978." Avoid using the same verb, such as "presents," to open every sentence.

16. Many text and professional books carry nearly identical titles (for example: Algebra, Vol. 1, etc.). It is important to mention the level of any book covering a general subject. Example: "Introductory text at undergraduate level," or "Suitable for graduate-level courses and for professional reference." Information about the level of the book will often be found in the author questionnaire.

17. Read the entire description of the book given in the author questionnaire before starting to write copy. Often, the first several paragraphs are general information, and the factual information about the book is buried in the last paragraph, or even the last sentence. Frequently, the author's own description of the book is all the copy you'll need. If the author says it well, use his or her wording; do not attempt to rewrite. After all, who should know the book better than the author?

3:04　　Copy You Write for One Market May Be Inappropriate for Another: Here's Why

You prepare and send a mailing to a book's primary market and it works. You try the same mailing to a secondary market and it doesn't. Why?

The answer, according to Ed Nash,* is that you have to consider the book as more than one book. Speaking before the Professional Publishers Marketing Group in New York on 18 May 1982, Nash explained that a mailing to a book's primary market may require a totally different copy approach than when the mailing is offered to a different market. He added that a technical book deals not only with

*Nash is author of the highly acclaimed *Direct Marketing* (New York: McGraw-Hill, 1982). He is also head of direct marketing at BBDO (Batten, Barton, Durstine & Osborn).

a rational need but also with a psychological need—namely, self-image—for the security of knowing the book is there should the need for it ever arise.

3:05   Copy Incentives That Help Increase Response

1. Offer a premium with a minimum dollar volume purchase, such as $50 or more, for three titles or more, etc.
2. Offer a discount for all orders before a certain date, or a prepublication price.
3. Indicate that prices are guaranteed to a fixed future cutoff date.
4. Include a free trial examination offer.
5. If payment is required with order, offer a full refund if not satisfied.
6. Offer credit-card charge option.
7. Include a toll-free 800 number for telephone orders.
8. Ask for the order. Refer to order form or envelope in your mailing in one or more prominent places.
9. Repeat the offer on the order form or card.
10. Include an extra order form, or a combination order form and order envelope.
11. Offer free shipping if order is prepaid.
12. If postage and handling charges are required, offer a flat charge for "up to two or three books," providing a saving if more than one book is ordered at the same time.

**3:06   More Copy Tips That Improve Effectiveness
in Direct-Response Promotions**

- If your direct response offering includes a free examination offer, include on your order form a space for a signature of the buyer. It's a publisher's protection should the buyer later claim he or she didn't order the book.
- Include an expiration on your direct-response book offers and state in your offer that prices are guaranteed until that date.
- Include a credit-card payment option if the books are high priced or may exceed your company's mail credit limit.
- Include routing instructions with your direct-response mailing to companies or institutions so it will have the benefit of a pass-along readership.

**3:07   Importance of Coupon or Order Form
in Direct Response**

Top direct-response copy professionals consider the order form or coupon the most critical ingredient of any direct-response promotion. Some top copy pros, says Ed Nash in *Direct Marketing* (McGraw-Hill, 1982), favor starting a copy assignment with the order form or coupon. Another leading mail order consultant, Lawrence Chait, advised in the February 1983 issue of *Direct Marketing* magazine that successful catalog houses give the order blank more attention than any other ingredient of the promotion.

Here are some tips for the order form or coupon when you are planning a direct-response promotion:

1. Its primary purpose: make it as easy as possible for the customer to order.
2. It must be completely understandable. If a subscription update service or a special offer is involved, make the terms completely clear, or your form will deter potential buyers.
3. It should repeat any special offer that is made in the body of the advertising copy. The reason: The reader of your promotion may tear out the advertisement order coupon or the mailing order form for later response. If the offer in the body of the copy is not repeated, the reason for removing the order form or coupon may be forgotten when the customer is ready to mail it back.
4. If you invite credit-card payment, provide complete information for how you wish information to be furnished.
5. It should include full information on shipping and handling charges and sales tax.
6. If you absorb shipping charges on prepaid orders, do you consider a credit-card payment as a prepaid order? If not, does coupon state this?
7. If you offer a free examination period, is this repeated in the order form?
8. If you have an 800 telephone number, have you included it?
9. If offer has an expiration date, has this been included?
10. If prepayment is required, does coupon mention conditions for returns?
11. Does coupon or order form allow sufficient space for customer's full name and address?

**3:08   Recommended Copy Elements for Coupon
or Order Form in Book Offerings**

1. Company name and address on all order forms/coupons. If the form is a business reply envelope, it is sufficient to have name and address on the mailing face.
2. International Standard Book Number (ISBN) for each title on

order form as identification check. If no ISBN is used as identification, use catalog number or order number.

3. Author/title/volume number/edition/series name (where space permits). If space is very limited, supply at least ISBN/order number or key/author name.

4. Book price, consistent with price shown for same book elsewhere in ad or promotion piece. If no firm price is available, show a tentative price and indicate that it is tentative.

5. Sales tax requirement as applicable.

6. Terms of payment available:
   (a) Prepayment required or credit-card option
   (b) Open credit: invoice sent with book(s)
   (c) Optional cash prepayment

7. Statement of postage and handling charge as applicable.

8. Statement of free examination period.

9. Statement of returns policy on prepaid orders.

10. Future availability dates on not yet published titles.

11. Expiration date of offer.

12. Disclaimers as applicable (see entry 3:09):
    (a) Price subject to change without notice
    (b) Territorial restrictions, if any
    (c) Requirements for international orders

13. Appropriate campaign/mailing list/media keys for tracking.

3:09   Order Form Disclaimers, Restrictions, Conditions: Copy Options

PAYMENT:

☐ Examination copies not sent to post-office box addresses without prepayment.

☐ Payment must accompany orders with post-office box addresses.

☐ If order totals $_____ or more, enclose _____% partial payment, or attach company/institutional purchase order.

☐ Prepayment required. Price includes shipping.

☐ Orders from individuals must be accompanied by payment.

☐ Foreign payment must be in U.S. currency, by U.S. bank draft, international money order, or UNESCO coupons.

☐ Prices are payable in U.S. currency or its equivalent.

☐ Add $_____ handling charge for books.

☐ Bill us plus postage, or Check enclosed, less 5%, postage prepaid.

☐ Charge orders are not considered prepayment.

☐ MasterCard/VISA orders are considered prepayment.

☐ All major credit cards are accepted.

PRICE:

☐ Price subject to change without notice.

☐ Minimum charge order: $_____.

☐ Price guaranteed until (date).

☐ U.S. prices are subject to exchange rate fluctuations.

OFFER:

☐ Offer valid in United States only, or Offer good only in United States and Canada.

☐ Order cannot be processed without your signature.

☐ Order subject to acceptance by (publisher).

☐ Offer expires (date), or Prices good until (date).

☐ Order subject to credit department approval.

☐ Order includes both basic and additional upkeep service such as new editions or additional companion volumes, or I do not want upkeep service.

☐ Premium offer extended for cash-with-orders only.

☐ Continuation order may be cancelled at any time without penalty or obligation.

DELIVERY:

☐ Please allow _____ to _____ weeks for delivery.

☐ If order cannot be filled within _____ days, payment will be refunded.

☐ If address is a post-office box number, give street address; we ship by UPS.

SPECIAL REQUIREMENT:

☐ When ordering by letter or purchase order, please attach this form completed.

3:10   Twenty-five Action Headings You Can Use on Your Order Forms

No matter how effective the copy is in your promotional efforts, it's the order form that ultimately produces the results. The chances for a reply or order form to be used are greatly increased if you include a heading that urges some kind of action. Here are samples of 25 action headings which you can use with your professional and scholarly book offerings.

1. Check and Return This Form Promptly
2. Clip Coupon. Mail Today
3. Don't Delay! Mail This Card Today
4. 15-Day Free Examination Offer
5. Fill in and Mail Today
6. Fill Out Now. Mail Coupon Today
7. Free 15-Day Trial Examination
8. Handy Mail-Order Coupon
9. Just Mail the Card Today
10. Mail Card at No Risk—Send No Money
11. Mail Coupon for "On Approval" Examination
12. Mail Coupon for 15-Day Free Trial
13. Mail Your Order Today
14. Order Now for Immediate Shipment
15. Order Today! Money Back if Not Fully Satisfied
16. Satisfaction Guaranteed or Your Money Back
17. Send No Money—Mail Coupon Now
18. Send Now for Free Examination
19. Special No-Risk Offer
20. Tear Off and Mail This Card—NOW!
21. Examine 15 Days at Our Risk—Rush Coupon
22. Mail No-Risk Coupon Today
23. Mail This Card for 15-Day Free Trial
24. Send No Money—Just This Card
25. Mail Free Trial Coupon Today

3:11   How to Maximize Results in Direct-Mail Copy: Ten Tips from Infomat*

1. Use short paragraphs and short words. Make your sentences and paragraphs flow. Ignore good grammar when you have a good reason. Don't be afraid to start paragraphs with *And, But, However,* etc. Make liberal use of bullets.

2. Experiment with different types of headlines. Then pick the ones you find most appealing, and boil them down to one, combining the best parts of each.

*From Infomat Inc., mailing list and direct response consultants, 25550 Hawthorne Blvd., Torrance, CA 90505.

3. Drop the warm-ups in the opening sentence of your promotional letter. Avoid starting letters with openings such as "As a college professor, you know how textbook costs are climbing every day . . ."

4. Offer all the reasons you can for doing business with your imprint. Work it into your copy as early as you can.

5. Sell benefits, not features. Readers buy advantages, not products. Stress buying points when you have sufficient points to stress, and save the features for the accompanying flier.

6. Give readers of your ad or letter news, or information of value that goes beyond what your product offers, where appropriate.

7. Utilize testimonials or review excerpts. They help build credibility.

8. Include credit-card option and toll-free 800 number as part of your offer.

9. Promise satisfaction or money back, if payment is required with order in your offer. It's a critical factor in getting people to send in money for something they may not be sure of, or to someone they don't know.

10. Ask for action. Good copy that fails to ask for action is not likely to get any.

3:12   Before You Can Write Copy: What Format to Select

If your copy responsibilities also include selection of a promotion format, here are some useful guidelines to assist your selection of the right format for your planned promotion.

- For fastest response to a planned direct response promotion, do an individual or "solo" promotion piece for one book.

- If you can't afford a single book promotion and you have a number of related books, try a card deck. The loose-deck format gives very fast response—about 50% within four to five weeks after you mail.

- If time is not important, try a catalog. This format will produce responses over a much longer period, has pass-along readership, and gives a higher-quality response—probably because you can include more descriptive copy than you would put on a postcard in a deck.

- If you're going to an audience that is familiar with your imprint and you want a quality response, try a self-mailer.* You can make it as large or small as you want and are unhampered by copy limitations. You'll get the bulk of your responses within 12 weeks from your mail date.

*This presumes no payment is required with order. If you require payment or a formal purchase order on company stationery, or written request on institutional stationery, your mailing format will have to be one that will permit enclosure of a business reply envelope.

**3:13   When Project Involves Inside and Freelance
Writers: Uniformity Guidelines**

A leading publisher of professional and reference books regularly uses
a distinctive mailing format for many of its offerings—a 6″ × 9″ white
booklet envelope, with effective teaser copy on the mailing face and
containing individual fliers for various related titles.

Each flier is printed on a 7″ × 10″ sheet, folded in half to 5″ × 7″.
Because copy presentation is done both in-house and by outside freelancers, copywriters are encouraged to follow a style sheet which helps
maintain uniformity of presentation. The copy guidelines on this style
sheet follow:

If:	Emphasize:
—the book has selling points that you can best put across by highlighting with brief, bulleted copy; or the book includes physical components of special interest (number of entries, illustrations, tables, special material)	features
—the subheads in the contents are truly descriptive, and clarify the scope and depth of the book; the product is technical; organization of material is a feature of the book	contents (full)
—you have a good quote, a particularly impressive author, a single outstanding feature, something special to say about a new edition	a box
—the project lends itself to a really benefit-oriented or catchy headline, use one, giving it strength (not length) and space	headline
—you've got a lot to say about the product and want to break up large copy blocks for readability; strong benefits can be lifted from the body copy for better impact; "features" are not appropriate and you want to create visual interest (also consider bulleted body copy)	subheads
—a boldface word or two in each feature, for example—or main heads in a table of contents—will make the piece easier to skim and more persuasive	boldface highlights
—in addition to a photo of the book or its jacket, an illustration from the text would increase selling (not just graphic) impact (and always add a caption, e.g., "one of 700 precise diagrams that explain every step of the xyz process")	illustrations
—the book jacket is dull or difficult to photograph effectively; a spread (with caption) can illustrate a special feature of the book, such as number of illustrations, attractive organization, massive coverage	photo of an open spread

If:	Emphasize:
—the author's credentials are particularly significant in the field; accomplishments are likely to convince potential buyer of need for this book (if credentials are not particularly impressive, omit or abbreviate author blurb)	authors, editors
—book is part of a distinguished series, the outgrowth of a special research program, a revision or new edition of a standard in its field, etc.	background information

3:14 Copy Approach for a Letter Promotion

1. Your copywriting approach should be personal (as opposed to the impersonal approach you would use for space ad copy).

2. Picture yourself as a salesman working with the printed word. You are making a sales presentation in written form. Visualize yourself as being in an eyeball-to-eyeball confrontation with your intended customer.

3. As a worker with words, you should keep your dictionary, thesaurus, and dictionary of synonyms close at hand and use them often. Do not be afraid to experiment with new words and phrases, even though more often than not you will be toning down your letter copy, rather than embellishing it.

4. Avoid touching too many bases in your letter. The ideal is to present and stick to one theme, even if it is only to draw attention to a wide selection of books you are offering in the same mail package.

5. Keep your copy honest, factual, free of superlatives, believable.

6. Avoid criticism of any competitive work, even if the work you are promoting has a strong competitor in the same subject area. (You can usually get around this by featuring those strong points in the published work you are promoting that are weak or are lacking in the competitive work.)

3:15 Eight Text Tips That Make Mail Promotions More Readable

1. Keep lines short. Because most people read words in clusters, a short line is easier for the eye to pick up than a long one. Eye-camera studies have shown that text is more readable if the columns are the width of 40 characters or less.

2. Keep margins ragged right. Text looks less formal and more inviting when set ragged right rather than flush right, although studies indicate no difference in readability.

3. Use a type face with serifs. Sans-serif typefaces are more difficult to read and make it easier for the eye to skip lines in text. (For headlines, however, a sans-serif face can be used, as there is little likelihood that the eye will jump to another line.)

4. Use lowercase type for headlines. Headlines set in lowercase can be read faster than headlines set in all capitals or initial capital letters.

5. Leave widows in. "Widows open up copy, let in a little more space," says one expert. "The opinion that you must avoid widows is an old wives' tale."

6. Conserve on color. Sometimes a touch of color, perhaps just in a headline, or an occasional spot here and there is more effective than a heavy mix of colors.

7. Favor darker-color ink for text. Where different colors of ink are used, use the darkest color for text and other reading matter, such as the contents.

8. Avoid reverse type. Reverse type is much more difficult to read than black on white for text matter, but can be used for a short blurb, feature, or headline.

3:16 University Press Direct Mail: One Marketing Manager's View

The following comments were made by Harlan Kessel, Marketing Manager, University of California Press, at the Third Annual Meeting of the Society for Scholarly Publishing, San Francisco, June 1981.

> There are a few points I'd like to make about direct mail. First, there should always be a special offer . . . There really isn't a mailing piece produced at [our] Press that doesn't contain some kind of special offer . . . almost always extra discount. It's rare that we don't offer less than 20% discount on a mailing piece . . . Second, we strive for more "introductory" or special post-publication prices, the kind of price that says on the flap "$19.95 until (specific date); $25.00 thereafter." This device provides an extra six months for special promotion and advertising. Third, we dropped the practice of free postage [including both] postage paid business reply envelopes [and] free postage for cash in advance orders.

3:17 A Seasoned Professional Offers Copy Approach for Almost Every Situation

This entry was written by Norton C. (Ned) Baron, a former Prentice-Hall executive responsible for trade, business, professional, and technical promotions. He has also taught retail advertising copy and sales promotion at New York University.

Baron, in this entry, offers a copy approach useful in the writing of copy in almost every situation. He calls it the "jujitsu" approach. He says that any audience, even one as discrete as "executives in a company's financial management," includes a variety of needs and frames of reference, and the "jujitsu" approach, if properly executed, can help address each segment effectively. Baron's contribution follows:

> Copywriters often are up against writing situations in which two or more audiences are being addressed. For example, a book on accounting systems might be offered to accountants, who will use the book in serving clients, and to executives in a company's financial management.
>
> Because of the emphasis in copywriting guidelines on the use of *you* and *your*, most copywriters will write ". . . will magnify your company's profits." Some, if they are informed that part of the mailing will be going to accountants, will add a sentence about fee profits for the accounting office, or will want to do a separate letter for the CPA.
>
> Simply by changing "*your* company" to "*the* company" this problem can be resolved. Here's why: Each recipient—the company executive, or the public accountant—understands which company is meant. Because each brings to his reading of the letter his own frame of reference, the company man knows you are referring to his company, and the public accountant knows "the" company is the *client*.
>
> This is the simplest illustration of what I call "jujitsu" (in which the strength and weight of an opponent are used against him). And it is this reliance on the "strength and weight" of the prospective buyer—his "knowledge and experience"—which can be employed to lead to a sale.
>
> This also eliminates the possibility of "patronization." It is patronizing to tell an experienced accountant he can increase his fees by ordering your book. It is not patronizing to say that the book will show him how to do a better job for his clients, or will help him take on new clients.
>
> He will make the "more fees" conclusion himself . . . and the more tellingly because it comes from his "strength."
>
> This approach, essentially, to leave unsaid what the reader can most readily supply for himself, can be explored in many channels. One productive result is that, by encouraging the copywriter to look for "jujitsu" attacks, he is forced to think very carefully about the *semantics*—how the reader understands the copy, given the reader's frame of reference. This can only lead to better, more profitable, selling copy.
>
> Essentially, I believe that guidelines to better copywriting for book promotion should not be concerned so much with the various fields into which book publishing may be divided by one publisher or another, but more with general applications.
>
> The differences in one kind of promotion to another has much more to do with strategy—such as the selection of lists or list segments, timing, pricing, terms, and so much more.

3:18   Routing Instructions as Part of a Promotion: Guidelines for Writing

Inevitably, some of your mailings will be of interest to more than one individual or department within the organization or institution to which your mailing piece is addressed. For this reason, it is often useful to include routing instructions on the face of your mailing piece, on the cover of a catalog, or on the faces of individual enclosures in a mailing package.

BASIC ROUTING INSTRUCTION

The most basic type of instruction is to add the words "Route to:" along with several blank lines, thus:

Route to: _____

_____

_____

TARGETED ROUTING INSTRUCTION

Where your mailing is targeted to two or more job titles or functions, you should specify the desired targets rather than leave blank lines, thus:

Please route to: ☐ Advertising Manager

☐ Copy Chief

☐ Publicity Manager

LIBRARY ROUTING SLIP

Another wide application is the inclusion of a library routing card or slip with mailings to academics or individuals who can influence library approaches. Copy on such routing devices may be for a specific title, in which case complete information on the title is included on the routing slip, or an open recommendation accompanying a multiple-book offering, thus:

TO THE LIBRARIAN

I recommend that the following books be ordered for the library

Author _____ Title _____

Author _____ Title _____

Author _____ Title _____

From _____ Dept/Title _____

THIRD TYPE OF ROUTING DEVICE

In addition to the basic or targeted routing instruction on the face of the mailing piece or on the face of individual enclosures in the mailing package, and the separate library routing slip, there is a third type of routing device which has been used by some book marketers with great effectiveness. Plan to have a second, duplicate order form or card in the mailing package and include at the top of the duplicate order form this instruction:

Please pass along to a friend or colleague

3:19   Copy Guidelines for Card-Deck Promotions

The key to successful copy for card-deck book offerings is that your copy must be appropriate for the audience, promise substantial benefits or help to the recipients in their occupations, be reasonably priced for what it appears to offer, and be available for a suitable free-examination period without obligation to the recipient.

If your copy oversells, returns will be extremely high. If the copy makes an offering to an individual when normally the product is purchased by the library, it will be difficult to trace response if, indeed, any is forthcoming.

Because response-per-card is small in a typical deck of 50 or more cards, you should have an offering priced at least $25 or higher so that it will be possible to attain a break-even point even when response is small.

High-priced reference works that require a lot of explanation and loose-leaf publications with various types of ordering options do not lend themselves easily to the very restricted space of a postcard. You can overcome this space limitation only if you opt for a double card folded in two, or a triple card folded into thirds. However, this can be very costly.

One way around the severe copy limitation is to have copy on both sides of the card and rely on the recipient to provide return postage and mailing envelope. Be sure your offer is a very good one or response can be very small with this type of reply bottleneck.

You can overcome the modest copy restrictions only when you have a book so well known in the field that the title is its own advertisement. McGraw-Hill has done this by listing only titles of well-known handbooks mailed to professionals in the field of the handbooks.

Wiley has listed as many as 28 book titles on the single card in a card deck. However, the deck offering was made to subscribers of a journal and the titles listed on the card in the deck represented titles advertised and described in the previous.issue of the journal. The headline on the 28-title card stated "Free 15-Day Examination of these Wiley-Interscience Books Advertised in Sept. Issue of *Journal of Chemical Education*."

**3:20   Card-Deck Copy Devices Used
to Encourage Multiple Orders**

Two different approaches have been used with great effect to entice multiple orders with a card-deck book offering. In a loose-deck mailing by Amacom book division of the American Management Association, a separate folder was enclosed titled "Multiple-Order Form," which listed all the books in the card deck. At the bottom of the multiple order form was this copy:

Affix peel-off label from envelope in this space.

The card-deck recipient then had the option of mailing back a card from the deck or checking off the title on the order form, affixing his or her name label, and mailing back. A postpaid return envelope was also enclosed.

Aspen Systems, in one of its loose decks, tried a different multiple-order approach. At the top of each of the 79 cards in its deck was a boldface number and adjacent to the number the copy "Available for FREE Examination." An extra card in the deck, under a heading "Time Saver Reply Card," provided a convenient way of ordering more than one publication (Figure 4).

3:21   Catalogs: Various Types and Their Uses

Other than the general catalog, offered by most publishers in various formats, there are various types of specialized catalogs with special requirements.

SUBJECT CATALOG

The subject catalog is a useful reference that enables the scholar, instructor, or professional to find available titles under subject headings that cater to his or her special interests.

MAIL-ORDER CATALOGS

These periodic publisher offerings deal with forthcoming titles and best-selling books from the backlist in special areas. Most mail-order catalogs have self-covers and can be mailed without envelopes. In some instances, the back cover serves as the removable order form. Mail-order catalogs work best when they include effective headlines and excerpts from reviews from well-known publications in the field, as well as a postpaid order form insert.

SEASONAL CATALOGS

These usually provide detailed listings of titles for the forthcoming

Time Saver Reply Card

Each publication has been assigned a number which is placed at the top of each card. Just **circle** the corresponding number(s) of the publication(s) you wish to receive on 30-day approval.

1	9b	18	27	36	45	54	63	71
2	10	19	28	37	46	55	64a	72
3	11	20	29	38	47	56	64b	73
4	12	21	30	39	48	57	65	74
5	13	22	31	40	49	58	66	75
6	14	23	32	41	50	59	67	76
7	15	24	33	42	51	60	68	77
8	16	25	34	43	52	61	69	78
9a	17	26	35	44	53	62	70	79

Send Today for 30-Day FREE Examination

☐ Please send _____ copy(ies) of this book immediately. After using it for 30 days, I will either honor your invoice, plus postage and handling, or return the book and invoice with no further obligation.

☐ Bill me ☐ Bill institution P.O. Number _____
☐ Payment enclosed. Maryland orders add 5% sales tax.
  (Aspen pays postage and handling)

Affiliation _____

Name _____

Title _____

Address _____

City _____

State _____ Zip _____

3   BSIA

FIGURE 4 This extra business reply card included in an Aspen Systems card deck was for use in ordering examination copies of more than one publication. It is keyed to numbers on the 79 cards for individual books. Note that two volumes which were available in both cloth and paper editions had "a" and "b" designations for the different bindings.

season (usually a six-month period), and more often than not they coincide with a spring or fall list.

SPECIALIZED CATALOGS

In some major houses, specialized catalogs are issued for different outlets. A trade catalog, for example, is issued in the spring and fall expressly for bookstores and wholesalers. Some publishers issue library catalogs, whereas others produce catalogs for accounts in non-traditional outlets, for industrial training purposes, or for educational purposes.

3:22   Uses of Letter Introduction in Publisher Catalogs: Examples

Most publisher catalogs open with a table of contents and ordering information. However, a number of publishers favor a letter-type introductory message at the front of the catalog, usually with a salutation and signed by a titled individual. Here are examples of four such letter approaches from different publishing establishments.

PRENTICE-HALL SEASONAL BUSINESS CATALOG

Letter opening on inside front cover is headed by caption line "A MESSAGE FROM THE PRESIDENT ..." under a large photo of the divisional president. Letter opens "Dear Customer:" and bears signature, name, and title of divisional president.

LEARNED INFORMATION, INC., CATALOG

Letter opening on inside front cover is in lower half in a hairline rule box. It opens with "Dear Colleague:" and describes publications in the catalog. It also invites the reader to suggest new publications and gives a phone number. It bears signature, name, and title of the company president.

SPRINGER-VERLAG MATH SEASONAL CATALOG

Letter on first right-hand page describes content under the heading "New Math Introduction." It has no salutation. It invites suggestions, comments, or proposals, and bears signature, name, and title of Mathematics Editor. Contents are on the three pages following.

THE FREE PRESS BUSINESS-ECONOMICS CATALOG

Letter on inside front cover opens with salutation "Dear Executive:" and describes the imprint's business-economics program (Figure 5). It highlights certain titles and programs covered by the catalog and closes with signature, name, and title of Senior Editor. No contents are listed. However, subject headings appear over certain pages in the catalog.

3:23   Direct-Mail Announcement for a Directory Publication: Copy Essentials

- Features
- Important new information not previously included
- Change in size from previous edition
- Expanded fields of coverage, if any, in new edition
- Number of new entries
- Number of changes in preexisting entries

Dear Executive:

You probably know that human resources development is a booming micro-economy within business these days. But do you know how big? A recent study estimated that American companies spent over $1 billion on training and development in 1982.*

The size of this commitment may be startling, but it makes perfect sense. Most corporations realized long ago that the single most critical factor in their success was the caliber of their personnel. Knowledge and expertise can be taught in almost every area, and improving managerial performance is of direct benefit to the individual and the company alike.

The Free Press has for many years been a leader in the publication of books designed to help business executives develop. Our books on planning (from strategy to execution), management, personnel, communication, and the new technologies have helped thousands of information-hungry executives enrich their careers.

This year, more than ever, The Free Press offers a broad-based list of authoritative books that will help executives in every area of business. In the field of **strategy,** Michael E. Porter offers real-world applications of his renowned competitive strategy, first conceived in a MBA course at the Harvard Business School *(Cases in Competitive Strategy).* In **executive development,** John P. Kotter, also of H.B.S., focuses on the management styles of 15 of the nation's most accomplished executives, zeroing in on the specific skills managers need to make it to the top *(The General Managers).* And in **manufacturing and production,** Richard Schonberger shows how to apply Japanese purchasing, inventory, assembly-line, and quality control techniques at the actual operating level of U.S. manufacturing plants *(Japanese Manufacturing Techniques).*

Then there are the longtime Free Press success stories: Bernard Bass's revised and expanded edition of *Stogdill's Handbook of Leadership,* Richard Sloma's *No-Nonsense Management,* and *Competitive Strategy* by Michael Porter (now in its twelfth printing).

This year also marks the inception of Macmillan's own supervisor training program, initiated with the cooperation of the National Management Association. This 10-part videotape-and-text seminar allows first-line supervisors to participate in up to 140 hours of interactive audiovisual training. The program is designed to teach effectiveness in management, communication, interpersonal relationships, counseling, leadership development, and other supervisory skills.

In sum, these pages contain a multimedia curriculum on the necessary skills and information to get ahead on the job. Please look through them carefully. We're sure you'll see why hundreds of companies are already using our materials in their training seminars and workshops.

Sincerely,

Robert Wallace
Senior Editor

*Based on a survey of *Training and Development Journal* readers.

FIGURE 5 Letter in catalog of The Free Press, a Division of Macmillan Inc., is signed by senior editor. Use of typewriter typeface and a simulated letterhead would have helped.

- New chapters/sections added, if any
- Contents current as of (give most recent date)
- Excerpts from reviews of previous edition(s)
- Awards or special honors won by prior editions
- Advantages over competitive works
- Compelling benefit-oriented headline
- Order form
- Sharp illustration of directory to support copy
- One or more sample pages or entries
- Scope: areas covered
- Types of indexes, if more than one or specialized

**3:24   New Edition of Encyclopedic Reference:
Announcement Copy Elements**

- Feature major benefit of new work on announcement cover or envelope.
- Include good reviews of previous editions.
- State clearly whether work is updated version of previous edition, or an entirely new work.
- State what percentage is new if a revision of a previous edition.
- Give some indication of time lapse since publication of previous edition.
- Stress changes in the field since the previous edition, especially if it is the first new edition in many years.
- Indicate whether editors/authors of new edition are same as for the former edition. If they are not, give the credentials of new editors/authors.
- Indicate whether new edition is in same style/format as previous edition. If it is not, spell out format and major changes.
- Indicate whether bibliography has been updated and what percentage consists of new entries.
- Mention any awards or approvals or recommendations by library or professional groups won by previous edition(s).
- List new features that are included in this edition.
- State what exclusive features this edition contains.
- If new edition is larger as well as revised, state how much larger it is than the previous edition.
- Indicate whether new edition replaces former edition or augments it.
- If new edition augments earlier edition, indicate whether earlier

edition will continue to be made available, and, if so, can it be obtained at a combination price with new edition.

- If new edition is a multi-volume work, indicate whether it will be published at one time or in separate volumes. If separate volumes, at what intervals.

- If published at one time and very high priced, can provisions be made for extended time payments?

- If published serially, is rate of publication and expected completion date indicated?

- If published over an extended period, is there a special subscription price for a commitment to purchase the entire work?

**3:25   Writing an Effective Sales Letter:
Tips on Assembly and Content**

1. A letter is easier to read if the paragraphs are of different lengths rather than all the same. A one-line paragraph is effective in adding emphasis to a preceding one that is much longer. Six lines is a good *maximum* length.

2. Make certain that the thoughts expressed in the copy have continuity from paragraph to paragraph. This will help to ensure holding the reader's interest from start to finish.

3. Letter copy written in a conversational tone is much more readable (and believable) than formal or carefully structured copy, which may have a stilted quality.

4. If your aim is a conversational type of letter, have it read to you and let your own ears be the judge of whether you have hit the mark. If it doesn't sound right to you, go back to the typewriter and try again.

5. Simple sentences are easiest to read. They will be comprehended more quickly than compound and complex sentences.

6. Simple words go with simple sentences. One direct-mail expert estimates that a good letter should have 70 to 80 one-syllable words for every 100 words in a letter. This may prove difficult in promoting technical and scholarly books and journals, but it is worth the effort.

7. Be sure your letter copy follows a logical sequence, reads in a conversational way, maintains a "you" attitude throughout, and makes no exaggerated or unbelievable claims.

8. Start with a short opening sentence that captures the reader's attention at once.

9. If your letter carries over to more than one page, break in mid-sentence or, preferably, in mid-word to maintain reader's interest from one page to the next.

10. Leave right-hand margins of a letter unjustified (ragged edge) to give the letter a more personal look.

The following points apply only if the letter is not supported by other advertising:

11. If the book or journal has a lot of important features, describe them in a column with asterisks, bullets, or numbers, rather than burying them in paragraph-style copy.

12. Underline key benefits or important features so they will be more readily noticed and remembered.

13. If your letter runs longer than one page and the budget does not permit a two-page letter, run second-page copy on the back of the first page, or use the back for the order form.

14. If you do not use a business reply card or envelope, a simple order form built into the lower portion of the letter will often pull just as good a response as a separate order enclosure.

3:26   Highlights of a Successful Letter: Checklist

A successful letter

—has the personal look of an individual-to-individual communication.

—has something newsworthy or timely to say and captures interest up front.

—is printed in a typewriter face so it looks like a letter.

—avoids flush left and right paragraphs—has some indented paragraphs—has underlines under some of the important points—has some of the features of the offer starred or bulleted.

—has paragraphs which are short, easy on the eye, and interesting.

—has a personal closing signed by someone if it opens with a salutation.

—stresses *you* rather than *we* or *I*.

—gives sufficient information so that the reader can make a judgment to take the action the letter requests.

—states the offer in a clear and understandable manner.

—asks for the action you desire from the reader: return the enclosed card, request free prospectus, enter a subscription.

—makes it easy for the reader to take the action you request: It mentions an enclosed BRC or BRE (or both), invites a toll-free 800 call, offers credit-card payment option, etc.

3:27   Use of Underlining in a Letter: Guidelines

- Use underlines to call attention to important words, phrases, or sentences.

- Use underlines as a substitute for what would be set in italic or boldface type.

- Use underlines to synthesize the letter's message for those who scan rather than read.

- Use underlines sparingly. Too much underlining can detract from a letter's readability.

3:28   Questions to Ask Yourself When Writing Promotion Copy

"These are questions I always ask myself or anyone else who writes for me," says Julie Zuckman, for many years journals promotion manager at MIT Press and currently circulation manager for *Technology Review*. "They are general points to keep in mind no matter what kind of promotion copy one is writing."

1. Have you spelled the author's name(s) and the title of the book correctly?

2. Did you double-check the spelling of proper nouns if you got them from someone else?

3. Are the headlines short and to-the-point, or cutesy/clever?

4. Did you include the Table of Contents? Would it have been a better idea to include it rather than write a boring paragraph?

5. Are the essential points bulleted or otherwise made obvious?

6. Did you avoid using the following tired words: important, interesting, relevant, hands-on, authoritative, up-to-date.

7. Did you avoid the passive voice:
   NOT   Included in each chapter is a problem set.
   BUT   Each chapter includes a problem set.

8. Did you let the copy sit around for at least a few hours before editing and submitting it for review?

9. Did you think about why someone would want to use this book rather than what *you* thought was interesting about it?

10. Did you triple-check the price and ISBN/ISSN?

11. Did you double-check the author's professional or academic affiliation in case he moved since he filled out the questionnaire?

12. Did you use quotes whenever possible to describe the book or journal's best features?

13. Did you remember to include the name of your company somewhere in the piece?

**3:29   Pitfalls of Direct Mail Letter Copy:
How One B&P Publisher Coped**

Over 30 years ago, when I was a student of advertising, I was taught that the basic ingredients of a successful advertisement were A∗I∗D∗A, that if your presentation carried these four elements your ad couldn't miss. The elements were:

Attention (your advertisement must attract attention)

Interest (your advertisement must arouse interest)

Desire (your advertisement must create desire)

Action (your advertisement must urge some action)

Generations of advertising copywriters have been raised on this infallible "rule" of good advertising. Yet, this same "rule" of good advertising, which the copy "pros" rely on, in the case of business and professional book advertising often can help "unsell" the prospective buyer.

How can this happen? It's easy! The copywriter, no matter how well trained as a *copywriter,* is not an expert in the field of the advertised work and thus, in his or her zeal to add "sell" to the copy, may easily overstate, make false claims or otherwise mislead, or make unprofessional statements that will turn off the sale.

Add to this the possibility that the copywriter doesn't have command of the jargon of the subject area the book covers, and the writer of the direct-mail letter can often tell the recipient by the wording of the copy that he or she (and indirectly the author of the book) does not know the subject.   .

HOW ONE B&P PUBLISHER COPED

One major publisher of business and professional books sold mainly through direct-mail sales letters avoided the errors of misstating the author's words by making the main thrust of their sales letters a series of "for instances."

These "for instances" were obtained by asking the author for a short statement giving three or four problems which might very likely be in the minds of the recipients of the sales letter at the moment they received it, and what the book had to offer to solve each problem.

Since this was written by the author in the language of the field, with the nuances that the author would employ if face to face with the prospective book buyer, there was no way the copy could "unsell" or turn off the prospective buyer of the book.

Said the longtime promotional head of this organization, "If we had asked our authors to write the sales letter, they would have balked. But many, in response to our simple request for three or four 'for instances,' were actually writing the most vital, the most credible substance of our letters. All we had to do was refrain from completing the effort with phony salutations, patronizing openings, etc."

3:30   Features and Benefits in Copywriting: Difference Between

I consulted with a number of seasoned professionals who have hired and trained copywriters. They all cited a common failing among publishing copywriters: a difficulty in determining what is a feature and what is a benefit. "And," adds one, "they fail to make it clear how the feature yields up the benefit."

"In writing a sales letter," says another, "the copywriter should develop a list of benefits to be claimed in the copy, and develop a headline (or the opening sentence in a letter which has no headline) in which the best benefit should be featured. He should then let the others fall in place later on."

Says another copy pro, "It takes some drilling and some thinking to determine what is a feature and what is a benefit, and often the copy ends up feature-laden, with practically no benefits presented."

Following are examples from book and journal promotions in which stated features have been accompanied by benefits yielded:

Product	Feature	Benefit
Journal	A wide range of refereed articles geared to the interests and concerns of this exploding field	Enables you to keep up to date on the best contemporary research and analysis being done in the field.
Business Periodical	Covers latest developments in (seven business disciplines)	Use the knowledge learned from our pages to solve problems, maximize opportunities, skirt dangers, outperform competition, and above all, *to get ahead*.
Handbook	New, revised, updated, and expanded edition	Gives you instant access to all the information you'll need to meet the professional challenges of the 80's.
College Textbook	New chapters on leasing, capital management, financing, current assets, and international finance	Specifically designed to help your advanced students understand the logic underlying financial management.
Professional Reference	Eight hundred information-packed pages	Gives you instant access to the precise information you want.

3:31   Tips on Letter Copy for a Consumer How-To Book

These copy insights for consumer-oriented books are offered by a professional whose direct-mail book offerings sell in the tens of thousands. The informal remarks were made for a direct-mail workshop conducted by the author of this book at the NYU Summer Publishing Institute in New York in 1983.

> When you're selling a book by mail to a consumer, you have to spell out what's in it for the consumer. . . . Get to the "meat" and spell out the benefits. . . . Get the reader's attention immediately and hold it all the way through page 1 so that he will turn to page 2. . . . And talk convincingly in your copy all the way until you wrap up your offer on page 4. . . . Go heavy on the book's benefits; your letter should be a heavy laundry list that mixes benefits to the reader with the ingredients in the book. . . . Give specific examples of the benefits—tell what's in the book and how it works.

3:32   Personalizing Sales Letters: Guidelines

WHEN TO USE

If your market for a particular book or journal is limited, and you must convert a substantial number of the available prospects, a personal or personalized sales letter is worth considering.

BENEFITS

A personal letter generally attracts greater attention from prospects than standard circular material. The recipient's name appears on the envelope, on the letter, and in the salutation. It says, "We have a special message for you." Once you have captured the recipient's attention, however, you must retain it. This you do by presenting a strong benefit in the first paragraph of the letter, followed quickly by supporting evidence that your offering delivers on the stated benefit. It is important to bear in mind that, with a personal or personalized letter (unlike a usual sales letter or circular), once you let your prospect's interest wander, you're unlikely to get it back.

Personal or personalized letters are particularly effective when the recipient's need for the work or periodical is not immediately apparent. They would be less effective with a generalized major reference in a particular field, such as an encyclopedia. But they would be strong producers of sales for peripheral publications, covering specialized aspects of a major field that may not be in the prospect's main area of interest. They are also useful for certain college textbook promotions and to provide correspondence support for the field sales force (see 6:08).

3:33   Difference Between Personal and Personalized Letters

If you place the recipient's name and address and the salutation on a letter, you are using a *personal letter;* that is, it is addressed directly to a person.

If, in addition to putting recipient's name and address and the salutation in a letter, you also make reference to the recipient by name in the body of the letter, you are using a *personalized letter*. A personalized letter is considered more effective than a personal letter.

3:34 Types of Personalized Letters Used in Publishing Promotions

THE FILL-IN OR MATCH LETTER

In this format, the body of the letter is printed, and the address and salutation are typed in manually. The advantages of this type of personalized letter are that small quantities can be handled readily and mailed out quickly; the disadvantages are the possible unavailability of typing services and the high cost of hand work.

WORD PROCESSOR LETTERS

These are produced on machines that can be set up to produce either fill-in or fully typed letters. The less expensive is the fill-in process. Letters and envelopes are produced on continuous forms, or feeding mechanisms are added to the basic word-processor equipment allowing the insertion of individual, personalized sheets and envelopes.

COMPUTERIZED LETTERS

Until recently, the personalized quality of computerized letters was not high. Accordingly, they found their major application with such publishing organizations as Readers Digest, which used the name of the prospect as an attention-getting device on a four-color letter-circular combination, but made no attempt to simulate personal letters. In professional-book publishing, there is strong evidence that personalized letters must look like a personal message to be effective. Recently, however, there have been major advances in the field, so that computers can produce high-quality, personal-looking letters.

3:35 Special-Offer Mailing Has Lessons for Copywriters: A Case Study

The prospectus for a multi-volume business reference, received in the mail, lacked one important ingredient. Nowhere in the elaborate 16-page 8½″ × 11″ booklet was there any mention of price.

A search of the 9″ × 12″ mailing envelope disclosed an order card nestled in the bottom. On the card, there was copy for a special pre-publication offer with a $50 saving.

When queried, the publisher said price had been intentionally omitted because the prospectus was printed in a large quantity for both pre- and post-publication use. Copy about pricing and the special offer had been omitted for reasons of printing economy.

Thus the special offer appeared only on the business reply card under the headline "Special Prepublication Offer," along with copy about the saving and the price.

This promotion offers several important lessons to copywriters and promotion planners:

1. Whenever you plan a special offer, be sure there is special teaser copy on the envelope that highlights the nature of the offer so that recipients know about it up front and have an incentive to look for it inside the envelope, in whatever form it may be.

2. The special offer, if independent from the main prospectus or flyer, should at least be equal in size to the accompanying promotional piece so it will be seen and removed at the same time.

3. If the response card or reply envelope for the special offer is to be loose in the envelope, have it nested into the main enclosure.

3:36 Direct-Mail Tips for Promotion Copy to Overseas Markets

- No book offers are made on free trial examination basis.
- All book sales are non-returnable.
- Specify a flat shipping charge in ad copy and include a separate one for air shipment and a separate one for surface shipment.
- In lieu of add-on shipping charge for overseas shipments, show a marked-up U.S. price for international shipments shipped surface mail (add-on charge only when air shipment is requested).
- Avoid American slang in your copy.
- Avoid use of new buzz words from specialized fields in your copy.
- Avoid colloquialisms.
- Avoid abbreviations.
- Avoid symbols and slashmarks; they tend to be misunderstood. For example: Instead of $25/Volume, say $25 per Volume.

3:37 Attempt to Hype Professional Group Fails: Lessons for Copywriter

The acronym for the Art Libraries Society of North America is *ARLIS*. Its members are career professionals in the field who know the subject well and also the names of all the important individuals within it.

A letter promotion to this group offered a newsletter that would provide an exclusive and unique source of information about art. The letter to the ARLIS membership opened with "Dear ARLIC member:" It did not mention the author's credentials.

Said an ARLIS member who received the offering, "It immediately turned me off; they couldn't even get the organization acronym straight." He had discarded the piece without reading it and stated he doubted whether any other ARLIS member had reacted differently.

This experience offers several valuable lessons to the copywriter:

1. When you address a professional group, be sure the group's name or acronym is spelled correctly.

2. When you write copy to a group of professionals in a field in which they are known to excel, avoid hyperbole and superlatives; it turns them off.

3. When selling information to professionals about their own field, identify the author as someone known or affiliated with that field, or with solid credentials that will be recognized and accepted by those within that field.

3:38 A "Secret" Ingredient That Can Give Your Copy Lasting Appeal

Over the years, successful copywriters have learned to utilize a "secret" that can make copy stand out and have lasting usefulness. The "secret": Include something that the recipient will want to retain for its perceived value or usefulness.

A promotion writer at McGraw-Hill found that a cookbook offering sold well when a certain recipe was included with the copy. When the recipe was replaced, the offer failed to score—until the recipe was reinserted.

A writer at Macmillan found that including a chart of historic dates (taken from a text) when included in a college promotion converted his mailing piece into a poster that was displayed and ultimately led to adoptions.

In the book club field, Leonard Malleck, director of Times Mirror Book Clubs, has long adhered to this same philosophy in the promotions for his specialized book clubs.

The idea is to make the special-interest book club mailing piece a valuable and useful document that will contribute to the reader's interest in the subject even if they don't buy the book offered. This copy approach, Malleck says, establishes a rapport with the book club customer that ultimately pays off in sales.

Other successful copy ingredients for the specialized book club mailing, according to Malleck: longer copy rather than shorter; lots of detail—these are activities the readers love; lots of illustrations; and the promise of the "real thing" when the readers of the promotion piece get the book.

3:39 **Has Look of Prepub Offer, but Small Type Says "No":**
Case Study

The early 1984 solo book promotion for a professional manual was a
four-page letter (11″ × 17″, folded to 5½″ × 8½″) under a simulated
letterhead, topped by a strong headline and a clear 3½″ high book
illustration. The headline led off with "—an up-to-date, comprehensive
guide. . . ."

It had all the earmarks of a prepublication offer—such phrases as
"Limited-time-offer—Save $17.50," and "Until March 31, 1984, you
can order . . . [at a] savings of $17.50 from the list price. . . ."

But it wasn't a prepublication offer, as I discovered in reading the
three lines of seven-point type under the illustration giving bibliographic details. One of the notations, in lightface type, was the publication date: 1980. It was a four-year-old book.

Review quotes in the letter from respected sources suggest the work
was an excellent one. However, the "up-to-date" wording in the headline, together with the limited-time saving to a certain cutoff date,
initially misled this reader into thinking this was a new book. I recommend avoidance of any copy approach that could be misinterpreted
as this one was.

4

Copy Approaches Used in Promotions by Various Presses

4:01   **Examine Output: Easiest Way to Tap Skills
of Leading Practitioners**

Where are all the good teachers of book promotion? As a general rule,
you'll not find them in university lecture halls, or even on seminar
panels. Chances are, they're hard at work in their offices, shirt sleeves
rolled up, busy applying their skills and their knowledge to the day-
to-day work that is going out into the mails.

How can one tap into their skills? Merely by examining the work
they turn out. If you want to improve your copy skills, you must first
learn what good copy is, then learn to recognize it, and lastly watch
how others are doing it and learn from their good (or bad) examples.

In the chapter following, we examine a number of specialized copy
approaches for the lessons they offer. Virtually all of the copy approaches reviewed reflect some aspect of printed promotion that
copywriters are, can be, or will be at some time concerned with. By
matching these approaches with your own, you have some standard
for evaluating your own performance, or for revising your approach
if you think the sample says it better than you do.

Bear in mind that the big successful presses employ high-caliber
talent, and the copy approaches of their promotions demonstrate this
talent in action.

You'll find here copy approaches for different types of order forms, for a highly regarded loose-leaf publisher's anniversary sale, for a university press sale, for an encyclopedia prospectus, for a prominent publisher of books on business and investment, for the several scientific publishers, and for a publisher who sells books by substituting teaser headlines for book titles on his catalog cover. Each example offers valuable lessons. By reading these examples, you will not only be learning, but also acquiring the practice of evaluating the competition's literature.

**4:02   Copy Approach for Multi-Purpose Order Form:
W. H. Freeman and Co.**

The centerfold of a W. H. Freeman and Co. annual mathematics catalog had in the centerfold a two-page bind-in on postcard stock. The 8½″ × 11″ page consisted of three removable perforated reply cards, each with a different approach.

CARD NO. 1

The first (postpaid) card addressed itself to the instructor with this heading, "For Possible Class Adoption." It contained this copy: "I am teaching the course described below, for which this text may be adopted. Please send me a complimentary copy."

CARD NO. 2

The second (postpaid) offered "for examination and possible class adoption, complimentary copies of (low-priced) Scientific American Offprints."

CARD NO. 3

The third (not addressed or postpaid on reverse side) was headed "For My Personal Use" and indicated that if the books purchased were adopted for classroom use the publisher would cancel or refund the charge. It offered a 15% discount and required payment with order. The reverse side of card No. 3 was blank, except for a single line of copy stating: "For Your Personal Library."

**4:03   Copy Approach for Multi-Audience Order Form:
MIT Press**

When writing order form copy for a catalog or promotion that will require different types of responses from different audiences, it is useful to design a multi-purpose form. A good example of such an all-purpose order form is the one used by MIT Press in its catalogs. The copy in the order form:

— states that orders from individuals must be accompanied by check, money order, or credit-card number.

— offers refund in full if the customer is not satisfied and returns the book within 10 days.

— requires that libraries and institutions using the order form attach a signed purchase order.

— specifies that textbook examination requests must be on departmental stationery and sent to a special department at MIT Press.

**4:04   Copy Theme for Anniversary Sale Offering:
Matthew Bender & Co.**

An appealing and successful inventory-reduction theme was used by Matthew Bender in 1982: it used the occasion of its 95th anniversary for a sale in which a wide range of much higher priced books were offered for a limited time, for $95 each.

The No. 10 outer mailing envelope bore this copy: "Help Us Celebrate Our Anniversary: Matthew Bender 95th." The promotion used two different envelopes—one for previous buyers and one for prospects.

The customer envelope bore this added copy over the address label: "Thanks for being our customer!—Look inside for a special money-saving offer."

The prospect envelope bore this added copy, angle-printed across the first third of the envelope: "What does $95 buy?—Plenty, if you act now. Look inside for details." The Bender return address was printed on the back flap of the envelope.

The inside package contained a four-page letter explaining the reason for the sale. The copy read: "We're celebrating our 95th anniversary with a special offer for you!" An accompanying four-page enclosure, same size and stock as the letter, listed 52 offerings normally priced at $120 to $170. Where the normal prices were listed, they were crossed out by simulated handwriting in red-ink overprint on black that stated "now $95."

A postpaid business reply card bore this head: "95th Anniversary Special Offer Order Card." The respondent was asked to circle the numbers corresponding to the numbered offerings.

A separate box on the order card asked the respondent to check off: "( ) I do not want Additional Upkeep Service." Another check box bore this copy: "( ) Save 10%. Full payment (plus applicable sales tax) is enclosed. Amount enclosed $ _____ ." The order card also bore an expiration date for the offer and a 30-day return privilege.

4:05 **Copy Approach Used in Sale Catalog:**
Columbia University Press*

The cover (Figure 6) of the 8¼″ × 11″ sale catalog features the name of the Press over two thirds of the two-color cover, a drop-out of PMS 252 (purple). In smaller size type as a banner across the lower third are three statements, purple on white:

1. 1983 Book Sale

2. Savings up to 90%

3. Free Bonus Books worth up to $40.00

A black surprint line over purple in lower right-hand corner has sale cutoff date: SALE ENDS JULY 31, 1983 (catalog mailed 1 April 1983).

The inside pages are in three-column format under running subject page heads. Individual columns also have their own subject headings in boldface. Book cover illustrations, each about 2 inches high, are scattered throughout the catalog, one or two per page. The largest percentage of copy descriptions are review excerpts in quotes with sources in italics. Many entries are listings only with no descriptive copy.† A separate price line is given for each entry in catalog, list price at left in lightface type and sale price at right in boldface. All entries and headings are printed in black ink.

The sheet comprising the back cover is the order form (Figure 7). Entries are numbered in parentheses to left of title on the inside pages of the catalog, and ordering is by entry number. Over 500 titles in the sale catalog are listed on the order form in six vertically ruled columns. Each column has a write-in space for quantity, catalog number, and sale price for each entry, all in 7-point type.

Ten numbered "Terms and Conditions" appear on the back cover order form under the instruction: *Read and Complete this Form.* Among the terms: minimum order of $10 and return of entire back cover order form. Individuals must remit check, money order, or indicate payment by bank credit card. A $2.00 postage and handling charge is printed on the order form; libraries and institutions must attach form to purchase order and pay actual postage and handling.

A separate box on the order form states "Earn up to $40 in Free Bonus Books." Copy states: If your order is $30 or more, you are eligible to receive FREE bonus books. Indicate the value of your bonus by placing a checkmark in the box below that corresponds to your Total Payment Due, and find the value of your bonus in the adjacent column. You can choose books in this catalog (at sale price) that total the value

---

* Sale catalog includes titles of New York University Press.

† Each listing includes page count, but no publication date. Titles from New York University Press are identified in italics after the page count.

FIGURE 6   Front cover of Columbia University Press sale catalog is printed in purple and white.

SALE ENDS JULY 31, 1983

QUAN-TITY	CATALOG NUMBER	SALE PRICE	QUAN-TITY	CATALOG NUMBER	SALE PRICE	QUAN-TITY	CATALOG NUMBER	SALE PRICE	QUAN-TITY	CATALOG NUMBER	SALE PRICE	QUAN-TITY	CATALOG NUMBER	SALE PRICE	QUAN-TITY	CATALOG NUMBER	SALE PRICE
	565	7.50		587	4.50		609	2.50		630	15.00		655	5.00		680	63.50
	566	7.50		588	8.50		610	5.00		631	7.50		656	5.00		681	125.00
	567	5.00		589	7.50		611	6.75		632	9.95		657	12.50		682	15.00
	568	10.00		590	5.00		612	4.00		633	20.00		658	3.95		683	25.00
	569	5.00		591	2.50		613	8.00		634	8.95		659	30.00		684	25.00
	570	4.50		592	15.00		614	3.00		635	8.00		660	6.50		686	7.00
	571	4.00		593	7.50		615	4.00		636	30.00		661	20.00		687	10.00
				594	5.00		616	4.00		637	50.00		662	5.00		688	8.00
Economics				595	12.50		617	4.00		638	5.00		663	5.00		689	15.00
	572	7.50		596	12.50		618	7.50		639	10.00		664	5.00		690	10.00
	573	5.00		597	10.00		619	3.00		640	15.00		665	7.95		691	3.00
	574	8.00					620	9.00		641	30.00		666	5.00		692	3.50
	575	5.00	**Political Science**				621	4.00		642	7.00		667	15.00		693	30.00
	576	4.00		598	3.50		622	5.00		643	5.95		668	5.00		694	5.00
	577	5.00		599	10.00					644	5.95		669	14.50		695	13.50
	578	2.50		600	8.75					645	2.50		670	4.95		696	3.50
	579	7.00		601	5.00	**Science**				646	10.00		671	7.50		697	3.50
	580	7.50		602	8.00		623	12.00		647	12.50		672	18.00		698	7.50
	581	3.00		603	7.50		624	9.95		648	20.00		673	5.00		699	7.50
	582	3.00		604	5.00		625	9.50		649	20.00		674	10.00		700	7.00
	583	15.00		605	4.50		626	10.00		650	6.00		675	5.00		701	3.00
	584	10.00		606	3.00		627	25.00		651	5.00		676	20.00		702	5.00
	585	2.00		607	20.00		628	15.00		652	8.00		677	32.50		703	10.00
	586	7.50		608	7.50		629	5.00		653	10.00		678	32.50		704	5.00
										654	3.00		679	32.50		705	18.50

Read and Complete this Form
Terms and Conditions

1. Payment via check, money order or bank card (Master Charge or Visa/BankAmericard) must accompany order.
2. Libraries and other institutions that submit purchase orders must attach this order form to their purchase order. They will be billed for the actual additional postage and handling charges.
3. Minimum order $10.00.
4. This entire form must be returned. Savings apply only to orders received on or attached to this order form.
5. Your order will be sent to your name and address as it appears on the mailing label unless you indicate otherwise above the mailing label. **Please do not remove original label.**
6. Publisher reserves the right to limit quantities.
7. Allow four to six weeks for delivery.
8. Much of our stock is limited. Please return your order as soon as possible to avoid disappointment.
9. All sales final. **Sale ends: July 31, 1983. No orders can be accepted after this date.**
10. This offer applies only in the U.S. and Canada. All orders must be paid in U.S. dollars.

Total number of books checked by you on this form: _____
(count multi-volume sets as one book)

Total cost of these books: $ _____
There is a postage and handling charge of: $ 2.00
TOTAL PAYMENT DUE $ _____

If your Total Payment Due is $30.00 or more, you are eligible for FREE Bonus Books. See the Bonus Book information on this page.

☐ Enclosed is my check or money order for Total Payment Due
☐ Charge my Total Payment Due to my credit card:
☐ Master Card　☐ Visa　☐ American Express

Card no. _____Expiration date _____

Signature _____
(no credit card orders accepted without signature)

EARN UP TO $40 IN
FREE
BONUS BOOKS

If your order is $30 or more, you are eligible to receive FREE bonus books. Indicate the value of your bonus by placing a checkmark in the box below that corresponds to your Total Payment Due, and find the value of your bonus in the adjacent column. You can choose books in this catalog (at sale prices) that total the value of your bonus. Be sure to write the catalog numbers of the books you have chosen as your free bonus in the space provided.

My Total Payment Due is	and	My Bonus is Worth
☐ $ 30.00 to 59.99		$ 5.00
☐ 60.00 to 99.99		$10.00
☐ 100.00 to 149.99		$15.00
☐ 150.00 to 199.99		$20.00
☐ 200.00 to 249.99		$25.00
☐ 250.00 to 299.99		$30.00
☐ $300.00 or more		$40.00

· My free bonus selections are (write in catalog numbers only):

___ ___ ___ ___ ___
___ ___ ___ ___ ___
___ ___ ___ ___ ___

Return this entire order form in the envelope bound into the catalog or mail it to:

COLUMBIA UNIVERSITY PRESS
136 South Broadway
Irvington, New York 10533

If your address is incorrect, or if this catalog is not addressed to you, place an "X" through the label (please do not remove the label) and write your correct name and address in the space provided

Columbia University Press
136 S. Broadway
Irvington-on-Hudson, New York 10533

Non Profit Organization
Bulk Rate
U.S. Postage
PAID
Permit 7470
Baltimore, Md.

Copywriter's Handbook
Nat. G. Bodian
Box 000
Cranford NJ 07016

FIGURE 7　Back cover of Columbia University Sale catalog is the order form.

of your bonus. Be sure to write the catalog numbers of the books you have chosen as your free bonus in the space provided.

My Total Payment Due is	and	*My Bonus is worth*
( ) $30.00 to $59.99		$5.00
( ) $60.00 to $99.99		$10.00
( ) $100.00 to $149.99		$15.00
( ) $150.00 to $199.99		$20.00
( ) $200.00 to $249.99		$25.00
( ) $250.00 to $299.99		$30.00
( ) $300.00 or more		$40.00

My free bonus selections are (write in catalog numbers only):

──── ──── ──── ──── ──── ──── ──── ────

The order form also carries a boldface heading: "Sale Ends July 31, 1983." It states, "Return this entire order form in the envelope bound into the catalog." A No. 10 envelope requiring postage is bound into the centerfold of the wire-stitched catalog.

**4:06   Copy Elements of Encyclopedia Prospectus:
Harper & Row**

When Harper & Row launched the first edition of *Worldmark Encyclopedia of the States* in 1981, it chose as the launch vehicle a self-mailer, printed in two colors of ink. It folded to $11'' \times 8\frac{1}{2}''$. It unfolded vertically to reveal a fact-filled sheet measuring $11'' \times 29\frac{1}{2}''$ (three $11'' \times 8\frac{1}{2}''$ panels plus a 4-inch perforated flap at the bottom which bore a $4'' \times 5\frac{1}{2}''$ order card). Sixty thousand pieces were mailed and produced nearly 1,600 orders for a 2.63% response. The offering period was at a prepublication price of $54.95 and covered five months. (The mailing took place late February with a July 31 cutoff date for the prepub offer.)

Key copy elements:

• Emphasis on factual content and the large number of sources from which the contents were drawn.

• Use of format that found approval by major library media in response to companion encyclopedia.

• More than 20 individual features of the encyclopedia listed.

• Listings of types of answers the encyclopedia supplied, using 14 examples.

• Illustration of the volume at nearly 50% of actual size.

• Illustrations of sample pages and maps with text large enough to read.

• Listing of 50 subjects for which information was provided by state, territory, and dependency.

**4:07   Copy Approach Used in Business Books Catalog:
Dow Jones-Irwin**

Catalog format is a 6″ × 9″ self-mailer. The four-color cover, printed on coated cover stock, does not mention the word *catalog*. It says "Distinguished Business Books," and is dated Spring 1983. Under the cover are 48 numbered pages. The second cover lists the contents by subject. Under 19 subject entries with accompanying page numbers is a box featuring a large boldface toll-free 800 number and this copy:

> For Visa and MasterCard Credit Card Holders Only
> Call Toll Free
> (800) 323-1717
> Operator 21
> Illinois Residents Call 1 800 942-8881

The copy directly under the "Contents" instructs the reader "How to Order":

> Just select the books you want, detach and fill out one of the enclosed cards and mail to us. Please be sure to include the order number for each title ordered and give us your Visa or MasterCard number and sign the card. You will be billed through your charge card for books ordered plus $2.00 for the first book and 50¢ postage and handling for each additional book ordered.
> Save Postage and Handling Charges!
> If you wish to save postage and handling charges, kindly include your remittance with your order, and your books will be sent postpaid. Illinois residents please add 6% sales tax.

Two additional notes are included: (1) Books ordered and found unsatisfactory may be returned within 10 days of receipt for credit or refund, and (2) All books listed carry a trade discount to booksellers except for prices marked with an asterisk which are sold to booksellers at a short discount.

A double postpaid bind-in order card is stitched in between cover and pages, one at each end of the catalog. An author/title index appears on the last page.

Catalog pages are double-column with running subject heads (Figure 8). One title and book illustration is in each column, or copy in left column and illustration in right column. Each book listing carries page count, book number, and price. Publication dates are lacking throughout; however, some titles have a "NEW 1983" above or adjacent to the book illustration.

Running subject heads are in 24 point caps atop each page over a horizontal 2 point rule. Page numbers are centered at bottoms of pages. Copy for book descriptions is 9 point memphis medium, ragged right, 15 picas.

FIGURE 8 These pages from the Dow Jones-Irwin business books catalog illustrate the format used.

POSITIVE ASPECTS

All pages are on PMS 100 (light yellow) background on 50-pound white offset stock. Oversize clear illustrations, approximately 4 inches high, are against white backgrounds for sharp contrast. A good mix of features and benefits is presented in 100- to 150-word descriptions.

NEGATIVE ASPECTS

Publication dates are omitted on all but 1983 titles, and many others are older backlist books. Those indicated for 1983 do not show availability date within the year although the catalog was issued in the spring. Month of publication would have been advantageous for new titles, publication years for older titles. Also, no ISBN numbers or data helpful to the librarian were provided.

4:08 **Copy Approach for Spring Subject Catalog:**
Academic Press

The catalog is a 5½″ × 8¼″ wire-stitched booklet, with a 70-pound white offset cover over a 16-page catalog printed on 50-pound white offset stock. The catalog is a self-mailer, with a perforated back cover as mailing face and removable order form.

The front cover bears all copy in a single box as a reverse or drop-out of the one color of ink used throughout, brown (PMS 492). Copy reads:

Academic Press
Presents New Titles in
MATHEMATICS:
• Pure and Applied Mathematics
• Mathematical Engineering
• Computer Science

An Author/Title Index appears on the inside front cover, followed by a separate index headed *Journals*, followed by five journal entries, all on the last page.

Catalog subject headings run in bold reverse in bleed-bands along vertical edges of pages. Titles are attractively presented: Title, followed by author or authors, each name on its own line with affiliation directly underneath name. A clear, detailed description is given for each title. In some instances, copy is preceded by the words "FROM THE PREFACE." For new titles, "TENTATIVE CONTENTS" are given; for older works, complete contents are given.

For all titles, unlike most publishers who list such information at the bottom, publication date, pages, price, and ISBN are given directly under the author name/affiliation and before the start of the copy.

"ACADEMIC PRESS" is printed at top of each page, flush left on left pages, flush right on right pages, so that, if a page is removed from the catalog, publisher name will still be known by the bearer of the page. A good idea.

New titles are listed one on a page with ample white space above and below the entry. Only one page carries more than one title. A single conference proceedings volume, under contents, lists name of paper in lightface and initials and name of author in boldface with a colon separating name from article.

A postpaid removable reply card carries both the U.S. and London addresses. It offers payment by four popular charge cards. A line is also included which states: "( ) Payment Enclosed (add applicable sales tax)." A separate line states: "( ) Please check if you are an Academic Press or Grune & Stratton author."

An added paragraph for foreign orders carries this copy:

Foreign Customers: Payment must be made in U.S. currency, U.S. Bank Draft, international money order, or UNESCO coupons.
AP London also accepts payment to U.K. Postal Giro Account # 583 5356

Order card also carries this message: "STAY INFORMED: Please check the appropriate boxes below and return this questionnaire whether or not you choose to order at this time." Check-off boxes for 12 categories of mathematics follow, with a thirteenth option: "____ other (please specify) _____ ."

Spaces are given on the order form for quantity, ISBN, and Author/Title/Volume No. A reminder is added in boldface above the perforation: "Professional books are tax deductible."

**4:09   Distinctive Copy Embellishments in Four
Publisher Mail Promotions**

ELSEVIER

The 1983 Chemistry Catalogue of Elsevier Scientific Publishing Company, Amsterdam, The Netherlands, had this "filler" slotted into an empty space on one of its pages:

Visiting London?
A large number of our chemistry
titles are stocked by
Foyles Bookshop
119-125 Charing Cross Road
London W.C.2., England

MCGRAW-HILL

The broadside for the *McGraw-Hill Computer Handbook* makes it easy for the recipient to know quickly what's in it for him or her. In four prominent copy blocks, it identifies each of four possible audiences; it then goes on to explain what benefits the handbook offers each. The audience headings are described like this:

If you are a businessperson, an engineer, a scientist, or a technical or managerial specialist in ANY field —

If you are a computer enthusiast —

If you are a student —

If you are a computer professional —

ST. MARTIN'S PRESS

A four-page bind-in insert in the centerspread of the St. Martin's Press Spring-Summer 1983 Catalog carried this heading, followed by detailed entries of eight new titles under five different subject headings:

STOP PRESS!   STOP PRESS!   STOP PRESS!

These books were scheduled for Spring/Summer 1983 publication too late to be included in the main body of the catalog.

The insert was superimposed on a four-page removable bind-in order form which, when removed and folded into thirds, became a postpaid business reply envelope, returnable to the St. Martin's Press Reference and Scholarly Books Division.

DOW JONES-IRWIN

The Dow Jones-Irwin Summer Book Catalog for 1983 included a bound-in order envelope in the centerfold (which required customer postage). It used the normally blank area on the back of the flap to build its computer software prospect lists with a letter-type questionnaire. After the opening "Dear DJ-I Customer," these questions were posed:

- Do you own and/or have access to a personal computer?
  (fill-in spaces were provided to check or supply brand name)
- In what types of software are you most interested?
  (nine check-off categories listed)
- How do you purchase your software?
  (check-off answer categories: Computer Stores, Mail Order, Book Stores, Direct from Manufacturer).

"When you have completed this questionnaire," said the close, "please drop it in the mail. Thank you very much. —Dow Jones-Irwin."

4:10   Use of Stamps in Medical Promotions: Approach of W. B. Saunders Co.

A number of medical book publishers rely heavily on the use of stamps (postage-stamp look-alikes) to promote their titles. One such house, W. B. Saunders Co. in Philadelphia, uses a combination of fliers, stamps, and postcards. A new book announcement consists of a two-page flier on the new title, a sheet of stamps, and a postpaid order card on which four stamps can be pasted. The sheet of stamps contains related backlist titles on the same medical specialty as the new book being announced and folds into the mailing envelope.

Because medical book jackets do not reduce to a 1-inch height and remain legible, Saunders prints a black-bordered book outline on each stamp. Inside the book outline are printed the title of the book and the name of the author. Directly under the book outline on each stamp are given the page count, price, and order number. Directly above each book outline on the stamp, the year of publication or the word "NEW" appears in boldface.

Stamps will work best in your medical book promotions if you use titles that are recognizable because of the author's name or the number of previous promotions done on that particular title. This approach doesn't work well if you are trying to establish a new medical list; it's mainly a backlist promotion vehicle.

4:11   Teaser Headlines Replace Book Titles on Catalog Cover: Boardroom Books

Boardroom Books relies heavily on headlines to sell its business books and continually does it well. This example is taken from their fall 1983 sale catalog, a 24-page 8½" × 11" self-cover. Atop the cover the copy read, "THE SHREWD BUSINESS CATALOG."

Under the cover was a table of contents, *Reader's Digest* style. However, instead of article titles, each contents entry was a teaser headline for each business book entry (instead of a title) along with its catalog location. Here are examples of the first four of 24 entries for assorted business books:

> 1,688 of the best-kept secrets in America............... Page 2
> 2,000 ingenious strategies the "born salesman" uses
> intuitively.. Page 3
> Real estate money-makers that are almost too good to be
> legal... Page 4
> 232 productivity secrets.................................. Page 5

Inside the catalog, each of the individual offerings occupied a full page containing three columns of bulleted copy, representing most of the book's contents. Atop each page was a headline, which was usually an enlarged extension of the one on the cover, followed by a book illustration and a bulleted listing of benefits. At the bottom of each page was the list price in black ink, crossed out in red ink, and printed alongside it was the sale price, in either red ink or black ink. Most of the books were listed at $50 and sale priced at $29.95, although the highest priced volume was offered at half price at $37.50.

4:12   Mailer with Innocuous Copy and Solutionless Puzzle Lacks Impact: Case Study

One way to get a self-mailer read is to tie the copy on the outside to the special interests of the recipient. Another way is to place benefit or curiosity-arousing copy near the addressee's name that will lead the recipient inside.

Here's the case of a publisher's self-mailer in a scientific field that failed to do either.

The folded $5\frac{1}{2}''\times 8\frac{1}{3}''$ self-mailer covered the outside display panel in 72-point type with this message: "Maximum Likelihood for Good Results." Where teaser copy would normally go, adjacent to the mailing label, there was a mathematical puzzle.

I read the copy "maximum likelihood for good results" and wondered what its message was and whom it would turn on. And what of the puzzle? It took five lines of copy under the illustration to ask for a solution, but nowhere inside did it give a solution.

In my view, this 1983 copy effort suffered from a lack of imagination. It also reinforced my conviction that lackluster or gimmicky copy approaches should be avoided in direct-mail promotions of scientific books.

5

Working with Words:
How to Improve the Quality
and Readability of Your Copy

5:01   Over 50 Other Ways to Say "Book"

A study of dozens of publisher catalogs indicates that most copywriters prefer to fall back on "This book" to describe most entries. The fact is, with some imagination, there are scores of ways to say "This book" without using the word book. Here are over 50 of them:

account	guide	revision
aid	introduction	short course
analysis	introductory text	standard
approach to	learning aid	study
assessment of	manual	summary
best-seller	monograph	survey
bible	new edition	synthesis
collection	new version	text
collection of papers	offering	textbook
compendium	one-volume library	title
compilation	overview	tome
contribution to	practical guide	tool
course	presentation	training tool
directory	primer	treatise
discourse	printing	treatment
discussion	proceedings	unique look at
document	ready reference	version
edition	reference	volume
encyclopedia	resource	work
exposition	review	writing

If you insist on "book," consider these variations:

casebook	picturebook	sourcebook
guidebook	schoolbook	workbook
handbook	textbook	

5:02   Over 50 Action Verbs That Speed Readability of Your Copy

Where space is limited and you have much to say in a few lines, every word saved permits more space for pertinent features. You can speed readability by eliminating the "This book" sentence opening and get your message off to a fast start with an action verb. Here are 57 examples:

Analyzes	Documents	Presents
Assimilates	Elaborates	Provides
Assumes	Evaluates	Reflects
Attempts	Examines	Reinforces
Brings	Exhibits	Reports
Combines	Explains	Reveals
Communicates	Explores	Shows
Compares	Focuses	Spotlights
Compiles	Furnishes	Stresses
Considers	Gives	Suggests
Contains	Guides	Summarizes
Covers	Highlights	Surveys
Declares	Holds	Synopsizes
Demonstrates	Identifies	Treats
Describes	Illustrates	Unites
Details	Infers	Utilizes
Discloses	Offers	Verifies
Discusses	Organizes	Warns
Displays	Outlines	Warrants

5:03   Over 75 Descriptive Terms You Can Use to Describe the Book

accurate	definitive	extensively rewritten
authoritative	detailed	first
balanced	down-to-earth	first of its kind
basic	easy to comprehend	fully documented
best-selling	easy to follow	fundamental
classic	easy to understand	hands-on
clear	easy to use	heavily illustrated
compact	effective	helpful
complete	encyclopedic	highly successful
comprehensive	essential	how-to-do-it
concise	exhaustive	illuminating
convenient	expanded	important

in-depth	objective	state-of-the-art
indispensable	outstanding	successful
informal	perceptive	systematic
informative	popular	thorough
innovative	practical	time-saving
introductory	problem-solving	timely
invaluable	profusely illustrated	unified
jargon-free	remarkable	unique
lively	revised	updated
long-needed	self-contained	up-to-date
lucid	self-help	useful
monumental	self-study	valuable
much-needed	self-teaching	well documented
multifaceted	simple to use	well referenced
new	single source	well researched
nonmathematical	small	working
nontechnical	standard	work-saving

5:04   Jargon to Avoid in Copywriting with Examples of Correct Usage

Copy in professional and scholarly book promotion should be direct, sound natural, and not have a "dressed up" appearance if it is to be effective. Following are examples of jargon to avoid with examples of preferred usage.*

Avoid	*Use Instead*
a great deal of, a majority of	most
a number of	many
as a consequence of	because
commence	begin
demonstrate	show
despite the fact that	although
during the course of	during, while
end result	result
fewer in number	fewer
for the purpose of	for
for the reason that	since, because
from the point of view of	for
in a number of cases	some
in connection with	about, concerning
in order to	to
inasmuch as	for, as
initial	first

* Examples used with permission from *How to Write and Publish a Scientific Paper* (ISI Press, 1979) by Robert A. Day and from *Effective Writing for Engineers, Managers, and Scientists* (Wiley, 1966) by H. J. Tichy.

initiate	begin, start
in relation to	toward, to
in respect to	about
in some cases	sometimes
in terms of	about
in the majority of instances	usually
in the proximity of	near
in view of	because, since
is defined as	is
modification	change
necessitate	require
on the basis of	by
perform	do
prior to	before
subsequent	next
subsequent to	after
sufficient	enough
take into consideration	consider
the great majority of	most
the only difference being that	except that
through the use of	by, with
to summarize the above	in summary
utilize	use
with the possible exception of	except
with the result that	so that

**5:05   Two More Terms You Should Avoid—
Or Use with Caution**

To the examples of jargon to be avoided in the preceding entry I would like to add two more that are commonly used in consumer advertising in the mass media. With special exceptions, they do not belong in professional and scholarly book advertising. The two are "Act Now!" and the word "simply."

Ask for the order in an ad or a promotion? Of course—always! But you should never try to push the reader into a hurried decision unless you are able to reinforce your copy with a compelling reason such as an expiration date for a special offer, an impending price increase, etc.

I don't like the word "simply" for a different reason. It's usually used incorrectly, and in a way that insults the reader's intelligence. It may be all right to say "simply mail the enclosed order form," but I've seen instances time and again where the word "simply" accompanied a complex task such as the completion of a questionnaire which required addressing and postage.

If you must use these two terms, be sure you use them correctly. Better yet, avoid them altogether.

5:06   Way to Measure Clarity of Your Writing: A Useful Yardstick*

How clearly do you write? Is there a way to measure it? What is the level of your writing? If too abstruse, is there an easy way to defog it?

The answer to all four of these questions is "Yes."

A simple yardstick has been devised which you can use to make your writing clear and easy to read. It's called the *Fog Index.*

The Fog Index is based on a concept created by Robert Gunning. Head of a writing clinic and advisor to writers for newspapers and magazines and in corporations for over 25-years, Gunning trained thousands to write clearly by "Fog" indexing.

If writing is going to be part of your career in publishing, your personal library should include a copy of Gunning's *The Technique of Clear Writing, Revised Edition,* published by McGraw-Hill in 1968 (along with Rodale's *Synonym Finder,* mentioned elsewhere in this chapter). It explains the Fog Index and is fun to read.

5:07   Formula for Clear Writing: Fog Index Explained

Use the yardstick as a guide after you have written. Good writing must be alive; do not kill it with system.

> Robert Gunning, in *The Technique of Clear Writing, Revised Edition,* McGraw-Hill, 1968.

You can readily establish how clear your writing is by *fog indexing* it after it has been written. An understanding of the simple formula, which follows, will not only enable you to find out how clear your copy is, but also how you can make it even clearer. Just knowing the formula has helped me to write more clearly since I attended a Gunning writing seminar over 25 years ago.†

To find out the *Fog Index* of a piece of copy, follow these three simple steps:

1. List in a column the number of words in each sentence in the copy being measured. If you have a compound sentence, with separate

---

* Under the Gunning formula, the Fog Index of this entry is 7.7. For readability level, see the table in entry 5:07.

† When the fog indexing principle has been firmly established, the clear writing habit can become instinctive. For example, the opening entry (1:01) of *Book Marketing Handbook, Volume One,* published by R. R. Bowker, 1980, has a Fog Index of 10.4. The opening entry (1:01) of *Book Marketing Handbook, Volume Two,* published by Bowker in 1983, has a Fog Index of 7.6. Both volumes are by this author.

thoughts connected by commas or semicolons, count them as separate sentences. Total the number of words, and divide by the number of sentences in the copy. *This gives you the average sentence length of the copy.*

2. Count the number of words of three syllables or more *per 100 words.*

   a. Do not count words that are proper names.

   b. Do not count words that are combinations of short words (such as "stockholder" and "copywriter").

   c. Do not count words that are verb forms made three syllables by adding *-ed* or *-es* (such as *edited,* or *sentences*).
   This gives you the percentage of hard words in the copy.

3. To arrive at the Fog Index, total the answers from 1 and 2 above (average length of sentence *plus* percentage of hard words per 100). Multiply the total by .4. The result will be the Fog Index.

"Anyone," says Gunning, in *The Technique of Clear Writing, Revised Edition,* "who writes with a Fog Index of more than 12 is putting his communication under a handicap. . . ."

And he offers this advice to would-be writers of ad copy, "[people] don't *have* to read ads—particularly when there is news in the neighboring columns that is within easy-reading range."

Following is a table, from Gunning's book, which compares the Fog Index with reading levels by grade:

Fog Index	Reading Level (by grade)	Reading Level (selected periodicals)*
17	College graduate	
16	College, fourth year	
15	College, third year	
14	College, second year	
13	College, first year	
12	High school, fourth year	*Atlantic Monthly* and *Harper's*
11	High school, third year	*Time* and *Newsweek*
10	High school, second year	*Reader's Digest*
9	High school, first year	
8	Eighth grade, elementary school	
7	Seventh grade, elementary school	

* Magazine scores shown are from Gunning's book. However, the writing in the popular periodicals shown is tested every issue to ensure good readability levels.

5:08   How to Write with Short Words*

You do not have to use long words when you write. There are lots of short words you can use to say the things you want to say. It may take more of your thought to come up with them, but it can be well worth the time.

With short words, you get right to the point. They help you write what you want to write in a style that makes good sense. What you write can be warm, curt, brisk, trim. And have no doubt, those who read your words will know what you mean and like the clear, short words you have used to say it.

Short words can give vent to big thoughts. They can race, crawl, turn, snarl, soothe, shout. They can make you feel as well as see (the keen edge of a knife blade; the rich gleam of pure gold). They can cause one to take note (Now in Stock!; How to Get One Free), build a want (Own Your Own Home!), or stir one to action (Mail It Now!).

One can read short words with ease. Long words tend to stall the eye or block the smooth flow of what your words have to say. There is no doubt that those who write with short words can say what has to be said and say it well.

5:09   When Long Words Are Preferable to Short Words

... if a short word will function as well as a long one, a writer should generally choose the short one. But there is no point in replacing a polysyllabic word by three sentences of short words. ... If readers understand the long words and do not understand the short ones, the long words are obviously the appropriate choice.

—H. J. Tichy, in *Effective Writing
for Engineers, Managers, and Scientists,*
Wiley, 1966

There is no call to avoid a long word when a long word is more graphic than a short one; but business English is so rich in short words that, if you wish to be terse and have more need of punch than of polish, you can stick to words of one and two parts.

—George P. Metzger, in *Copy,*
Doubleday, 1926

5:10   Conciseness in Writing: Experts' Advice

Vigorous writing is concise. A sentence should contain no unnecessary words, a paragraph no unnecessary sentences, for the same reason that a drawing should have no unnecessary lines and a machine no unnecessary parts. This requires not that the reader make all his sentences short, or

---

* Inspired by "Words with One Syllable Work" by Joseph Ecclesine, in *An Almanac of Words at Play* (Willard R. Espy), New York: Clarkson N. Potter, Inc., 1975.

that he avoid all detail and treat his subjects only in outline, but that every word tell.

—William Strunk, Jr., in *The Elements of Style,*
3rd rev. ed, Macmillan, 1979

. . . use plain simple language, short words, and brief sentences. That is the way to write English . . . don't let fluff and flowers and verbosity creep in. When you catch an adjective, kill it. No, I don't mean that utterly, but kill the most of them—then the rest will be valuable. They weaken when they are close together, they give strength when they are wide apart.

—Mark Twain, quoted from Mary C. Bromage in
Writing for Business, University of Michigan
Press, 1965

. . . simple sentences are often used by good writers to relieve material which would otherwise be heavy with formality. . . . Reading tends to be hard if sentences average much more than 20 words in length.

—Robert Gunning in *The Technique of Clear Writing,
Revised Edition,* McGraw-Hill, 1968

5:11   **Some Common Problems in Copywriting**

The copywriter finds that certain problems constantly repeat themselves. A few of these are outlined below with suggested solutions, presented with permission from Herman M. Weisman's *Technical Correspondence: A Handbook and Reference Source for the Technical Professional* (Wiley, 1968):

Accept, Except
  Accept (verb) means to take when offered, to receive with favor, to agree to. *Except* (verb) means to exclude or omit; *except* (preposition) means with the exception of, but.

Access, Excess
  Access means approach, admittance, admission. *Excess* means that which exceeds what is usual, proper, just, or specified.

Adviser, Advisor
  Both are acceptable . . . *adviser* is used more frequently, but the spelling of *advisory* is the correct one.

Affect, Effect
  Affect is almost always a verb, meaning to influence or to make a show of. *Effect* is rarely used as a verb. As a noun, it means result or consequence.

Among, Between
  Among denotes a mingling of more than two objects or persons. *Between,* derived from an old English word meaning "by two," denotes a mingling of two objects or persons only. In current usage, *between* is used where the meaning denotes more than two objects or persons.

And/or
This expression is commonly used to show there are three possibilities to be considered: He offered his house *and/or* automobile as security for the loan. (He offered his house, or his automobile, or both as collateral.)

Beside, Besides
Beside means near, close by, by the side of. *Besides* means in addition to, moreover, also, aside from.

Can, May
Can expresses the power (physical or mental) to act. *May* expresses permission or sanction to act.

Could, Might
Could and *might* are the original past tenses of *can* and *may*. They are now used to convey a shade of doubt or a smaller degree of possibility.

Censor, Censure
Censor means to delete or suppress. *Censure* means to condemn or blame.

Center about, Center around, Center on, Center upon
In copywriting, the preferred is *center on* or *center upon*.

Catalog, Catalogue
If you prefer the second spelling, you are a traditionalist fighting a losing battle. (See 13:03.)

Compare, Contrast
Compare is used in two senses: (1) to point out similarities (used with the preposition *to*); and (2) to examine two or more items or persons to find likenesses or differences (used with the preposition *with*). *Contrast* always points out differences.

Complement, Compliment
Complement (noun) means the number or amount that adds up to the whole. *Complement* (verb) means to make complete, supplement, or supply a lack in. *Compliment* (noun) means praise or commendation. *Compliment* (verb) means to praise or to show regard for.

Continual, Continuously
Continual means repeated at frequent intervals. *Continuously* means uninterrupted.

Disinterested, Uninterested
Disinterested means fair, impartial, unbiased. *Uninterested* means lacking in interest or without curiosity.

Farther, Further
In copy, use *farther* when applied to physical distances. Use *further* when referring to degree or quantity.

If, Whether
If is used to introduce a condition.   *Whether* is used in expressions of doubt.

Imply, Infer
Imply means to suggest by word or manner.   *Infer* means to draw a conclusion about the unknown on the basis of known facts.

In, Into
In shows location.   *Into* shows direction.

Lay, Lie
Lay is a transitive verb meaning to put something down.   *Lie* is an intransitive verb meaning to rest in a reclining position.

Like, As
Like, the preposition, is used correctly when followed by a noun or pronoun without a verb. Like should not be used as a conjunction; *as* should be used instead.

May Be, Maybe
May be is a compound verb.   *Maybe* is an adverb meaning perhaps.

None, No one
None is commonly used to refer to things (but not always).   *No one* is used to refer to people.

Oral, Verbal
Oral refers to spoken communication.   *Verbal* has the general meaning of communication—written or spoken—which uses words.

Phenomenon, Phenomena
The plural form of *phenomena* is frequently misused for the singular *phenomenon*.

Principal, Principle
Principal is used both as a noun and an adjective. As a noun it has two meanings: (1) the chief person or leader; and (2) a sum of money drawing interest. As an adjective, *principal* means "of main importance" of "of highest rank or authority."   *Principle* is always a noun and means fundamental truth or doctrine, or the basic ideas, motives, or morals inherent in a person, group, or philosophy.

Slow, Slowly
Slow is both an adjective and an adverb.   *Slowly* is an adverb. As adverbs, the two forms are interchangeable, but *slow* is more forceful than *slowly*.

Than, Then
Than is a conjunction in clauses of comparison.   *Then* is an adverb relating to time.

Toward, Towards
The two forms are interchangeable.

5:12   **Nonsexist Alternatives When Writing
to a Mixed Audience**

Increasingly, the sciences and professions have a better mix of men and women. Consequently, the tendency to use "he" and "his" and other traditional sexist expressions when writing to mixed audiences should be avoided whenever possible, and nonsexist alternatives substituted.* Here are some suggested alternatives:

Traditional	Nonsexist Alternative
he	he or she, one, you
his	his or her
man	people, humankind
chairman	chairperson (optional)†
manhood	adulthood
workmanlike	businesslike
businessmen	business executives, managers
salesman	sales representative
workman	worker
foreman	supervisor
manpower	personnel, workers, work force

5:13   **Need a Word? Try** *The Synonym Finder*

Stuck for a word? Want a better or more precise way to say it? Turn to Rodale's *The Synonym Finder.* [*The Synonym Finder* by J. I. Rodale (revised by Laurence Urdang), 1979. Rodale Press, 33 East Minor Street, Emmaus, PA 18049].

This invaluable aid has served me through hundreds of writing assignments over the years and is highly recommended as a basic tool for every copywriter. I've worked with both editions. The current (1979) revised edition has more extensive coverage. However, I find myself relying on the 1961 first edition because of its larger, easier-to-read typeface. Perhaps a third edition will return to the larger typeface.

* Though not necessarily for engineers. ". . . fewer than 5 per cent of the over one million individuals employed in engineering are women," according to Carol J. Auster, professor of sociology at Franklin and Marshall College, writing in the 2 May, 1984 issue of *The Chronicle of Higher Education.*

† The National Association of Parliamentarians views "chairman" as the title of an office and not a person, and favors its continued usage.

6

The Word Processor:
Practical Tool for Copy Preparation

6:01   **Introduction to the Use of the Word Processor
for Copywriting**

If, as one anonymous writer put it, *training* is learning the rules and
experience is learning the exceptions, then this chapter should provide
an ideal introduction to the use of the word processor in the art of
copywriting.

The word processor is slowly making its presence felt in the advertising and promotion departments of many publishing establishments. However, for the majority of those who labor at the creation
of advertising and promotion copy in both large and small establishments—both commercial and institutional—the word processor as a
copywriting tool is still an unknown.

In the course of assembling the data for this *Handbook,* I located
and interviewed a number of publishing professionals who work with
and use the word processor in the preparation of advertising and
promotion copy and elicited their views, their feelings, and their experience with the WP.

The entries in this chapter outline, for the uninitiated, some of the
benefits of the WP for the copywriter (6:02) and as an overall item of
equipment in the advertising department (6:03). There follows a free-
wheeling discussion by a copywriter of the various uses he has found

for the word processor and of his adjustment from the typewriter to the WP (6:04). Next, an advertising and promotion manager from a Boston publishing establishment talks about his feelings while using the WP (6:05). Case studies are also included on how the word processor is used in a highly potent way as a tool of college textbook marketing (6:07), on how another textbook publisher uses the word processor for college textbook sales correspondence (6:08), and on how a book publicist uses it in the publicity department of a large commercial house (6:09).

If all of these entries seem to indicate that everyone loves the word processor, a counterbalance is provided in the comments of a British writer (6:06) who praises the WP as "the next logical step from the typewriter"; he then goes on to explain how he sees it as differing from a typewriter, and concludes by stating he still prefers the typewriter "and will go on using one as long as I can."

The entries that follow, then, give many rules, applications, and points of view designed to provide the reader with ideas on how to look at, think about, and work with the word processor to best advantage. Here are the rules. By your own use of the WP, you'll learn your own exceptions.

6:02   Benefits of Word Processor for the Copywriter

- Faster first drafts. Copy is less labored when you know you can edit easily later.

- Cleaner and more professional-looking presentation copy (provided your equipment includes a letter-quality printer).

- No more cut-and-paste. Words can be changed, paragraphs can be moved around with ease, and each draft looks "finished" so that its effect can be decided upon without confusion.

- More flexible than a typewriter. You can play around with different formats (for instance, indents on sales letters) without wasting time re-keyboarding.

- Compact, accessible storage. Keep everything in the computer memory for fast call-up for reference and rewriting.

- Faster, neater rewrites. Additions, deletions, alterations can be introduced with minimal effort, and new "presentation" copy generated.

- Less proofreading after first draft. Once copy has been keyboarded, only new elements must be read for typos.

6:03   Benefits of Word Processor
in the Advertising Department

- Avoids redundant copywriting. The same blurb can be used for multiple purposes.

- Saves copywriting time and expense. Bibliographic information can be reused and reference made to existing copy, even if new copy is required for a special slant.

- Decreases design and typography costs. Setting up a database compatible with today's typesetting technology, one planned for multiple use, can dramatically lower costs in these areas.

- Provides flexibility. Standing copy can be picked up quickly and adapted as required.

- Speed. Type and mechanicals can be generated rapidly from existing copy.

- Accuracy. Material need only be proofread once for accuracy, as new formats can be generated without re-keyboarding; errors can be corrected in the database as spotted and will not crop up repeatedly from manual pick-up sources.

- Marketing responsiveness. A data bank allows marketing managers to make quick decisions requiring printed pieces, to respond to marketing opportunities.

**6:04   A Copywriter Talks About His Experience
with the Word Processor**

A copywriter who works in the copy department of a large New York City commercial publishing house provided the following comments.

> I use it for everything from space ads to copy for book jackets, direct-mail pieces, and catalogs. The biggest advantage is speed and accuracy—the ability to edit right on the screen.
>
> There's really no comparison between the typewriter and the word processor. With a word processor, you have the ability to think on the screen as you are going along. I want to take something from the third page and move it to the first page—I do it. You can move things around.
>
> I've been using the word processor for 18 months. Before that, in my early months on the job as copywriter, I was using a typewriter.
>
> Every copywriter that has come into our department has gone from the typewriter to the word processor. I know of none that have had any difficulty adjusting. Most of the copywriters that go from typewriter to word processor have a fear of the computer itself. I, myself, don't understand the computer or how to use it. But if you learn the command keys or function keys on the top of the word processor keyboard, you have no trouble.
>
> The only disadvantage I can see for using a word processor in copywriting is the eye strain factor. You're staring at a screen all day long. I don't have a problem now, but some of the newer copywriters just starting out complain about the eye strain factor.
>
> What advice would I have for a newcomer just facing up to a word processor for the first time? I'd tell him (or her) it's a glorified speeded-up version of a typewriter, a faster way to type, to process the words. It really is just a typewriter with a screen, an electronic typewriter that allows you

to always have the words in front of you on the screen to do whatever you want to do with them.

I see these as some of the advantages of the word processor for a copy-writer:

- You have your speed.
- You have editing ability.
- You have ease of use.
- You can use a "search" key to correct or change a word anywhere in your copy instantly without looking for it.
- You have reliability. Mine (a Wang) is very reliable. There is very little downtime, maintenance is minimal.
- The keys themselves have the same feel and touch as a regular type-writer.

6:05   An Ad Manager Talks About His Experience with the Word Processor

The writer of this entry is George W. Pratt III, advertising and pro-motion manager in the Law Division of Little, Brown and Company, Boston.

> Copywriting is a rather personal experience. Copywriters have their own ways of doing things. Some prefer pencil and paper, some the Smith-Corona. Whatever works for you is probably what you should be doing.
>
> I've had good success using a word processor for certain kinds of copy-writing. I find it to be an efficient way to keep my copy all in one place, and it's always in its most recent form. I can get a printout of what I'm working on, and it's always clean and exactly as I remembered it. I don't have to worry about losing my rough notes, or my first draft. I can make corrections as I go, add paragraphs in context, delete bad copy, etc. And, at any time, I can print out a copy of what I've got so far.
>
> I particularly like the word processor for letters. I can get a decent picture of how my letter is going to look in print while I'm still working on it. For copy that will include substantial graphics, however, the word processor may be a less effective tool. However, if I'm working on more than one project at one time, the word processor keeps everything where it should be. Anything I wish to work on will be presented to me in the form it was last in when I saw it. Also, output can be formatted to simulate actual appearance, making checking for length, etc., a bit easier. As an organizer for a busy copywriter, the word processor can't be beat!
>
> From the creative standpoint, I have not found using a word processor to be a road block. In fact, I can just go ahead and write and not worry about anything else because I know it's all being stored for later revisions or work. The word processor does not intimidate me and that's important.

6:06   Processor Denotes Progress, but One Writer Offers Opposing View

The word processor, wrote Christopher Priest in *The Bookseller* (14 April 1984)

. . . is the next logical step from the typewriter, just as that was once an improvement on the pen, which in turn replaced the quill.

A processor displays words in the form of electronic images on a screen. From a writer's point of view, the words are therefore simultaneously fixed and fluid. They are fixed because they look permanent, like typewritten words . . . but at the same time they are fluid because the program allows letters, words, sentences, even whole paragraphs . . . to be deleted with the touch of a key, or replaced, or moved around . . .

. . . the defending argument [is] a word processor actually helps a writer in the act of composition because it enables the text to be reconsidered, rephrased, rewritten, without the chore of either hand corrections or endless retyping. All writers produce drafts that need extra work, and a word processor facilitates it.

. . . a word processor is not a better or more efficient kind of typewriter; it is a profoundly different type of machine . . . writers who are thinking of moving into the new technology should reflect on the fact that these machines have been designed by computer people, not by other writers. Everything about word processors bespeaks the computer "mind."

For [some] of the reasons I stated above, I suspect the spread of writer-operated processors will be to the general detriment of the quality of writing . . . I still prefer a typewriter and will go on using one as long as I can.

The author of this volume, having done all of his writing on a manual typewriter since his days as a journalist in World War II, takes the same view as Priest. I learned to write while looking at a sheet of paper wrapped around a rubber roller, to let the clicking of the keys serve as an idea stimulator, and to edit with a pencil rather than a special key on a keyboard.

However, for the newcomer just starting, the word processor is fast becoming an everyday basic tool. It is likely to replace the electric typewriter, just as the electric machine made the manual typewriter obsolete.

Those whose writing careers start with a word processor will see it as a basic work tool and cultivate their own writing skills so that they embrace the keyboard and screen as the logical way to write.

6:07   Use of Word Processor as a Tool
of Textbook Marketing

One college textbook publisher uses the word processor as a marketing tool in a highly potent way. When numerous complimentary copies of a textbook have been sent out to potential adopters, the word processor is used to follow up with a personalized letter to each recipient, reminding them that the comp copy was sent and asking if they are considering the book for adoption or need additional help in making an adoption decision.

The procedure involves putting the names of the comp copy recipients into the (Wang) processor, and merging them with a stock standard letter that can be universally applied to all book titles. In spaces provided, the word processor is programmed to provide the title of the book under consideration and descriptive matter on that book.

It is interesting to note that a separate database contains catalog descriptions for all titles on the publisher's list. When the word processor requires a book description, it is linked to the catalog database, and the descriptive matter stored in the database is drawn into the letter.

The result is output to an IBM laser printer, and each letter produced has the appearance of an individually typed original.

Still another word processor receives the name and address of the professor and produces addressed enveloped. Letters are then hand signed and mailed.

6:08   Use of Word Processor for College Sales Correspondence Support

At one textbook house, the word processor is used extensively to provide correspondence support for the field sales force. When a college rep has called on a professor regarding a particular text, he or she then requests that the home office send the professor a personalized follow-up letter.

At the home office, there are a number of separate "stock" letters stored in the word processor which have been prepared beforehand. Such letters are individually numbered, so that the sales rep can ask for Letter 7, Letter 8, etc., to get the desired letter sent to the particular professor.

Some of the stored letters are used without change. Some require the addition of special copy which the rep may also request—add-on lines or phrases such as "Sorry I missed you on my last call" or "I've taken the liberty of ordering you a comp copy of (title) and will see you on my next visit."

A separate program will spell out certain abbreviated words or word forms in addresses. For example, the word "Dept." will be spelled out as "Department," and words such as "Col" or "Coll" spelled out as "College" or "U" as "University."

The word processor correspondence support program has been very effective.

6:09   The Word Processor as a Tool of the Publicist

The word processor has become an indispensable tool in many publishing publicity departments. It is used in three key ways:

1. To process releases and book review lists
2. To assemble and prepare news releases
3. To prepare personalized letters to book reviewers and media people

In the publicity department of one multi-line professional publishing establishment, all of the addresses of book review sources are kept online by subject. Says the publicist there:

> We have a state-of-the-art list and we really take advantage of it.
>
> I maintain a "control" list by subject in a binder and the addresses are all on line in the computer. When I do a review list, I check off the publications I want to send review copies to and call them up on the word processor as necessary.

USE FOR WRITING RELEASES

The publicist continues:

> I also use the word processor for writing my releases. The word processor has incredible flexibility. I can turn a word into a paragraph as my thoughts are being organized and move those thoughts into paragraphs and flip flop them as I please at the touch of a button. Since I started with the word processor, I don't have to cut and paste my notes anymore when I'm preparing a release. I hardly ever use my rubber cement anymore.
>
> How do I write my releases on the word processor? I use it for everything from "soup" to "nuts." When I start to prepare the release, I take out the bibliographic file and go through it.
>
> Those notes I think will be helpful are put into the word processor. Then I shuffle them around and turn them into the final press release. Once I have the press release written, I pull it out of the letter-quality printer and have it reproduced by offset on our standard news release letterheads.

INTRODUCTION TO WORD PROCESSOR

The publicist, a journalism school graduate, says he made the switch from typewriter to word processor while a student working on the school paper. He sees the transition for a writer from typewriter to word processor as "a very natural transition."

What would he tell a newcomer considering the use of a word processor?

> The first thing is to make a complete inventory of your lists used and all your text processing needs, and then to think of what input a word processor will have. You have to think of how word processor technology will supply what you need and how you can use the word processor to achieve it. Having established both your needs and how a word processor will fill them, the next step is to shop around for a word processor to meet those needs.
>
> Today, the word processor meets all the fundamental needs in publishing publicity—lists, releases, personalized letters. In my view, this is the only way to do it.

7

Headline Writing for Specialized and Business Books

7:01 Headline Writing for Book Promotion Copy: Essentials, Guidelines

The selling message may be superb, but if no one stops to read it, you've wasted your time...

Edwin Nash in *Direct Marketing,*
McGraw-Hill, 1982.

All copy pros agree that if you fail to capture the reader's attention with your headline, you won't have much luck getting the rest of your copy read. David Ogilvy calls the headline "the telegram which decides the reader whether to read the copy."

The fact is that the headline is a vital component in any type of book promotion. Whether in an advertisement or as a teaser on a mailing envelope, it must generate instant interest if it is to be successful.

Of headlines for printing advertising, Victor O. Schwab wrote in *How to Write a Good Advertisement* (Harper, 1962): "There are two principal attributes of good headlines. They select from the total readership of the publication, those readers who are (or can be induced to be) interested in the subject of the advertisement. And they promise them a worthwhile reward for reading it."

For direct-mail headlines, Edwin Nash says in *Direct Marketing,* "The headline must instantly flag down prospective buyers and intrigue them with an offer, a broad benefit or need fulfillment, or a curiosity-provoking specific selected from the body of the advertisement."

So, picking up on Schwab's theme, in print advertising your headline may have more general appeal while at the same time aiming at that segment of the broad readership for which the copy is intended. Conversely in direct mail, because you can select your audience with pinpoint precision, your headline must be more precisely targeted.

What should your headline do? Here are a few things to bear in mind:

- Attract the reader's attention.
- Lead the reader into reading the copy.
- Be clear in its meaning.
- Be reasonably short in length.

A lot of what your headline has to do may relate to the position your publishing establishment enjoys in its field. If your house enjoys a preeminent position in a particular field and you're advertising to practitioners within that field, a simple headline like "New Books from (Your Imprint)" may be sufficient to attract wide readership.

If you're offering a specialized book to a specialized audience, your headline may have to work harder—to promise an important benefit, offer needed information or new insights or the results of recent research in a professional area.

How do you learn to write good headlines? By copying the best efforts of others. You learn by studying and copying good examples until you get a feel of what a good headline should be. Then you'll probably prefer to do your own thing.

7:02   Ten Questions to Ask About a Headline

1. Does it naturally lead into copy?
2. Does it select its audience?
3. Does it have clear, unambiguous words?
4. Does it utilize punctuation for emphasis (leaders, underlines, italics, exclamation points, quotation marks)
5. Does it sound believable?
6. Does it, by typesize and spacing, stand apart from the copy?
7. Does it command attention, stop the reader?
8. Does it avoid punctuation which stops the reader, such as a period?
9. Does it have a relationship to the copy?
10. Does it have psychological appeal?

7:03   Key Ingredient Used in Winning Headlines

Involve the reader in your headline if you want it to be effective.
That's the lesson indicated in an examination of a list of winning
headlines in Victor O. Schwab's *How to Write a Good Advertisement*
(Harper, 1962). A personal pronoun appeared in nearly two-thirds of
the 100 examples cited. The words *You* or *Your* appeared 45 times; *I,
Me,* or *My,* 11 times; *We* or *They,* 7 times.

The same psychological principles that made these headlines effective for general audiences may also be applied to book and journal
advertising aimed at specialized audiences. Involve the reader in the
headline, link him or her with the benefit your ad copy offers, and
your advertisement will be read.

**7:04   Headline Tips That Increase Readership
of Professional and Scholarly Book Ads**

- If your headline words trigger an emotion in the reader or respond
  to a "want," there is a good likelihood he or she will read the ad:

    Engineers in fast-changing fields want to be current

- If your headline draws the reader into the opening sentence of the
  ad copy, your ad will be read.
- When your headline stresses the book's principal benefit to the
  potential buyer, he or she is likely to read further.
- When your press's imprint is familiar and respected, its inclusion
  in the headline will enhance readership:

    New ... from The MIT Press

- When your headline identifies a specific segment of a periodical's
  readership that the books will appeal to, they are more likely to
  read the ad:

    New Titles on Personal Computing ... from Hayden

- When the books in the ad aim at a specific level of a segment of
  the audience, indicate both audience and level:

    New Advanced Physics Texts ... from Addison Wesley

**7:05   Tips on Headline Writing from a Member
of the Copywriters Hall of Fame**

David Ogilvy, member of the Copywriters Hall of Fame, and one of
the most prolific writers on modern advertising technique, offers these
tips for headline writers:[*]

---

[*] Entries 1, 3, 5, and 7 are from his best-selling *Confessions of an Advertising Man* (New
York: Atheneum, 1963). Entries 2, 4, 6, and 8 are from *Ogilvy on Advertising* (New
York: Crown, 1983).

1. The wickedest of all sins is to run an advertisement without a headline.
2. Headlines that promise the reader a benefit work best.
3. Avoid using negatives in headlines.
4. Specifics work better than generalities.
5. Tricky headlines—puns, literary allusions, and other obscurities—are a sin.
6. Headlines get five times the readership of body copy.
7. Avoid blind headlines—the kind that mean nothing unless you read the body copy underneath; most people don't.
8. Putting a headline in quotes increases recall by over 25%.

7:06   The Two Approaches of an Advertising Headline

A headline, wrote Victor Schwab in his classic *How to Write a Good Advertisement,* must promise the interested reader a worthwhile reward for reading the advertisement. This can be done through two approaches—a positive one or a negative one.

The positive approach, says Schwab, "manage(s) to convey in a few words, how the reader can save, gain, or accomplish something through the use of [the advertised offering]."

The negative approach, he adds, "point(s) out how the reader can avoid (reduce or eliminate) risks, worries, losses, mistakes, embarrassment, drudgery, or some other undesirable condition through the use of [the advertised offering]."

7:07   Tips on Headline Writing from John O'Toole

John O'Toole, head of one of the world's largest advertising agencies—Foote, Cone & Belding—and one of the top copy professionals of the post-World War II era, offers these views on effective headline writing in his thoughtful and enjoyable *The Trouble with Advertising* (New York: Chelsea House, 1981):

- Headlines should be vigorous. . . . I rejoice in active verbs.
- Headlines should sing. . . . enjoyable to read, easy to remember.
- They should be short. . . . The shorter the better.
- Headlines should be involving [involve the reader].
- Headlines should march, dance or skip with effortless grace, memorable cadence and revelatory insight.

7:08   An Exhaustive A to Z Compendium of Headline Ideas for Specialized and Scholarly Books

Advance your career with _____

Advice on every facet of _____
All the basic techniques you need
The all-new edition of the classic best-seller
A _____ approach and exceedingly clear explanation that _____
At last!—Practical Guidance on _____
At last, a _____-oriented view of the subject

A basic, down-to-earth guide to _____
A basic down-to-earth guide to _____ for _____
A basic rundown on what you need to know about _____
A basic but thorough rundown on what you need to know about _____

Be a better _____ in _____
Benefit from the experience of leading experts
This book makes it easier than ever to _____
The book that can help you become an expert in _____
Brings together data from _____ and _____
Brings you up-to-date on important recent developments
Brings you up-to-date on methods to _____
Brush up your technique with this new guide

Catch up on the latest _____ techniques and their applications
Catch up with sweeping technological changes in the industry
Catch up with the latest _____ techniques and their applications
A clear, concise and highly readable account
A clear, concise way to learn all you need to know about _____
A clear, easy-to-follow introductory text
A clear explanation in nonmathematical terms
A clear nonmathematical guide to _____
A clear, nonmathematical how-to-do-it guide
A clear, nontechnical account for _____
A clear understandable presentation of _____
Complete coverage of _____—in one volume
Complete coverage of techniques, applications, methods, and equipment
Complete, easy-to-read coverage of _____
Complete information on _____
A complete introduction to _____
A complete single-source guide to all aspects of _____
A complete survey of the field
A comprehensive and in-depth review
The most comprehensive and up-to-date text of its kind
A comprehensive overview of _____
A comprehensive synthesis of the subject
A concise basic guide for _____
A concise, illustrated introduction to _____
A concise introduction to _____
A concise state-of-the-art review
A concise yet thorough account

Consistent commonsense guidelines for any questions you may have on ———

Concrete, sensible guidance on ———

Covers the complete range of ——— and ———

Current, authoritative information you can use

A current, comprehensive, and authoritative perspective

The current state-of-the-art review

The definitive handbook on ——— ... compiled by ——— top professionals

Detailed guidelines for ———

Detailed help on ——— practices and procedures

Detailed information for more effective ———

Discover new ——— techniques

Discover the latest advances in ———

Discover the latest concepts in ———

An easy-to-follow approach to ———

An easy-to-understand book that shows you how to ———

An essential guide for engineers who ———

Essential guide to ———

Essential information for ———

Essential reading for ———

The essential reference for ——— in ———

An essential tool for ———

Everything you need to know about ———

Everything you need to know to understand the mysteries of ———

An excellent source of information and ideas on ———

Exhaustive guide to the practical applications of ———

Expanded ... More useful than ever before!

Expert advice for anyone involved in ———

Expert new solutions to practical problems

Extensive data on the ——— aspects of ———

Fast answers to ——— questions

Field-tested techniques to solve your ——— problems

Fills the gaps in ——— literature with one self-contained comprehensive volume

The first book to cover these new theories

First book to treat all aspects of ———

First complete guide to ———

The first comprehensive guide for ———

The first full-scale study of ———

The first in a new series

The first in-depth book on this subject

The first new edition in ——— years

First-of-its-kind guide

The first self-contained guide to ———

First time in book form—Important new material for/on ———

A fully illustrated up-to-date guide
A fundamental resource for _____

Gain a basic understanding of current concepts in _____
Gain a better understanding of _____
Gain a better understanding of all aspects of _____
Gain a better understanding of the theory, design, and application
  of _____
Gain a comprehensive understanding of _____
Gain a deeper understanding of _____
Gain a fuller understanding of the principles and techniques needed
  for _____
Gain an in-depth understanding of _____
Gain quick access to _____ expertise
Gain a solid introductory understanding of _____
Gain a working knowledge of _____
Get a detailed overview of _____
Get instant answers to questions on _____
Get the latest data on _____ research techniques
Get the latest developments in _____
The greatest collection of _____ ever assembled under one cover
A guide to the principal methods of _____

Handy reference and self-study review of _____
Help for anyone involved in _____
Helps you to isolate, measure, and solve _____ problems
How to apply _____ to _____
How to better understand the _____ of _____
How to choose and use _____
How to cope with problems of _____
How to effectively use _____
How to get maximum benefits from _____
How to get the most from _____
How to keep up with _____
How to set up and use _____
How to use _____
How to use _____ techniques in your work

Ideal for teaching and self-study
An ideal handbook for _____
The ideal ready reference for the nonspecialist
Ideal ready reference to the _____ of _____ and _____
An ideal reference and learning aid for researchers and students
Ideal reference tool for _____
Ideas you can use immediately
An important new sourcebook ... with more information on the sub-
  ject than any other available work
Important, ready-to-use facts on _____
Improve your ability to apply _____ to _____

Improve your ability to apply _____ technology to your _____
Indispensable for anyone involved in _____
The indispensable guide for the entire field of _____
An indispensable manual for everyone concerned with _____
An indispensable reference for everyone involved in _____
The indispensable reference for the industry
Information for virtually all uses of _____
Information you can put to immediate use
Innovative ideas to correct, eliminate, and minimize _____ problems
Innovative ideas to eliminate or minimize _____ problems
Instant access to information on every aspect of _____
An instant-answer reference guide to help you in _____
Instant answers to questions on _____
Instant answers to your _____ questions
Let internationally known authorities bring you up-to-date on recent
    advances
Keep up-to-date in this exploding field
Keep up-to-date with _____
Keep up-to-date with this latest edition
The key elements you need to know to _____

The latest developments in _____
Latest edition of an established classic
The latest ideas and research on _____
The latest technology to help you solve _____ problems
A leader in the field brings you up-to-date on _____
A leading authority shows you better ways to _____
Leading experts share their experience on advanced techniques
Learn about the latest techniques and equipment for _____
Learn how to get the most out of _____
Learn practical uses of _____ in your work
Learn the "Hows" and "Whys" of _____
Let _____ authorities reveal and integrate the latest thinking and
    research for you
Let the experts show you new solutions to practical problems in
_____
Let the experts show you new solutions to practical problems in your
    work
A logical, multiapproach explanation of the theory of _____
A lucid nonmathematical explanation of _____

Master essential skills for _____
Master the essential skills for coping with _____
The master problem solver for every phase of _____
A mine of information
More exhaustive, more useful than ever before (new edition)
The most complete guide to _____ available / ever published
The most comprehensive treatment of topics pertinent to _____

Most extensive collection of _____ information available in a single volume
A much-needed reference (of) (on) (for) _____

A new and refreshing guide devoted to _____
A new approach to _____
The new "bible" of _____
New edition of a standard guide / of an industry classic
A new edition of this authoritative guide
Two new guides in a series devoted to _____
New ideas for _____
New information on _____ research
A new, informed approach to _____
New methods to _____
A new, more realistic approach to _____
New revision / edition of a classic
A new strategy for solving _____ problems
New techniques to help you improve your _____
New techniques to help you solve problems in _____
A new way of tackling _____ problems
Now in one convenient volume—Basic source material for _____
Now you can understand and use _____

Offers you all current knowledge—with special money-saving features
On-the-job instant-answer reference work for coping with everyday problems
A one-volume examination of the basic principles of _____
A one-volume library on _____
This one-volume reference covers the entire field
The only comprehensive treatment of _____
The only reference on the subject
The only resource on _____ you need
Over _____ pages packed with detailed techniques on every aspect of _____

A pioneering analysis of current research in _____
Powerful new skills for increased job effectiveness
Powerful ways to solve tough _____ problems
Practical details on key elements of _____
Practical guidance you can use to _____
A practical guide to _____
A practical guide to every aspect of _____
A practical guide to a variety of _____ methods
Practical guidelines to help you _____
Practical help on _____
Practical help on how to _____
Practical in-depth coverage of _____
A practical introduction to the entire _____ industry
Practical "know-how" to help you _____

This practical manual helps you understand the basics of _____
A practical new approach to _____
Practical, proven ways to _____
Practical ready-to-use help on all aspects of _____
Practical step-by-step advice
Practical, tested ideas for every _____ need
A problem-solving approach to _____
Profit from the experience of experts
Profit from the experiences of _____ experts
Provides you with a thorough understanding of the _____ of _____

Quick answers to your _____ questions
Quick, expert answers to your _____ questions

Ready reference or self-study course on _____
Recommended practices and data for _____
Refresh your knowledge of _____
Refresh your memory . . . sharpen your skills with this exhaustive review of _____
A refresher on the principles of _____
Now!—A refresher of the principles of _____
Revised and expanded to reflect new developments
Now revised and expanded
Revised and updated guide to _____
Revised version of a widely acclaimed professional reference

Save time looking up facts about _____ by using the single source
Save time with this major reference for _____
A self-contained guide to _____
Now!—Share the experience of _____ of the nation's top authorities on _____
Sharpen your skills in _____ with this self-study guide
Shows _____ how to use _____ to _____
Shows you the skills you need for _____
A simple, concise, complete guide to _____
A simple, direct, and practical book that shows step-by-step the "how-to" of _____
A simplified guide to _____
A simplified, illustration-packed reference covering the full spectrum of techniques
A single comprehensive source covering every facet of _____
The single source for anyone who wants to _____
A single source for everyone who want to _____
The skills you need for _____
A solid introduction to _____
Now!—Solve any _____ problem with these tested methods
A sourcebook and manual of _____ for _____
A sourcebook of useful data and techniques

A staff of experts brings you help on every important area of _____

The state-of-the-art in _____
A state-of-the-art synthesis of current information
State-of-the-art techniques for _____
Stay on top with the latest developments in _____
Step-by-step guidelines for _____
Step-by-step guidelines for us _____
Successful, time-tested methods for _____
Summarizes the existing knowledge of the subject

Takes the mystery out of _____
Teach yourself to _____ with_____
Time and money-saving solutions to your _____ problems
A time-saver you'll use every day in _____
A time-saving one-volume reference that summarizes existing knowl-
    edge of _____
A time-saving reference on _____ for _____
A time-saving source of current information
A time-saving way to catch up on current ideas
A timely and informative new look at _____
A total systematic approach to _____

A unified approach to _____
A unified treatment of _____
A unique and practical approach to _____
A unique new approach to _____
An unparalleled overview of _____
Up-to-date, accurate information on _____
Up-to-the-minute "inside" information on _____
Update your _____ "know-how"
Update your _____ knowledge of
Updated!—A classic work for _____
An updated and expanded edition of the "classic" in the field
A useful text for working _____

Valuable help for the _____
Valuable information on _____
Valuable lessons on _____

Want a better, more comprehensive background in _____ ?
Ways to benefit from _____
A wealth of techniques for dealing with _____
What you need to know to _____
A work-saving, problem-solving guide to _____
A working aid for _____ that stresses _____
A working reference for _____
A world authority explains _____ so you can understand it

Your complete guide to _____

Your desktop guide to the basics of _____

Zero in on over _____ tested techniques in _____
Zero in on time and money-saving techniques in every facet of
_____
Zero in on your problems in _____ with these tested methods

**7:09   Business Book Headline Writing Often Difficult:
Here's Why**

There is a tendency among authors of business books to build the
headline into the title. As a consequence, while it is relatively easy to
find powerful benefit-loaded selling headlines in the advertising and
promotion of professional and specialized books, these are rare for
books in business, investment, and finance.

The scarcity of good headlines for business-oriented books was discussed with book copy pros who had their own theories for this phenomenon.

Said one: "You can't sell business-type books with benefits." Because
of the sophistication of this audience, she said, "You have to capture
their attention and their imagination."

Said another, "The reason there are so few good headlines for business books is that most of the promotion is written by people who
don't have the least idea of who buys business books and why."

The entry following offers a sampler of some good business book
headlines. A reading provides ample reasons why they were effective.

7:10   A Sampler of Effective Business Book Headlines

Secrets used by top tax professionals

Everything you need to know about real estate to make money in
today's market

The best tax shelter in America

How to increase sales without increasing expenses

How to reduce the dange of a tax audit

For managers on the rise who want to be executives at the top!

Let 38 experts show you how to do it right

How to preserve your money—come hell or high water

The job you want is out there. The way to get it is in here . . .

Successful strategies to help you in your business

Increase your earning capacity by almost 30% within 6 months . . .

Why some people almost always make money in the stock market

**7:11   Business Publisher Learns How to Make Headlines
Believable: Case Study**

The business journals publisher had used the same self-mailer in promotions over a long period and it always worked well. It was built
around a headline: "Find out FREE why more than 50,000 tax experts
regularly turn to [name of journal]."

After two years, the piece was redesigned, and in place of the headline, several benefits were substituted stressing such copy appeals as:
"Save time," "Make more money," "Look good to your clients." These
new copy appeals were based on questioning of professionals in the
field on what they look for in new publication offers.

The redesigned piece failed to score. Unlike the earlier headline
claim, which "married" the claim to immediate supporting evidence
that it was true (. . . more than 50,000 tax experts regularly turn
to . . .), the new piece offered the right benefits, but failed to tie them
to a supporting authority.

The clear lesson from this study: When your headline and supporting
copy offer a benefit, give the promise credibility by tying it to a supporting authority.

**7:12   How to Make Long Headlines
More Interesting and More Effective**

The purpose of the headline is to lead the reader into the advertisement
or mailing piece. When it is too long, its impact is diminished or
counterproductive. Victor Schwab provided a precise formula for
length of headlines in his *How to Write a Good Advertisement* (Harper,
1962): "It is not wise to make a headline any lengthier than its primary
function actually requires."

Following are examples of long headlines used by three different
publishers for book promotions. In each instance, a series of step-by-
step procedures is followed through which I believe the effectiveness
of the headline was improved by shortening.

By following these procedures and applying the principles to your
own work, you will readily find that you can not only write effective
short headlines, but make them more interesting as well.

EXAMPLE 1

The original headline used (33 words):

> Introducing the first practical guide that shows you how your
> company—large or small—can have more representation in
> government . . . and a greater voice in federal regulation and
> legislation that affect your business. . .

Shortened to 19 words:

Introducing the first practical guide to help your company increase representation in government and influence federal regulation and legislation

Shortened to 12 words:

Practical ways to increase federal government representation . . . influence federal regulation and legislation

Shortened to 9 words:

Ways to increase federal representation . . . influence regulation and legislation

EXAMPLE 2

The original headline used (25 words):

Now you can achieve and increase your business success with hundreds of concise, practical answers to questions you face every day, if not every hour . . .

Shortened to 14 words:

Increase your business success with concise practical answers to questions you face every day

Shortened to 9 words

Concise, practical answers to questions you face every day

EXAMPLE 3

Teaser copy on the outer envelope is supposed to be the headline which gets you to look inside the envelope. It should be eye-catching, brief, and grab your interest instantly.

Here's one business book offering that, in my view, missed the boat entirely. If you consider all of the copy as a "headline," this one had over 100 words.

Original:

What kind of business is it in which—
- Someone will spend $100,000 . . . $200,000 . . . or even $500,000 to finance the sales of your product, at no interest rate whatsoever.
- Almost 100% of the time, your customers prepay your costs of selling to them.

- You get up to 10% second orders—before you've even delivered the original product.
- You can tax-shelter not only up to 100% of the profits you've made in this division—but also huge amounts of the profits you make in other divisions as well (all perfectly legitimate).

Believe it or not, it's your present business, selling your present products, THE NEW EASY WAY SHOWN YOU INSIDE!

Shortened to 10 words:

New, Easy, Profitable Way to Sell Your Present
Products . . . inside!

7:13   Why Many Textbook Ad Headlines Turn Readers Off

The textbook market is extremely competitive. Yet, in the advertising to college faculty, many prestigious publishers devote headlines not to book benefits or superiority, but to self-praise. The following examples indicate a sampling of actual headlines from "name" houses that tend to turn readers off:

The Best . . . from the Best

Don't Experiment . . . Use the Best!

The best science texts come from (imprint)

As the late Curtis Benjamin said in *Scholarly Publishing* (October 1971), "When bookmen extol the high values and noble uses of their product, no one listens. . . . Let us leave the praising of books to others."

By contrast, the advertising of many of these same houses for scientific and scholarly works does a far more effective job by listing only the imprint. Watch the ads in *Choice,* for example, and note the simplicity of headlines. You'll find such examples as:

New and Forthcoming Books from (name)

Just Published by (name)

New for Fall 1983 from (name)

This same principle holds true for textbook direct-mail promotion. Studies in both the United States and the United Kingdom show that college faculty depend heavily on publisher direct mail for information about new texts and will look at a publisher mailing even if it has a weak or ineffective headline. Abbott Friedland, a veteran book marketer, while based at Princeton University Press summed it up nicely, "Anytime we advertise . . . we emphasize the (Princeton) imprint. The book(s) in that ad becomes incidental."

**7:14   Ingredient That Increases Headline Readership:
Study Result**

The more specific your headline benefit, the more it is likely to increase readership of your advertisement. This was the finding of the Laboratory of Advertising Performance at McGraw-Hill Research in a study of a one-page advertisement prepared for *Electrical Construction and Maintenance.*

Various attendees at an electrical construction show were given a copy of the ad to score, but each got only one of three different headlines used.

- The first headline made a general statement which implied the user of the advertised products would benefit.
- The second headline was somewhat more specific but the benefit was expressed as a generalization.
- The third headline promised a benefit and used precise numbers to support the benefit.

Result:

1. Headline with IMPLIED promise of savings
   Definitely would read   67.8%

2. Headline with GENERALIZED promise of savings:
   Definitely would read   72.3%

3. Headline with SPECIFIC promise of savings:
   Definitely would read   75.6%

7:15   Review Quotes as Headlines for Backlist Titles

When you're promoting backlist titles that have already been reviewed, forget about writing headlines and let the reviews say it for you. Go through your reviews and select a good quote (or assemble one). You can be sure the review quote attributed to a prestigious journal will carry more weight with a scientist or scholar than anything a publisher might say.

Here are examples of review quotes as headlines from an engineering card deck received at the time of writing:

"enthusiastic and unlabored treatments . . ."—*Applied Optics*

"A clear, illuminating account."—*Physics Bulletin*

". . . well organized, well presented, succinct, well written . . ."
                              —*Optical Engineering*

". . . very useful and readable . . ."—*Nature*

". . . authoritative . . . strongly recommended."—*Choice*

8

Copy Fitting: How to Write Copy to Fit Space Available

8:01   Copy Fitting: Defined and Explained

Copy fitting is the determination of what amount of typewritten copy will set in a particular type size and face to fit a precise area. It is also establishing how much typeset area a given piece of typewritten copy will occupy.

For the writer of advertising and promotion copy, often the available area has been pre-established, like an advertisement which will occupy half a page, has $3\frac{1}{4}" \times 10"$ of open or "live" space, and into which you must fit a headline, descriptions of six books, and a signature—possibly also a coupon order form.

A knowledge of copy fitting will enable you to write precisely the correct amount of copy and to avoid costly overset.

In direct-mail promotion, there is more available space and the need to write in such precise amounts is not as great; nevertheless, often a flier of a particular design winds up with a lot of overset composition which results in copy-cutting and resetting.

Acquiring the habit of writing to fit for every job means a greater efficiency in writing, and considerable savings in composition. It requires only that you acquaint yourself with this basic information.

1. The particular typeface and size to be used.

2. Width in which line is to be typeset.

3. How many lines of set type it will take to fill available space.

4. How many letters or typewriter characters are required to fill one line.

8:02   When There's Too Much Composition:
Ways to Avoid Resetting Entire Job

Even with the best of copyfitting skills, you still have too much copy for the space available and you wind up with too much composition. What can you do with the overset to get it all in without resetting the text, or omitting one or more important titles? Here are some ways to save the overset:

1. See if copy will read as well with the last sentence of one or more paragraphs omitted.

2. Omit the last paragraph of one or more blocks of text—if it does not seem to affect the preceding descriptive matter.

3. Check whether a lengthy multi-paragraph block of copy will read as well with the opening paragraph deleted. Sometimes it may read better!

4. Leave overset text matter intact and reset book titles in a smaller type size.

5. Omit or shorten headline. Often a two-line head can be converted into a one-line head or shortened to one line.

6. If both book description and contents are given, omit the description and use contents only. On texts and some scientific works, contents are often all that is necessary.

7. If an advertisement includes both coupon and 800 telephone number, omit coupon and use 800 number only, in large type.

8. If an ad headline runs full width of the page, shorten to run across half the page width, possibly in a smaller size of type, and use the saved space for text matter.

9. Photographically reduce all composition by a small percentage.

8:03   Fitting Copy with Precision for Your Advertising
and Printed Promotion

This entry will enable you to fit copy, with reasonable precision, for any desired area in an advertisement or printed promotion. It should be born in mind that depth and width for most type areas are stated in picas or inches. However, depth for type itself, and the spacing in between, is stated in points.

TO MEASURE DEPTH

There are 72 points in an inch. Since type sizes are given in point size, a line of 9 point type will occupy ⅛ inch of depth. Thus eight lines of 9 point type will occupy 1 inch of depth in an ad or layout. Conversely, nine lines of 8 point type will occupy 1 inch. The spacing between lines is also expressed in points. Thus if 8 point type is spaced or leaded 1 point, its depth measurement would be the same as though it were set in 9 point type.

TO MEASURE WIDTH

While a type area may be stated as so many inches wide, most line widths are given in picas. A pica measures 12 points in width. There are 6 picas to the inch. Thus a 3-inch wide line would be stated as 18 picas. Line widths are often stated in fractional picas. As the conversion table (8:07) indicates, a line measuring 3⅛ inches in width would be stated as 18.75 picas.

EXPLANATION OF CHARACTER COUNT

The term *character count* means the number of typewritten characters, including letters, numbers, punctuation marks, and spaces that, when set in a given typeface and size, measures exactly 1 pica (⅙ inch). While most typewriters have the same number of characters per inch, in typeset composition, the number of characters per pica may vary from one typeface to another, even when set in the same type size.

The tables given in entry 8:04 provide the average number of typewriter characters per pica for most typefaces, set in lowercase type. If composition is to be in uppercase type, the count is usually about a third less. The tables are based on machine-set composition. Photocomposition may vary by about 10% from the numbers shown.

LEADING AS A FACTOR IN DEPTH OF TYPE

In typography, the term leading (pronounced led-ing) means the spacing between lines of type. Leading, or spacing between lines is stated in points. Thus 8 point type, leaded 2 points, would have the same depth as a line of type set in 10 point type. When a block of copy falls short of a desired depth, one may "spread out" the copy by opening up spaces between lines, between paragraphs, or both. Sometimes, just leading an opening paragraph by 1 point (for eight or nine lines) will stretch a piece of copy to precisely the desired length. Or, leading 2 extra points between paragraphs may improve readability of a block of type set solid.

HOW TO ARRIVE AT CHARACTER COUNT FOR A TYPEFACE

In copy fitting you fit to a specific typeface and size. The character count for most typefaces and sizes is available in a book of typefaces.

If none is available, you can determine the character count yourself by finding a sample of the typeface you have in mind and figuring it out. Here's what you do: Count the number of typewritten characters in several lines of printed type. Measure how many picas those lines consist of: three lines 4 inches wide would be 12 inches or 72 picas. Divide the number of picas into the total number of characters in those three lines. That will give you the average character count per pica for that typeface and size.

Your designer has specified a type area 3 inches wide by 3 inches deep. The job calls for 8 point Times Roman. Follow these steps:

1. You establish that the character count for 8 point Times Roman is 3.1 characters per pica.

2. You know that 3 inches of depth equals three times 72 points (per inch) or 216 points of depth. Since a line of 8-point type will only occupy 8/216 of the available space, you determine that it will take 27 lines to fill the entire 216 points. Your line is 3 inches wide which translates into 18 picas. For Times Roman, the character count is 3.1 per pica. By multiplying 3.1 times 18 picas per line, you have 55.8 characters per line.

3. You set your typewriter to accommodate 55-character line width and type no more than 27 lines, and this will translate into a block of 8 point Times Roman which should be exactly 3 inches wide and 3 inches deep.

   Suppose instead of 27 lines, the copy runs to only 24 lines and you want it to fit the 3-inch depth precisely. You can make up the missing 24 points (3 lines × 8 points per line) by leading each of the 24 lines by 1 point, or asking that the 24 lines of 8 point type be set on 9 point body. You can also leave the 24 lines set solid, but ask that the 24 lines, consisting of four paragraphs, be leaded an extra 8 points between paragraphs.

WORKING WITH THE COPY-FITTING TABLES

The universal copy-fitting tables which follow 8:04 give character counts for 6 point through 12 point type sizes. Once you have obtained the character count for any typeface or for the typeface specified for the job at hand, use the appropriate table to locate the correct typewriter margin settings and you're ready to start fitting copy to any desired area.

The character counts in the tables cover most line lengths up to 30 picas. Should you have to deal with a longer line, look up the character count for a line in the table half its length and double it.

8:04   **Converting Typewritten Characters into Type:
Tables**

If you wish to fit copy to any desired area, the following will guide
you to the correct typewriter margin setting for virtually any typeface
set in type sizes from 6 to 12 point. If you know the type size and
approximate number of characters per pica for the typeface in which
the copy is to be set, refer directly to the table for that type size. By
glancing at the column at the extreme left (the desired copy width),
you will find on the corresponding horizontal line the correct margin
setting.

Conversely, if you do not know the typeface or size and have a finite
amount of copy you wish to fit to a certain area, you can use the copy-
fitting tables to establish what type size in any given face will be
required for the job. For example, assuming you have a block of copy
with 500 typewritten characters and a copy area of 20 picas by ⅝ inch
deep, here is how you could determine the type size that would be
appropriate. Assume the desired typeface is Helvetica. In 6 point Helvetica has 3.5 characters per pica. A 20-pica line would utilize 70
characters. If ⅝ inch is approximately 45 points (⅝ inch times 72 points
to the inch), you could get seven 6 point lines into the ⅝ inch area.
Seven lines would utilize 490 characters, or just about the total 500
units in the copy. Specifying 6 point Helvetica for the job would give
you a precise fit on the first setting.

Pica	Average Number of Characters per Pica for 6 Pt. Type												
Width	3.1	3.2	3.3	3.4	3.5	3.6	3.7	3.8	3.9	4.0	4.2	4.4	4.8
1	3.1	3.2	3.3	3.4	3.5	3.6	3.7	3.8	3.9	4.0	4.2	4.4	4.8
10	31	32	33	34	35	36	37	38	39	40	42	44	48
12	37	38	39	41	42	43	41	46	47	47	50	53	58
14	43	45	46	48	49	50	51	53	55	55	58	62	68
16	50	51	52	54	56	58	59	60	62	63	67	71	78
18	56	58	59	61	63	65	66	68	70	71	75	80	86
20	62	64	65	68	70	72	73	76	78	79	84	89	96
22	68	70	72	75	77	79	81	84	86	87	92	98	106
24	74	77	78	82	84	86	88	92	94	95	100	107	116
26	81	83	85	88	91	94	95	100	101	103	109	115	126
28	87	90	91	95	98	101	103	108	109	111	117	124	134
30	93	96	98	102	105	108	110	116	117	119	126	133	146

Pica	Average Number of Characters per Pica for 7 Pt. Type											
Width	2.6	2.8	3.0	3.1	3.2	3.3	3.4	3.5	3.6	3.7	3.9	4.0
1	2.6	2.8	3.0	3.1	3.2	3.3	3.4	3.5	3.6	3.7	3.9	4.0
10	26	28	30	31	32	33	34	35	36	37	39	40
12	31	33	36	37	39	40	41	42	43	44	47	48
14	36	39	42	43	45	47	48	49	50	51	55	56
16	42	44	48	50	52	54	54	56	57	59	63	64
18	47	50	54	56	58	60	61	62	64	66	71	72
20	52	55	60	62	65	66	68	71	72	73	79	80
22	57	61	66	68	71	73	75	78	79	81	87	88
24	63	66	72	74	78	80	82	85	86	88	95	96
26	68	72	78	81	84	87	88	92	93	96	102	104
28	73	77	84	87	91	94	95	99	100	103	110	112
30	78	83	90	93	97	101	102	107	107	110	118	120

Pica	Average Number of Characters per Pica for 8 Pt. Type											
Width	2.3	2.4	2.6	2.7	2.8	2.9	3.0	3.1	3.2	3.3	3.4	3.5	3.7	3.8
1	2.3	2.4	2.6	2.7	2.8	2.9	3.0	3.1	3.2	3.3	3.4	3.5	3.7	3.8
10	23	24	26	27	28	29	30	31	32	33	34	35	37	39
12	28	29	31	32	34	34	36	37	38	40	40	42	44	47
14	32	34	36	37	39	40	42	43	45	47	47	49	51	54
16	36	38	42	42	45	46	48	49	51	53	54	56	58	62
18	41	43	47	48	50	51	54	55	58	60	60	63	65	70
20	45	48	52	53	56	57	60	61	64	66	67	70	73	77
22	49	53	57	58	62	63	66	67	70	73	74	77	80	85
24	53	58	62	64	67	68	72	73	77	80	80	84	87	93
26	58	62	68	69	73	74	78	79	83	87	87	91	94	100
28	62	67	73	74	78	80	84	85	90	93	94	98	101	108
30	66	74	78	80	84	86	90	92	96	100	101	105	108	116

Pica	Average Number of Characters per Pica for 9 Pt. Type									
Width	2.1	2.4	2.5	2.6	2.7	2.8	2.9	3.0	3.2	3.3	3.4
1	2.1	2.4	2.5	2.6	2.7	2.8	2.9	3.0	3.2	3.3	3.4
10	21	24	25	26	27	28	29	30	32	33	34
12	25	28	30	31	32	34	35	35	38	40	41
14	29	32	35	37	37	39	41	41	45	46	48
16	33	37	40	42	42	45	46	47	51	53	55
18	36	41	45	47	48	50	52	53	58	59	62
20	40	46	50	52	53	56	58	59	64	66	69
22	44	51	55	57	58	62	64	65	70	73	76
24	48	55	60	62	64	67	70	71	77	79	83
26	53	60	65	68	69	73	75	77	83	86	90
28	57	64	70	74	74	78	81	83	90	92	97
30	61	69	75	79	80	84	87	89	96	99	104

Pica Width	Average Number of Characters per Pica for 10 Pt. Type												
	2.0	2.1	2.2	2.3	2.4	2.5	2.6	2.7	2.8	2.9	3.0	3.1	3.2
1	2.0	2.1	2.2	2.3	2.4	2.5	2.6	2.7	2.8	2.9	3.0	3.1	3.2
10	20	21	22	23	24	25	26	27	28	29	30	31	32
12	24	25	26	28	29	30	31	32	33	34	36	37	39
14	28	29	31	32	34	35	36	37	39	40	42	43	45
16	32	34	35	37	39	40	42	43	44	46	48	50	52
18	36	38	40	41	44	45	47	48	50	51	54	56	58
20	40	42	44	46	48	50	52	54	55	57	60	62	65
22	44	46	48	51	53	55	57	59	61	63	65	68	71
24	48	50	53	55	58	60	62	64	66	68	71	74	78
26	52	55	57	60	63	65	68	70	72	74	77	81	84
28	56	59	62	64	68	70	73	75	77	80	83	87	91
30	60	63	66	69	73	75	78	81	83	86	89	93	97

Pica Width	Average Number of Characters per Pica for 11 Pt. Type									
	2.1	2.2	2.3	2.4	2.5	2.6	2.7	2.8	2.9	3.0
1	2.1	2.2	2.3	2.4	2.5	2.6	2.7	2.8	2.9	3.0
10	21	22	23	24	25	26	27	28	30	30
12	26	27	28	28	29	31	32	34	36	36
14	30	32	32	33	34	36	37	40	42	43
16	35	36	37	38	39	42	43	45	48	49
18	39	41	41	42	46	47	48	51	54	55
20	44	46	46	47	49	52	54	57	60	61
22	48	50	51	52	54	57	59	62	65	67
24	53	55	55	56	59	62	64	68	71	74
26	57	59	60	61	64	68	70	74	77	80
28	61	64	64	66	69	73	76	79	83	86
30	66	69	69	71	74	78	81	85	89	92

Pica Width	Average Number of Characters per Pica for 12 Pt. Type											
	1.7	1.8	1.9	2.0	2.1	2.2	2.3	2.4	2.5	2.6	2.8	2.9
1	1.7	1.8	1.9	2.0	2.1	2.2	2.3	2.4	2.5	2.6	2.8	2.9
10	17	17	19	20	21	22	23	24	25	26	28	29
12	20	20	22	24	25	26	27	28	29	31	33	34
14	24	24	26	28	29	31	32	33	34	36	39	40
16	27	27	30	32	33	35	36	38	39	42	44	46
18	31	30	33	36	37	40	41	42	44	47	50	52
20	34	34	37	40	42	44	45	47	49	52	56	57
22	37	37	41	44	46	48	50	52	54	57	61	63
24	41	40	44	48	50	53	54	56	59	62	67	69
26	44	43	48	52	54	57	59	61	64	67	72	74
28	48	47	52	56	59	62	63	66	69	73	78	80
30	51	50	56	60	64	66	68	71	74	78	84	86

8:05   **Copy Fitting Less Precise with Photocomposition: Variables to Consider**

No copy-fitting formula is 100% accurate. Vivian Sudhalter, former creative head of the McGraw-Hill Professional and Reference Book Division, cautions that in photocomposition a new set of variables tends to make existing copy-fitting procedures less precise. When first queried, she suggested a 10% allowance as a rule of thumb for variables in copy fitting. However, she proposed one should also take these points into consideration in determining a fit:

- The conscientiousness of the type house
- The size of the face (the bigger the size, the more the runover)
- The character of the face (the more extended, or "blockish," the more the runover)
- The pica width of the line (the longer the line, the better the fit)
- Whether the copy is justified (it shouldn't happen, but machines seem to be lazy with hyphens and there's more runover with unjustified lines)

8:06   **Quick Rule-of-Thumb for Estimating Copy Length**

You're writing copy for an ad and the "live" area or area in which your descriptive matter must fit measures 3 inches wide by 6½ inches deep exclusive of headline and signature. How much, roughly, can you write in a given type size to keep within this area?

Here's a quick rule-of-thumb formula to guide you in your efforts. It's called *the square-inch method.*

1. Determine the number of square inches of type area (in this instance you will have 19½ inches).
2. Find a block of copy set in the same typeface and size in which the ad will be set and draw a pencil or pen outline around 1 square inch. Pick an example where composition has been set solid, i.e., without spacing between the lines.
3. Count the number of words in that 1 inch block.
4. Multiply times number of square inches available. The answer is the approximate maximum number of words of copy that can be written to fill that area.

In this example, let's say you've selected 8 point Helvetica as your sample. You count about 25 words in a 1-inch block. You have 19.5 inches of type area in the ad times 25-words-per-inch gives you about 488 words. With 10 words to the line in your sample, you have to write about 48 lines of copy.

8:07   **Inches to Points and Picas: Conversion Table**

Measurement in inches	Equivalent in points	Equivalent in picas
$\frac{1}{32}$	2.25	0.1875
$\frac{1}{16}$	4.5	0.375
$\frac{1}{8}$	9	0.75
$\frac{1}{4}$	18	1.5
$\frac{1}{2}$	36	3
$\frac{3}{4}$	54	4.5
$\frac{7}{8}$	63	5.25
1	72	6
$1\frac{1}{4}$	90	7.5
$1\frac{1}{2}$	108	9
$1\frac{3}{4}$	126	10.5
2	144	12
$2\frac{1}{8}$	153	12.75
$2\frac{1}{4}$	162	13.5
$2\frac{1}{2}$	180	15
$2\frac{3}{4}$	198	16.5
3	216	18
$3\frac{1}{8}$	225	18.75
$3\frac{1}{4}$	234	19.5
$3\frac{1}{2}$	252	21
$3\frac{3}{4}$	270	22.5
4	288	24

9

Copy Techniques and Approaches for Books in the Sciences, Engineering, and Medicine

. . . a technical book deals not only with a rational need, but also a psychological need—namely, self-image—for the security of knowing the book is there should be the need for it ever arise."

Ed Nash, speaking at PPMG
Meeting in New York, May 1982.

Scientists are, by training, skeptical. Schooled in the empirical method, they doubt, they question, they probe. Their credence is not easily secured.

from "An Executive Summary of a Study
of Scientific Publications" by
McGraw-Hill Research, 1983

9:01 Writing Copy for the Technical Book: Guidelines

Faced with the task of writing copy for a technical book, the less-experienced often find it difficult to extract essential information and to present it in a logical sequence. The job becomes even more difficult when a wealth of information is available, and the writer has been asked to limit his copy to perhaps 100 to 150 words of description. These guidelines will be helpful:

1. Open with a short, one-sentence description. It should provide the basic essence of what the book is all about, so that it will suffice if all the other copy following is omitted.
2. Briefly present the book's principal benefits. Emphasize those that are new, unique, or unusual.
3. State the primary focus of the book.
4. Mention the book's principal audience(s) or level of presentation.
5. Mention the book's special features or characteristics: indexes, tables, illustrations, appendixes, etc.
6. Whenever possible, avoid repeating words used in the title or subtitle. Often they are self-explanatory. Use the available space to SELL by showing how this book does its job better than its competitors, or fills a real need in the field.
7. In summarizing material which is essentially incomprehensible to the nonspecialist, it is safest to draw your descriptive copy directly from the main headings of the Table of Contents. Paraphrase as little as possible. Condense by elimination, rather than rewording.

9:02 Copy Appeals to Scientists and Engineers

The physical sciences are characterized by rapid technological turnover; consequently, a professor's learning remains useful for a relatively short period of time . . . scientists respond by spreading their learning efforts over their careers and by learning only that which is more or less immediately useful.

John M. McDowell (Arizona State University)
in *American Economic Reivew,*
September 1982.

Professor McDowell's statement bears an important message to those seeking useful copy appeals for messages directed to scientists and engineers. Whenever it is possible to do so, stress the currentness of the information offered. If a new edition, how it differs from the prior edition. If competitive with a previously published work, what new or more recent information it offers that was not in the other work.

Scientists have a need to be knowledgeable about what other researchers in their field are doing. Scientists will recognize the benefits in copy which stresses the timeliness and currentness of the material offered.

Engineers, especially those out of school for a number of years, want to be informed on state-of-the-art developments—information that will help them avoid professional obsolescence. They will buy books that offer detailed coverage in areas of special interest.

9:03 Engineers Tell Why They Buy Books on Engineering Subjects

A practicing engineer will usually buy a book on an engineering subject from personal or employer funds for these three reasons:

- To help solve an immediate engineering problem
- To help update professional skills or knowledge
- Because he or she feels threatened on the job by lack of knowledge and thinks the book will help

Six practicing engineers offered these suggestions during a 1981 discussion on the subject with marketers from McGraw-Hill. In addition to citing these factors as reasons for buying engineering books, they also indicated that book promotion for important engineering books should focus on those critical chapters that are important to a prospective buyer and not on those that build up to or elaborate on the important contents.

9:04 R&D Scientists and Engineers Will Buy from a Contents Listing: Study Result

A 1980 study, conducted by the Institute for Scientific Information, carried an important message for copywriters of advertising for scientific and engineering books aimed at the research/development market: This audience will readily buy a book from a listing of contents only, without descriptive copy.

The ISI study probed the book-buying patterns of subscribers to its *Current Contents,* most of whom are in various research and development branches of science and engineering.

Current Contents is published in seven editions by discipline. The study surveyed a statistical cross-section of the 35,000-subscriber base. Each *Current Contents* issue carries the contents of recent issues of scientific and engineering periodicals. Along with the contents of the periodicals, each issue also carries the contents of selected new, pertinent scientific books in a section titled "Current Book Contents."

"Current Book Contents" includes an ordering coupon and invites subscribers to order the books listed directly from the ISI office. Three-fourths of those responding to the survey reported that they bought books on the basis of the contents listings in "Current Book Contents."

9:05 Twelve Traps That Reduce Effectiveness of Sci-Tech Book Advertising

1. Do not advertise a book as "new" if it is not of the current year or season.
2. Do not advertise a book without including a publication date.
3. Do not advertise a book without a price or at least a tentative price.
4. Do not advertise a sci-tech book without including its full subtitle.
5. Do not advertise an edition about to be superseded without giving some indication of the new edition's availability.

6. Do not advertise a symposium proceedings without identifying it as such.

7. Do not advertise a book with an old edition illustration if the new jacket or artwork for same is available.

8. Do not advertise a book at the old price at a time when prices are about to be increased, without a cutoff date or a price increase disclaimer.

9. Do not advertise a book with a mock-up illustration which is not reflective of the true size / thickness of the actual book.

10. Do not advertise a book for which no ordering provision has been made on the accompanying order form.

11. Do not advertise a book for which the copy is highly technical until it has been cleared with author, sponsoring editor, or a competent authority.

12. Do not advertise a book as *paperbound* if it has a non-conventional binding, such as spiral binding. Specify type of binding; *paperbound* is assumed to be perfect binding.

9:06   Hard Sell and Sci-Tech Ad Copy

When your advertising asks for the order right out front with a price and a place to buy and with "NOW" included in the copy, that's hard-sell advertising.

Lewis Kornfeld, in *To Catch a Mouse, Make a Noise Like a Cheese*, Prentice-Hall, 1983.

Early in my publishing career as a writer of promotion copy for scientific and technical books, I encountered Ben Russak, who had just established American Elsevier Publishing Company.

"Avoid hard sell," Russak advised, "if you want to be successful in this area of publishing." I did. And I was. And 20 years later I am able to recall and write about it.

If you write or plan to write ad copy for scientific, technical, and scholarly books, this is still good advice.

9:07   Basic Differences in Copy Approach
Between Scientific and Business Books

The basic differences in copy approach between the scientific book and the business book, says Peter Hodges, a leading book marketing professional, "is that engineers and scientists read out of curiosity about their field, while business people read out of fear that they may have missed something.

"In science copywriting, sell the content."

"In business copywriting, sell the benefits."

**9:08   Clearing Up the Confusion Between "Scientific"
and "Medical" Books**

In some publishing establishments, medical books are integrated into
a general science publishing program. In such houses, copywriters
make little or no differentiation between promotional copy for medical
books and other scientific works.

In medical publishing establishments, or in houses where there are
special copywriters just for medical promotions, such copywriting is
seen as different or special because of the highly specialized nature
of the audiences and markets to which medical books are directed.

Confusion as to when a book is a scientific book and when it is a
medical book exists primarily in houses that have integrated science/
medical publishing programs. To clear up this confusion, we asked a
veteran medical marketer what differentiated a medical book from a
scientific work. This was her answer:

> A medical book is designed for someone in medical practice or research. It
> must have clinical application, i.e., apply to the care of people who are
> sick, and be of interest to practitioners, nurses, or students.

9:09   Copy Guidelines for Medical Book Promotions

1. Use normal language where specialized medical terminology can
   be avoided.
2. Stress benefits: "well illustrated," "200 full-color illustrations,"
   "covers these key features," etc.
3. Medical people will respond to good headlines, brief copy, benefits.
4. Table of contents is a must in medical promotion. If the doctor can't
   see the book, the list of contents is the next best thing. *Show* what's
   in the book; don't tell what's in it.
5. The stature of the author in his or her field or specialty is a very
   important point to cite.
6. Affiliation with a prestigious institution also carries weight, especially if the author is not well known.
7. Talk about the book, not about the field.
8. Newness of offer is the greatest appeal. Feature new books and new
   information offered for greatest effectiveness in medical direct-mail
   promotions.
9. If your mailing is to doctors, a "P.S." at the end of the letter usually
   will get read before the body of the letter. When writing a promotion
   letter to an MD, save an important feature for the postscript.

9:10   **Copy to Engineers Addresses Readers' Fear,**
        Offers Many Benefits: Case Study

One of the primary reasons engineers buy books on engineering subjects is that they feel threatened by lack of knowledge and think books they buy will help (see 9:03).

The copywriter for the Mechanical Engineer's Book Club (McGraw-Hill) skillfully addresses this fear in a 1984 book club membership solicitation. The headline copy proclaims "9 reasons why membership . . . is essential to the professional who wants to stay on top of changing technology."

The reasons are then briefly stated with strong benefit-oriented copy that makes repeated use of "you" and "yours," as the following excerpts indicate. The italics are mine.

1. *You* save on every book *you* buy.
2. [Selections] give *you* continuing access to the latest books in *your* field.
3. *You* will immediately begin to participate in [a plan] that allows *you* . . .
4. *You* are given a far wider selection . . . than *you* would find in most bookstores.
5. *You* keep abreast of fresh ideas, new information, current developments.
6. *You* always have a . . . free examination period . . . return any book that doesn't meet *your* needs . . . *Your* account . . . credited.
7. [Main selection shipped if no receipt of] *your* reply card [with] alternate selections *you* would like to receive, or *your* desire not to receive a book that month. . . .
8. . . . *you* will receive regular bulletins . . . no obligation or commitment on *your* part.
9. . . . *you* will be sent a separate brochure [with] "special books for *your* special interests."

9:11   **Copy Benefits for Bookstore Promotions**
        of Scientific and Technical Books

1. Emphasize those titles that offer trade discounts.
2. Offer paperbound editions of popular titles at trade discount.
3. Offer spring and fall combination specials (as on a 10- or 25-book assortment) at higher-than-usual discount.
4. Mention the availability of an Agency Plan with a preferential discount.
5. Offer to give a good discount on single-copy special orders.
6. Offer to accept collect calls or a toll-free 800 number on special orders, and promise fast fulfillment.
7. Offer a cash discount with prompt payment.

8. Offer free freight with prepaid orders.

9. Offer to drop-ship to special order customers.

10. Offer the name of a contact person who can be called through a toll-free number for book pricing and availability information.

**9:12   The Social Science Research Monograph:
Promotional Copy Approach**

The social science research monograph represents a theoretical, speculative, or substantive contribution to social science knowledge and generally can be promoted to a widely varied audience that includes policymakers, researchers, practitioners, and intelligent, well-informed laypersons. Your promotion copy should aim to convince the potential reader that the book makes a significant contribution to social science, explain the implications of the research presented, and stress the permanent value of the book for archives. If the book offers numerous citations to other relevant research, the number of literature references should be mentioned; as should the number of tables or appendixes if either is an important or sizable part of the book's content.

10

Copy Approaches for Book Promotions to the College Market

___

10:01 Copy Approach in Textbook Promotion Letters

Textbook promotions involving a single book are often very simple. This is especially true of upper-level texts where the number of prospects is often very small. Many such promotions consist of an $8\frac{1}{2}'' \times 11''$ offset letter printed on a letterhead in one color of ink. Some have a "built-in" coupon as part of the letter; others are accompanied by a return order card or envelope for examination requests.

Such letters usually stress benefits to the student and emphasize contents, features, and supplements for instructor and student. If mailed prepublication, they also give availability date—an important aspect of any college promotion. They might also cite advantages over competing texts. Letters are printed on one or two sides of the sheet, often with the coupon on the back. The primary intent of any such letter is to get the professor to request an examination copy of the book.

10:02 When You Promote Professional Books to Academics: Copy Guidelines

Academics are accustomed to receiving complimentary copies of books aimed specifically at the adoption market. However, many publishers not specifically in the textbook market often promote their professional references to college faculty. When they receive a request for a complimentary or "desk" copy, they are at a loss as to how to respond.

On the one hand, their policy is not to give away copies of professional books or imported co-editions. On the other, they fear the loss of a possible adoption. One way that such situations are handled is to send the book on 60-day free examination.

The publisher informs the instructor that the book requested will be sent under three options:

- If the book is adopted and the publisher so notified, the instructor may then retain the book as a desk copy.
- The book may be returned within 60 days and the invoice will be cancelled.
- The instructor may retain the book for his or her personal library and remit payment, usually at an academic discount.

Publishers using this procedure usually set a minimum-copy requirement for adoptions. Most require an adoption order of ten or more copies. A few require eight or more. One publisher sets the minimum at five.

Here are examples of copy approaches used by six different publishers in promotions that included college faculty:

EXAMPLE ONE:

> Is either of these books a possible selection for your course? We'll be glad to send you a copy to look over at your leisure on a 60-day on-approval examination. If you subsequently order 10 or more copies for classroom use as a required text, return the invoice with notification of the bookstore order and we'll cancel it. Retain the copy of the book as your desk copy. Or, purchase the book for personal use at our academic discount. (Of course, you may return the book in saleable condition with the invoice, thereby cancelling the charge.)

EXAMPLE TWO:

> We acknowledge receipt of your request for a complimentary examination copy of (title) to consider for adoption in (course name) course you offer at (institution). We consider (title) a reference work rather than a classroom text and have not set aside a supply of complimentary examination copies for general distribution. If, however, you order a copy for your personal library, we will be pleased to extend our 10% academic discount. Should you subsequently adopt this book for your course and place an order for 10 or more copies, we then will cancel the

charge billed you for the book, and the copy you purchased would in effect become a complimentary desk copy.

EXAMPLE THREE:

Please send
1. Title/Author _____
2. Title/Author _____
3. Title/Author _____

For Possible Adoption

Send on one-month approval. Charge will be cancelled upon adoption of 10 or more copies. Please notify us within the 30-day period, and retain approval copy for desk use.

Course Title:

Date Course Offered:

Usual Enrollment:

Author of Present Text:

For Personal Reference

( ) Bill me at (____%) educational discount
( ) Payment herewith, less (____%) educational discount

EXAMPLE FOUR:

As the nature of the book you requested prohibits gratis sampling, we will be pleased to offer it on approval at our customary academic discount. If you decide to adopt the title for your class and subsequently ten or more student copies are ordered through your bookstore, we will be glad to cancel the charge and have you keep the book with our compliments.

EXAMPLE FIVE:

Please send the following book(s) for 30 days free examination
Author and Title:

( ) For possible class adoption
( ) For my personal reference library

Books shipped for 30 days examination will be billed to you at (____%) educational discount. If adopted for class use in quantities of 5 or more, simply return our invoice or invoice number and the charges will be cancelled, and you may retain your book as your desk copy.

Note: On requesting an examination copy, please give course title, usual enrollment, and present text.

EXAMPLE SIX:

( ) For my personal library
( ) For possible class adoption
Please send at my professional discount of (_____%). If 6 or more copies are ordered for my class, I shall notify you to cancel the charge for this copy.

Course Title:

Semester course given:

Approx. enrollment:

Present text:

Titles wanted:

10:03   What Professors Look for in College Textbook Promotions: Study Result

A leading publisher of college texts now operates under a well-defined mail promotion program that evolved through a combination of in-house research and work by its large staff of college travelers.

The program is both time and money saving and extremely cost effective. It was launched with a field research program by its travelers who questioned college professors about what they looked for in a brochure for a college textbook, i.e., what would prompt them to open a brochure that they received in the mail from a publisher. From this study, involving 60 to 70 travelers, this finding emerged:

1. What the professor wants to know immediately is the name of the book, the author, and what course the book is for.
2. The second most important part of a college promotion should be a complete table of contents.
3. The third most important part of any college textbook promotion is a business reply card, something that is easy to tear out or remove and send back to the publisher.

"Out of this study," says a product manager from this publishing establishment, "we found that creativity in college brochures was not worth the money we were spending on it. What was needed for good college promotions was good solid copy and a good headline."

Prior to the start of the college promotion study, the publisher called in a number of free-lance artists and had a number of basic design formats prepared that would be suitable for college textbook promotions. The different formats were shown to college professors by the college travelers and their opinions were solicited.

What the college faculty reactions indicated was that a professor sees a brochure as a vehicle for getting a book. Anything else that the publisher puts into a college brochure should be there solely to reinforce that primary objective.

But it is the business reply card that really makes the brochure work. The sole aim of all the copy is to get the professor to return the business reply card. (Some professors prefer to contact the college rep directly, rather than to mail back a card, especially if their interest is immediate, as it frequently is around book adoption time. A useful adjunct to the order card is a toll-free 800 number.)

In the case of the publisher making the survey, every request card received is treated as a lead. The card is forwarded to the traveler and he is asked to visit the professor, so that the mail advertising is directly coordinated with the sales efforts of the travelers.

10:04   Suggested Copy Approach When Major Textbook Is Involved

If you're dealing with a large-volume major text where the promotion copy will be a critical factor in the book's success, and you have a substantial amount of promotion planned, here is a way to prevent problems.

Prepare a bank of copy on the text in a number of variations from a short two- or three-line blurb all the way up to a major large-scale presentation. When you have prepared five, six, seven, or even ten or more copy variations, run them past the book's author or authors for prior approval.

Subsequently, when any type of promotion is planned, go to the copy bank and utilize one of the approved copy variations, or some combination of two or more. When you have to prepare a handout, a poster, an ad, or any type of presentation, you have a ready source of written material that you know will be right the first time.

10:05   Pitfalls of Writing Textbook Promotion Copy: Advice from a College Traveler

A long-time college traveler (now an editor) offers this word of advice to writers of textbook promotion copy:

> Be aware of what your reading market is when you sit down to write copy.
>
> A lot of copy for college texts gets written in liberal-minded Eastern cities and the copywriter tends to ignore more conservative attitudes in some areas. Sometimes he or she loses track of readership in the small Midwest towns where they don't share these liberal views and may be inclined to find some copy offensive.
>
> It should also be kept in mind by copywriters that a lot of their copy will be directed to many colleges which have religious roots or bases, and attempts at jokes or humor may not be viewed in the same light as was intended by the writer.

A case in point was a text I handled on human sexuality which included frontal nude illustrations. Some colleges with religious orientation were offended and sent the book back.

Women's rights is another highly sensitive area where copy, unless carefully screened, may have a negative impact.

I repeat, be aware of your market and its sensitivities before you write. This is critical for any copy intended for the college market. Never forget that you are writing copy for the "chooser" of the book and not the ultimate reader.

10:06   Copywriting Practices of a Leading Textbook Publisher: Interview with Marketing Manager

A textbook marketing manager describes his practices as follows:

The in-house copywriting in most houses that publish texts is adequate. But for extra-special work, there are good writers. But they are hard to find or too expensive [two "name" agencies at the time of this writing were charging $60 or more per hour]. In our house when extra-special copy is needed, we rely on outside free-lancers.

Most of the ones I've used have journalism degrees and work out of their homes. They'll work for a quarter to a third of what the big agencies charge.

We had previously paid for our promotional flyers by the job, but we felt the copy cost wasn't worth it—about $300–$400 for a single-title flyer—so we went for the free-lance route, which has worked out satisfactorily.

How do we work with free lancers? When we do a flyer, we work out a strategy of what we want to do. The product manager is responsible for the strategy. He calls in the free-lance copywriter and tells him, "Here is what we want to do. Here are the facts, and this is what our goal is for this piece. You give us the copy."

We have set a series of standard promotion formats for our brochures. We used to spend a lot of money on flyer design. Then we got some outside artists and had them design a series of formats that we now use.

The basic flyer format has a heading, a brief introductory paragraph, bulleted feature copy, and a table of contents. We did some research and found that the most important copy on a college brochure is the table of contents. The most important element in the copy is to identify the book and the market.

How do we work with a free-lance copywriter? Well, we have seven or eight basic ad formats. The product manager selects the format he wishes used for the brochure or flyer and gives the copywriter a dummy copy of the format desired.

Along with the dummy of the format, the product manager informs the free-lance copywriter of the strategy or purpose of the flyer. With it, he or she supplies selected data that the copywriter can use to extract the data needed for the flyer. This may include a copy of the author's questionnaire, or anything that may provide a source of useful information to the copywriter.

Armed with the dummy format, the strategy, and the source material, the free-lance copywriter is given about a week to complete the work.

10:07 The Actual Review as Promotion Copy: Guidelines

A review of a book in a leading journal in the field carries much more authority than any copywriter can lend to a piece of copy. When a book, such as an undergraduate text, has been given in-depth review coverage, it is virtually impossible to select precisely the right phrase to capture the essence of the review.

One alternative is to reprint the review in its entirety in your promotional flier on the book. Another is to reprint the review (with permission) as it appears in the periodical, and to mail it as a page reprint from that publication with a cover letter calling attention to the review.

Here is how one such cover letter was worded with a review reprint mailing:

Dear Professor:

The March edition of The Journal of Chemical Education carried a review of (title and author). In the event you missed seeing this review, we enclose a copy for your interest.

If you are presently teaching or intend to teach (subject of book), and have not received a copy of (repeat book's title), we would be happy to send you one.

Yours sincerely,

10:08 Use of Adoption Lists in Promotion Copy: Some Guidelines

Copywriters for college texts should take heed of the fact that listings of schools that have adopted a particular text are a useful sales vehicle, but that there are risks involved.

One of these, a college marketer points out, is that a listing of large prestigious universities may be counterproductive if you are promoting a textbook to small community colleges. On the other hand, if you are promoting to the large well-known universities and you include in your adoption list such names as Harvard and University of California at Berkeley, you are bound to impress.

Another element of risk in using such lists to be certain that the schools listed are actually using the book as a text. Some adoption lists tend to be inaccurate; a large order from a school bookstore might be for an evening continuing education course, rather than for an undergraduate text. Be sure of your sources when including adoption lists in promotion copy.

10:09   Obtaining Permission to Quote:
Follow-Up Letter After Comp Copy Was Sent

Good quotes from professors always strengthen a college textbook promotion. Many professors to whom comp copies of a text have been sent are happy to provide such quotes when requested to do so. Here is a sample of a follow-up letter one publisher sends *after* comp copies of the book have been sent. It asks for comments or suggestions and adds a check-off box stating, "You may quote me in your advertising."

[Publisher's Letterhead]

Dear Professor:

Recently we had the pleasure of sending you a complimentary copy of (title and author).

We would like to know if this text meets your educational needs. Your comments and suggestions at the bottom of this letter will be appreciated by us and helpful to our authors.

A self-addressed, stamped envelope is enclosed for your mailing convenience. Thank you for your cooperation.

Cordially,

(printed signature)

Name (typed)
Title

Name _____

School _____

Address _____

Department _____

Course title _____ Enrollment _____

Do you plan to use (book title) in your course? _____

If so, how? _____ text _____ reference _____ supplement

Will this book replace another book? _____ yes _____ no. If so, which one?

For what other course would this text be suitable? _____

Additional Comments / Suggestions _____

_____

_____

_____

_____

☐ You may quote me in your advertising.

_____

Signature

```
My comments on ...............................................................
                        Author or Editor                    Title




    ......... Date                      Name of course .........................
    May we quote you? □Yes   □ No       Level? □ Fresh. □ Soph. □ Jun. □ Sen. □ Grad.
    Will you adopt? □ Definitely □ Possible □ No   For use as: Req'd Main Text □ Recom. Reading □
    Decision date ...........................   Approx. Course enrollment? ..............
    Text used .............................

    Name (please print) .................................................................
    Dept. .....................................................   Position ................
    Institution ...................................................   Tel. ................
    City ........................... State ............. Zip Code ...............
```

FIGURE 9 This business reply card is typical of those sent out with complimentary copies of books by the Educational Sales Department of publishers.

10:10   Obtaining Permission to Quote: Card Enclosure with Comp Copy

Figure 9 is an example of a request to quote, printed on a $4\frac{1}{4}'' \times 6''$ postpaid reply card and enclosed with each comp copy mailed. Surprisingly, as with a number of such samples examined, there was no request for a signature on the card.

10:11   Delay in Publication of Important New Text: Copy Approach to Save Adoptions

The new edition of a major text has been delayed, and you're asked to prepare an announcement for college faculty announcing the delay. Here's a copy approach that worked for one publisher:

Dear Professor:

The new edition of (title) by (author), originally scheduled for publication in March, has been delayed until May. We would be most appreciative if you could hold your textbook decision until you have had an opportunity to examine this new text. We feel confident your interest and that of your students will be profitably served by your consideration of Professor (author's name) new edition.

Sincerely,

The Editors

10:12 Special Characteristic of Good Copy: Case Study

A well-written letter or piece of promotion copy has a special characteristic: it will stand the test of time. Copy that reads well and can hold its credibility many years after it was written is good copy. Further, good copy sets a pattern which can serve as a model for the writing of copy for similar works, with a minimum of change.

The letter following offers such an example. It was a personalized letter, addressed to professors of electric engineering by name, to introduce a new edition of an electrical engineering textbook in 1950. The writer and signer of the letter, Warren Sullivan, is currently Vice-President, Marketing, Publishing Group, John Wiley & Sons, Inc.

October 25, 1950

Dear Professor [name]:

We take great pleasure in announcing the publication of the third edition of Professor Kuhlmann's DESIGN OF ELECTRICAL APPARATUS on October 19th. The author and publisher have forwarded a copy to you with their compliments and you may expect to receive it within a few days.

This book will offer complete and practical methods for designing electrical machinery, with simple calculations for each type of machine, covering D-C machines, A-C generators and synchronous motors, and induction motors and transformers. The latter section has been extensively revised to include the method of determining the effect of saturation in leakage flux paths and the calculation of the deep bar constants and limits have been revised to conform to the latest practices.

Changes in work curves, the use of new design values, the inclusion of a design of a single phase power supply transformer, material on multiplex windings, equivalent diagram calculations for transformers and various types of rotors in induction motor design are special features of this edition. A removable appendix of about twenty-six pages, containing symbols and fundamentals is also included, to be inserted under a band inside the rear cover.

The author has taken special pains to emphasize the points that he believed would be of general interest, in line with the suggestions offered by former users. When you have had an opportunity to examine it with a view towards its applicability in your course, we will certainly welcome your comments.

Very sincerely yours,

Warren Sullivan
Acting Sales Manager

**10:13   Textbook Promotion Technique:
           Letter Written by Author**

A technique used with great effectiveness from time to time by college textbook publishers is the letter written by the author on his own institutional letterhead to potential adopters.

The reason such letters are effective is that academic educators are extremely peer conscious and will accept a statement by a fellow educator about a potential textbook more readily than they will accept an advertising blurb, signed or unsigned, from the book's publisher.

Here is an example of one such letter used with great success by the College Division at McGraw-Hill. It was written by the author on the letterhead of his school and addressed to "Dear Fellow Chemist and Educator."

Dear Fellow Chemist and Educator:

By this time you should have received from McGraw-Hill a complimentary copy of my new text, *Introduction to Chemical Analysis.* I am writing to thank you for considering the text for your course in chemical analysis.

I have spent a great deal of time preparing a text which I believe is the best available teaching tool for analytical chemistry. I would like to point out a few of the features of the text.

Chapter 6, entitled "Error in the Chemical Analysis and Sampling," is a discussion of several topics that are generally applicable to all methods of analysis. The text has been written so that Chapter 6 can be taught prior to Chapters 2 through 5 if desired. Nothing in Chapter 6 requires knowledge of the material covered in an earlier chapter. I think you will find the chapters on molecular spectroscopy, atomic spectroscopy, potentiometry, nonpotentiometric electroanalysis and chromatography (Chapters 8 through 13) to be particularly thorough and current. The separate chapter on curve fitting, the working curve method, and the standard addition technique (Chapter 7) is designed to demonstrate the general utility of those techniques.

Chapters 2 through 5, on chemical equilibrium, gravimetry, acid-base reactions and volumetric analyses, contain a balanced treatment of the important classical methods of analysis. The chapter on analytical automation and process-control analyzers (Chapter 14) is a brief introduction to the design and use of analytical equipment that is commonly used in hospitals, governmental laboratories, and industrial laboratories.

I have attempted to write an easily understandable text that covers the major areas of analytical chemistry. After you have had an opportunity to review the text (regardless of your plans for adoption), I would like to hear your comments. Specific suggestions are especially appreciated.

If you have not received a copy of the text, please write or phone (318-231-6737) me and I will see to it that you get one. For faster service, contact your local McGraw-Hill representative or Mr. James A. Dodd, Marketing Manager, Science and Mathematics, College Division, McGraw-Hill Book Company, 1221

Avenue of the Americas, New York, NY 10020. Thank you for considering the text and for your assistance.

10:14   Copy Orientation for Continuing Education Market

If you plan to promote to the continuing education (CE) market, your copy should be oriented to the segment of the CE market being solicited and the aims of the CE program. Essentially, CE courses are targeted to these four groups:

1. Professionals (doctors, teachers, engineers, business people, nurses) taking vocational or professional retraining courses
2. Persons attending school nights or weekends to obtain a college degree
3. Day students taking some courses at night to avoid conflicts in schedule or to get their degree more quickly
4. People taking recreational courses

TIMING AND TARGETING OF PROMOTIONS

Over half the courses in college or university continuing education programs are taught by daytime faculty members who may already be receiving your mailed promotions for courses they teach. Rather than risk duplication of effort by mailing to complete lists of CE instructors just in order to reach part-time faculty, consider instead mailing to the CE area coordinator for the subject or discipline, and group all your titles within that subject area in a single promotional mailing. (A list of CE coordinators by subject area is available from College Marketing Group.)

CE coordinators assemble the fall program during the summer months. Often they may decide on textbooks to be used in the school's CE programs. However, your promotion piece should ask them to route your mailing to the appropriate part-time or full-time instructor if they do not control adoptions.

10:15   Copywriting for the UK Academic Market

Two marketers at a prominent UK publishing establishment were asked what approaches or guidelines would be helpful in writing copy for the UK academic market. Their replies follow.

MARKETER ONE

Copywriting for the academic market in the UK should not be gimmicky. Good, straightforward, factual information is required and, of course, if it is a textbook, the level should be clearly stated.

MARKETER TWO

In writing copy for the UK market, it is important not to oversell, not to have too aggressive an approach. You have to give a very accurate picture of what the book contains.

If you're doing textbook copy, it is very important to give an accurate guide to the contents. Professors are not as concerned with where the authors are when they write as with what is in the book—where authors got their degrees is not important (though I understand that it is in the U.S.). And for college texts, the more straightforward the copy, the better.

10:16   Copy Approach Used to Request Return of Unwanted Comp Copies

Legally, a publisher has no recourse when he sends out comp copies to a professor for evaluation. And many professors augment their income in a modest way by selling the comp copies they receive. But here's one publisher who makes an effort to request the return of unwanted comps. His approach utilizes a book enclosure measuring $3\frac{3}{4}'' \times 5\frac{1}{2}''$ on which appears the following copy:

You can help the rising cost of textbooks!

The enclosed copy is being sent to you for adoption consideration. However, if you don't wish to consider it, please use this postage paid label to return the book to us. The book will then be available to a colleague for review. Your cooperation can have considerable impact on the price of textbooks.

Thank you.

The above slip-with-copy appears on a surface that is coated with dry-gum adhesive. The reverse side of the slip is a Special Fourth Class Rate merchandise return label (publisher pays postage due plus 20¢ merchandise return fee). Recipient need only moisten and affix slip to parcel to return book postage-free.

11

Copy Approaches
for Book Promotions
to the Various Library Markets

**11:01 Seven Copy Strengths That Increase Effectiveness
of Professional and Reference Book Promotions
to Libraries**

You can strengthen the effectiveness of your copy if it defines clearly
or emphasizes the following seven points:

1. Purpose, scope, and audience of book.
2. Timeliness of subject matter.
3. Advantages over other works in same field. Stress the newness of
   the contents, especially in rapidly changing fields or subject areas.
4. If a new edition, percentage of new material and/or revisions since
   previous edition.
5. Format of your book(s), if material is presented in a different, more
   convenient format than that of competing works.
6. Value of your book in strengthening a specific reference collection.
7. Credentials of author, especially if he or she is an authority in the
   field.

11:02 Copy Tips for Promotions to Librarians

- Librarians rely heavily on review excerpts for new reference works. However, excerpts are of minor importance when promoting a new edition of a widely held work.

- When editions of reference works are in both cloth and paper, include the paper edition in your copy; over 60% of librarians in a survey indicated they will buy paperbound editions.

- No selling can be done from promotion copy that lacks prices. If you cannot include a final price, use at least a tentative price.

- Avoid hype or any approach that will insult the librarian's intelligence.

- A clear opening statement is prerequisite in any library promotion, or the balance of the promotion piece will not be read.

- When promoting an expensive work, be sure to include author credentials unless the author is widely known as an authority on the subject.

- Avoid promotions to special librarians in areas outside their sphere of interest.

11:03 Promotion Copy to Public Libraries: Essential Ingredients

Whatever format a library promotion takes, one essential ingredient should be included: complete bibliographic information. These are some of the essential copy ingredients one director of a major public library looks for in library promotions from publishers:

- Publication date
- ISBN
- Catalog copy by subject, then by author
- Identification of new-title entries in the catalog as such, with both month and year of publication included

11:04 Credibility in Copy Approach to Public Libraries

Librarians resent a copy approach that will insult their intelligence. Library promotion copy should present facts, reinforced wherever possible by quotes from reviews or from recognized authorities. The copy should leave the purchase decision up to the librarian.

A publisher's praise of his own book is suspect by the librarian. Nor should copy push the librarian into a buying decision; it should at best suggest or recommend.

Here is an example of a copy block from a publisher's public library promotion, carried in large-size type above the publisher's order form:

> These books should be in every reference collection, no matter
> how large, no matter how small . . . they should find their places
> in special collections and in circulating collections as well . . .

In my view, the above copy would have been more impressive and
believable if it had carried an attribution from a librarian or a publication related to the library field.

11:05 Special Library Promotions:
Copy Approaches That Work Best

Unlike the public librarian who looks for complete bibliographic information, the special librarian is more concerned about having a
detailed description of the information package being offered and an
indication that the offering is up-to-date and reliable. Special librarians may assume that offers from some of the larger publishing houses
are current and reliable, but smaller houses have to offer more proof.
This can easily be done by including on all offers the publication year
(and month, if fairly recent) along with the author's business or professional affiliation and other credentials that imply authority or reliability.

Special libraries also buy paperback editions of peripheral reference
materials, so if you have these available, mention this in your promotion copy. Try to be as accurate as possible on availability dates
for major forthcoming works. If the work is to be a serial, be sure your
copy indicates the time span over which the serial will be published,
the number of volumes planned (if known), and the number of volumes
to be published each year. Also indicate whether the serial is sold by
subscription, whether the subscription price is guaranteed for the
entire work, and whether there is a subscription discount.

Another question your copy should answer in subscription offerings
is whether payment must be made up front for the special subscription
price, or whether individual volumes will be billed at the special subscription rate as each volume is published.

A final tip for promotion copy to special libraries: Always include
the name (and direct-dial number, if possible) of a responsible individual in your firm whom a librarian can call when there is a question
about one of your mail or advertising offers. Special librarians make
good use of the telephone and frequently order by phone.

11:06 Promotions to High School Libraries:
Copy Guidelines

- Write promotion copy that is simple and understandable.
- Keep book description short and, if possible, include table of contents.

- Biographical information on the author should be included, where pertinent.
- Include Library of Congress (LC) catalog card number.
- Supply Dewey decimal number, if possible.
- Show publication date, price, ISBN, and page count.
- Indicate whether the book is available in both paper and cloth.
- If your promotional offering includes many books, group them by subject.
- Include positive reviews; they will help the selection process.
- Include a simple checklist order form.
- Be sure to mention whether a title is an annual, serial, new edition, or part of a series; for series, give the name of the series.

11:07 Copy Ingredients Librarians Will Welcome in Your Advertising Copy

A 1983 report of the Council on Library Resources recommended that dictionaries, encyclopedias, and other reference books of lasting importance be printed on acid-free paper. It recommended, too, that the publisher indicate in the book below the copyright line whether or not the book had been printed on acid-free paper.

The report also called attention to librarian concerns about bindings, because with the widespread use of glue and adhesives for binding "many books fall apart almost before they get on the library shelves."

Sewing was cited as "the best method for longevity and openability," and the report encouraged publishers to use sewn bindings whenever possible for hardcover books.

It therefore makes sense, in your ad copy and other promotions to the library market, to indicate it if your books are printed on acid-free papers and have sewn bindings.

11:08 The Importance of Price in Library Promotion Copy

When you're preparing copy for an advertisement directed to the library market and you want it to generate book orders, the books in the offering should be reasonably close to their publication dates, if not already available, and the copy should contain prices. An exception is a prepublication offer which will produce orders months in advance of publication.

For most libraries, price is critical in any decision to order. It is an essential piece of information for this market, and no selling can be done from promotion copy that lacks prices.

If you are writing library promotion copy and your books lack prices, try at least to include a tentative price. It gives the librarian some idea of how much of a bite the book will take out of the budget.

**11:09   Copy Guidelines for Inventory Reduction
Sales to Libraries**

Inventory reduction sales are widely used by professional and scholarly publishers and even more so by university presses. The marketing manager of University of California Press, Harlan Kessel, told a publishing audience at the Society for Scholarly Publishing meeting in San Francisco in 1981 that "special offers are essential if you want to sell scholars books for their professional use. . . . Today's buyer of scholarly books is a bargain hunter."

These copy criteria will ensure that your sale offerings to libraries are successful:

1. Allow ample time for response: at least 90 days from date of mailing.
2. Offer discounts larger than those normally given by library suppliers.
3. Do not insist on prepayment.
4. If sales are final, indicate conditions under which returns will be permitted.
5. If quantities are limited and may not be sufficient for all, indicate available quantities to avoid disappointment.
6. If incentives are offered for special types of combinations of purchases, keep these within reason.
7. Utilize catalog format.
8. Clearly identify the sale offering on the face of the mailing envelope or catalog cover.
9. State the conditions of sale clearly in an easy-to-find location.
10. Use a special order form or reply envelope to identify readily orders from the sale offering.
11. Avoid mixing sale and nonsale offerings in the same mailing piece.
12. If older titles are offered, indicate whether these are superseded by new editions.
13. Avoid complicated layouts or type arrangements.
14. Keep the type area on the page to a modest width to allow for marginal notations.
15. Keep to alphabetical arrangement by author or editor under subject headings.
16. Always include the year of publication for each title.
17. Always include the ISBN for each title.
18. If the descriptive copy is short, include favorable review excerpts in addition to or in place of copy.
19. Have each entry clearly indicate the saving by showing both the regular price and the sale price.

20. Prominently state the range of savings on the sales announcement in terms of percentages, such as "50% to 80%."

21. Give a believable reason for the sale; avoid such frivolous titles as "Whale of a Sale!"

22. A check-off order form requirng only an "x" simplifies the ordering process and can increase sales.

23. If prepayment is required, state that library or institutional orders will be acceptable without payment or if accompanied by a purchase order.

24. Provide an incentive on shipping charges for orders over a certain size.

25. Offer an additional discount if orders reach a certain amount, or offer different added discounts if orders reach certain dollar levels.

26. If a bind-in order envelope is used, repeat the mailing address several places throughout sale offering, especially if the sale address is different from your usual address. This can encourage subsequent orders, that could be tied to the sale offering, after the order envelope has been removed.

11:10   Copy Incentives for Converting Annuals and Series into Standing Orders

A number of publishers of annuals and series offer special discount incentives in promotional announcements to encourage standing or continuation orders. Here are the copy approaches used by several.

GALE RESEARCH

> All Standing Order customers receive a 5% discount on all titles for which they have Standing Orders. This 5% discount will automatically be reflected on all invoices sent for Standing Order titles.

JAI PRESS

> For your convenience, we suggest the placing of a Standing Order for our Research Annuals so that you will automatically receive a copy of every new volume upon publication. Institutional Standing Orders will receive a 10% discount and your order will remain on file until cancelled.

PLENUM PUBLISHING CORPORATION

> Many of our series and treatises are eligible for Series Standing Orders which receive a special 15% discount on all future and

any previously published volumes. Standing orders eliminate unnecessary paperwork on your part (ensuring shipment of each volume immediately upon publication), and may be cancelled at any time. . . . This discount is only available in the USA.

**11:11   Copy in Library Catalog
to Encourage Pass-Along Readership**

In a prominent box facing the first page of listings in its library catalog, JAI Press includes this copy to encourage pass-along readership:

A Reminder. . .

Many people are responsible for library acquisition decisions. Once you have finished with this catalogue, we ask that you send it, along with your recommendations, to the appropriate library acquisitions staff member, departmental library budget administrator, or other interested book buyer.

The seasonal catalog issued by Elsevier Science Publishing Company, Inc., New York, includes this carefully thought out "Library Routing Memo" in the lower left-hand corner of the catalog's mailing face, which is its fourth cover:

LIBRARY ROUTING MEMO

Date Received _____

___ Acquisitions
___ Cataloging
___ Chief Bibliographers
___ Circulation
___ Collection Development
___ General Reference
___ Serials
___ Subject Bibliographers
___ Other / Add to Routing
___ Return To _____

11:12   Selected Copy Elements from Various Publisher's Library Promotions

All books are printed on acid-free paper and bound in a library-grade cloth
—ARNO Press

Please indicate quantity and title of your selections, accompanied by the UNIPUB order number, or an authorized purchase order.
—UNIPUB

Let our standing order plan go to work for you—and earn discounts of 20%.
—The Urban Institute Press

Libraries: All books in this catalog are available at a 10% library discount on direct orders to St. Martin's Press.
—St. Martin's Press

Each (NEW BOOKS) bulletin provides complete ordering information, including price upon publication and LC card numbers. Each title is available from your wholesaler or from McGraw-Hill.
—McGraw-Hill Book Company

The Library Wholesalers listed below participate in the Methuen Agency Plan for Wholesalers. They receive immediately on publication a representative selection of all new Methuen, Inc. titles. We hope this information will be helpful to you when ordering Methuen books.
—Methuen, Inc.

Note: All returns must be requested in writing and await a written authorization before returns can be made.
—Elsevier Science Publishing Co., Inc.

Prepublication pricess are shown for books that have not been published by presstime for this catalog. These books will be available in less than six months. Ordering now assures you that your books will be shipped at prepublication prices immediately upon publication.
—CRC Press. Inc.

Practically all Westview titles carry both ISBN and LC numbers. We participate in the Library of Congress Cataloging in Publication (CIP) program.
—Westview Press

11:13   Encyclopedic Reference Copy Appeals That Librarians Respond to: Survey Result

1. Quality of content
2. Currentness of information, timeliness of data

3. Authoritativeness: caliber of contributors

4. Reference source for quick answers to questions

5. Value as a starting point for information searches

6. Usefulness as a reference tool in a specific subject area

7. Convenience of format

8. Strengths in terms of competitive works (if any)

9. Quality of manufacture (binding, acid-free paper, etc.)

10. Value in terms of price

**11:14 Missing Copy Ingredients Doom Quality
Library Promotion: Case Study**

The book catalog was a slick, expensive-looking effort: coated stock, color illustrations, ad-agency quality copy. The titles, a collection of scientific and professional books, seemed to be on important topics. The mailing apparently had been made to libraries, since two special libraries contacted had both received the same piece.

But the originator of the offering was an unknown quantity. The company had as its name a series of letters (like XQZ Publishing). The address was a P.O. box number in a remote rural community. The letters forming the name of the company conveyed no particular meaning, and were not listed in the publisher section of *Literary Market Place.*

After only a minute's examination, I concluded that the professionally slick offering lacked the two vital ingredients which virtually ensured failure:

1. No author identification in the book offerings.

2. No publisher identification.

Librarians buy information rather than books. They buy information that will augment material already on hand in their collections, or which they feel confident will provide reliable, useful information for their clientele or reference needs.

A book on a scientific or professional business subject by an author who is not a well-known figure in the field and who is not identified as to his credentials or professional affiliation is not likely to be bought blindly "on faith" by a librarian, unless he or she can trust the integirty of the publishing house making the offering.

Librarians know who the major and reliable publishers are in their various fields of specialization. The reputations of these publishers create an aura of confidence and credibility in their offerings. And the librarians know there is recourse if they are not satisfied.

However, when an offering is from an unknown source with no credibility, and the books are by authors with no credentials, librarians justifiably are likely to be very wary. And even more so if books require prepayment.

If yours is a small or relatively unknown operation, and especially if your company name is one consisting of letters or initials, don't mail to any library unless your copy tells the recipient who you are. Why are you publishing? If your address is a post office box number, is there also a telephone number and name of a contact person who can be reached to answer questions?

A new, small, or relatively unknown house should, in my view, include in each promotion at least a terse "founder's whiskers" paragraph which tells who you are, why you are publishing, your affiliation if part of a larger organization, and any special credentials that your establishment or its members have. If your name consists of two or three intials and they mean something, state somewhere in your offering what they mean.

Establish your imprint, its identity, in every printed promotion. If your offering is superior and you have identity, librarians will remember your imprint in subsequent offerings.

Lewis Coser, in *Books: The Culture and Commerce of Publishing* (Basic Books, 1982), stated it well, "A publishing house's reputation is important . . . libraries rely on publishers with a reputation for, and a tradition of, publishing good scholarship."

12

Copy Approaches for Books in Business, Law, and Economics

12:01 Copy Approach for Books Aimed at Corporate Audience: A Marketer's Suggested Copy Approach

Says one marketer of books for corporate audiences—mainly staff and middle-management personnel:

> Keep your copy conservative. It should have an air of stability and practicality. Include in your advertising copy information a subordinate can comfortably present to a boss for consideration or approval. Copy emphasis for the corporate middle manager should be applications- and problem-oriented. If you're writing copy for books in such business areas as business data processing and accounting, your copy should be more conservative than for books on management, marketing, and investment.

12:02 Copy Approach for Business Management Books: Editor's Comment

An editor of books for business managers, whose career in publishing began as a copywriter, offers these tips for business book copywriters:

1. Keep copy brief, specific, and utilize just enough technical jargon to

assure the potential buyer of the book's practical usefulness and relevance.

2. Many business managers think of themselves as very busy even if they are not. Consequently, they are not avid readers. Copy intended for this audience often requires a feature/benefit/advantage type of presentation. The most obvious example of this occurs in books where the copy promises the buyers/users that they will be more efficient if they employ the techniques contained in the book.

12:03   Business Book Copy Should Stress Advice and Information

There are five million Americans who think of themselves as managerial. These are prime prospects for any books you may be promoting on business management. The five million figure is the claim of John Kotter of the Harvard Business School in a *Wall Street Journal* article ("Business Is Hotter Than Sex, Book Publishers Find," 1 August 1983).

This vast audience, Kotter avers, is looking for advice and information. He says they have been "primed by some amount of business-school education—as undergrads, MBAs or executives in training programs."

The *WSJ* article, authored by Harriet Rubin, business books editor at Harper & Row, contains potential copy appeals from two other publishing professionals:

Claire Wyckoff, publishing and marketing director of the American Management Association Book Clubs Division, says that business books give the buyer an insight into how management works.

Bob Wallace, senior editor at Macmillan Free Press, points out that a consultant's book can often be bought for around $15 whereas his services might cost thousands of dollars.

Another sales appeal in business book promotions is tax deductibility. As with most other publishers' business book promotions, a line in each Wiley business book promotion states "Professional Books are All Tax Deductible."

12:04   Why They Buy Business Books: Thoughts from a Marketing Manager

Says the business books marketing manager at one large commercial house:

> Business is becoming like engineering. You must master a body of knowledge in order to work.
>
> It is becoming more *business* and less *organization*. In former times, the person who was a macho self-starter could work his way to the top and stay there. Today, these requirements are less important and the businessman, if he is to succeed, must match those qualities with a body of

knowledge in many specialized areas such as time management, budgeting, and perhaps some psychology or social psychology.

Business today requires a greater degree of sophistication from its managers. Established managers are realizing that they lack the sophistication of younger people just entering the business in such areas as basic computer theory, quantitative techniques in marketing, and more.

Managers will buy books that will keep them current on organizational realities, that will give them an understanding of the technical aspects of each new job as they move up the ladder. They will buy business books because they realize that knowledge is power.

12:05   Special Wording on Order Form Is Key to Repeat Sales for Annuals

A publisher of annual volumes for professionals in business, accounting, and taxation has a highly effective technique for selling upcoming volumes without risk.

On the order form for the initial sale, copy is included which states that new annual editions will be sent automatically unless the customer specifically requests on the order form that new annual editions *not* be sent.

Two to three months before each new annual is published, an address correction mailing is made to customers. No mention is made in the mailing of an upcoming new edition. If the form is returned and the customer indicates he or she is still at the same address, or indicates a new address, the new edition is sent.

12:06   Single Line of Order Form Copy That Increases Sales for Loose-Leaf Publisher

A New England publisher of loose-leaf books, annuals, and subscription services attributes a large measure of the company's success to a single line of copy in its direct-mail order forms.

The line, which appears in virtually all of its continuation offerings, says, "I understand that subsequent volumes in the series will be sent on approval."

If you are writing copy for offerings that include supplements or updates, or for serials, you might want to consider using this line. Of course, inclusion of such an "automatic" shipment could turn off potential buyers; you risk that possibility when it becomes a part of an order. To get around this, you might modify the line of copy to be an ordering option thus: "(   ) Please send subsequent volumes in this series on an approval basis."

Even though your publishing establishment may not send books on approval, you might want to make an exception in this type of offer, since the customer has already bought and paid for the first volume, establishing credit as a payer.

**12:07   Business and Management Books in Sci-Tech
Promotions: How to Integrate**

When planning sci-tech multi-book promotions, do not hesitate to include some of your better books on business and management. Scientists, engineers, and researchers, especially in such rapidly changing fields as science and electronics, are hungry for all types of information on management techniques, as well as other books that offer tips on career guidance or improvement of personal skills. Books on consulting, income tax guides, and the like are also of interest.

When you do include such non-related books, do not insert them among the technical books.* Instead, group them under a common heading *after* the technical presentations. Use headlines like: "Reference Sources for Your Professional Library," or "Useful Professional Reference Works," or "Professional Reference Works, Handbooks, Guides."

**12:08   Twist the Trite to Make a Headline Work:
Case Study**

Sometimes the headline in a business book promotion is almost exactly defined by the publication being promoted. "But what do you do," says Peter Hodges, book-marketing pro, "when this headline and its close variations have been used frequently before?"

An answer he suggests is to use it, but try to add a tag line. He cites the example of a real estate investor's deskbook promoted during 1982 at a time when the real estate market was in a very depressed state. The natural basic headline idea suggested something like:

"How to achieve maximum profits in real estate."

"But," adds Hodges, "although we wanted to stress profit, some consideration had to be given to the condition of the market. So we added: 'Tested strategies for successful investing in good times and bad.'

"The mailing worked. I think partially because we tried to make it relevant to the current fears of the prospect, and also because it was a bit different."

**12:09   Copy Technique When Product Is Unfamiliar
to Prospective Buyer: Two Case Studies**

When your copy assignment involves a product the prospective customer is unlikely to be familiar with, try relating it to something which is familiar. Two case-study examples of this approach are cited by Peter Hodges in successful promotions directed to tax accountants.

---

* This does not apply in card deck promotions where they may be randomly inserted.

STUDY ONE: FIVE-VOLUME TAX MANUAL

A couple of years ago, we were launching a major tax set of five volumes. How could we get across to the prospect the enormity of this major new work? One of the ways was to describe the new set as the natural successor of a well-known and well-regarded book published 50 years earlier and still actively in print.

STUDY TWO: TAX PLANNER CALCULATOR AND SOFTWARE PACKAGE

This example involved a Tax Planner which is a calculator that does tax planning. The tax accounting field was not familiar with this type of hardware and software combination. So I reached back to an advertisement I'd seen almost 25 years before to adapt the headline. The major sub-heading said: "As important to your tax practice as your telephone or photocopier." When each of these were innovations there were skeptics, but no more. So our prospects were able to understand the potential importance of our new product and also to feel that they were pioneers.

On the subject of pioneering, Hodges thinks most business people like to be up with the times, if they can be so without undue risk, so if you call on them to innovate in your copy, make them feel it's smart, but not dangerous.

12:10   Books as Premiums: Sample Solicitation Letter

Books can often be sold in bulk quantities to business and industrial firms for use as premiums. The premium book may be tied in with a related product, it could be a company handout because it illustrates company products or was written by an employee, or it could be a public relations gesture to engender good will among a particular audience.

The likely premium buyer may be someone whose products are mentioned in a particular book, or who sees its contents as a sales aid. In such special cases, the solicitation letter should be tailored to the specific situation. However, there are ways of generating premium sales through direct mail solicitation. Here is a copy approach used by one establishment:

Dear Premium Buyer:

If you are looking for an effective marketing vehicle that will not only identify and promote your products, but also have lasting value to your customers or prospects, you might want to consider using a book as a premium.

Many companies already use books as premiums in conjunction with the sale of their products. Some have found other applications for premium books—one company has its sales representative leave a book after a sales call. Of course the book bears their company imprint.

If you would like to investigate how your company sales program can benefit through the use of books as premiums, please contact us. We will be pleased to provide suggestions, suggest books, tell you of our quantity discounts. We offer a wide range of titles from our current list and can also supply special customized editions bearing your company name and logo.

Sincerely,

13

Copy Approaches Used
by Scholarly Presses

13:01 **The Most Frequently Used Promotional Vehicle
in Scholarly Publishing**

"The catalog," says Abbot Friedland, for over 20 years marketing
director at Princeton University Press, "is the single most frequently
used [promotional] vehicle in scholarly publishing."

I concur. A study of the direct-mail offerings of a number of university presses over a period of time overwhelmingly confirmed this
statement.

It is easy to understand why this format is favored. It works, and
given the limited marketing staffs and capabilities of most university
presses, combined with modest promotion budgets, the simplified catalog format is both economical and convenient. The major customers
of the university press are the library and the scholar, and press
offerings are varied. The catalog format combines a broad spectrum
of offerings in a way that makes it easy to distribute and easy to use
by the primary audiences for which it is intended.

TYPES OF CATALOGS

University press catalogs generally fall into four distinct types:

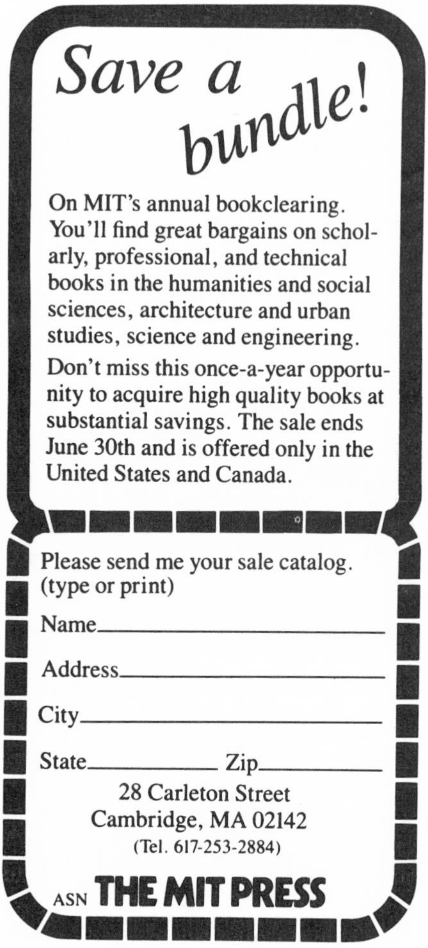

Save a bundle!

On MIT's annual bookclearing. You'll find great bargains on scholarly, professional, and technical books in the humanities and social sciences, architecture and urban studies, science and engineering.

Don't miss this once-a-year opportunity to acquire high quality books at substantial savings. The sale ends June 30th and is offered only in the United States and Canada.

Please send me your sale catalog. (type or print)

Name_____

Address_____

City_____

State_____ Zip_____

28 Carleton Street
Cambridge, MA 02142
(Tel. 617-253-2884)

ASN **THE MIT PRESS**

FIGURE 10 The *sale catalog* is an important vehicle for most university presses, and most university presses issue sale catalogs on a regular basis. However, to my knowledge, only The MIT Press actively merchandises its annual sale catalog in paid-space advertising. Above illustration shows the fairly standard format used to invite catalog requests. The advertisement "Save a bundle" appeared in the January 1983 issue of *Science News*. This ad copy varies little from year to year.

1. The annual catalog, a general offering of all titles in print through the current season and, sometimes, also listing books in preparation.

2. The periodic (sometimes annual) subject catalog, providing detailed information on all titles within a given area or related group of areas.

3. The seasonal catalog (usually Spring and Fall).

4. The sale catalog (see Figure 10).

A sampling of the copy approaches of selected university press catalogs will be found in the entries following.

13:02 The Use and Abuse of Copy in Scholarly Press Catalogs

Catalog copy style varies from one scholarly press to another. Presses with small lists may devote an entire page to a single title, sometimes even including cover and book illustrations. Others, especially where space is limited, may restrict copy to a brief listing of basic bibliographic data and ISBN and/or order number.

The longer descriptive entries provide detailed descriptions of the book and usually mirror the copy appearing on the book's jacket flap. They also pick up the jacket-flap author biography.

Some presses rely on excerpts from reviews or quotations from academic reviewers, omitting contents. Others rely heavily on the book's contents to tell its own story, sometimes with and sometimes without a one-sentence or very brief description. The latter format is the one used and favored by many commercial presses.

The heaviest buyers of scholarly books are academic libraries. They require little copy to be convinced that a particular title should be ordered. Many academic libraries place university press books at the top of the list in their standing orders to their library wholesalers.

How do academic librarians feel about copy in university press catalogs? Thomas M. Schmid, acquisitions librarian at the University of Utah, addressed the subject in a paper presented at the meeting of Western University Presses in Salt Lake City in October 1975 (see references at the end of this entry) when he commented:

> Why does any book need a description running to three hundred words or more? If the book is that hard to explain, it probably shouldn't have been published.
>
> Take a book on Pomeranian swine exports. . . . Any scholar who is going to buy the book, or ask the library to buy it, is already going to be *crazy* about Pomeranian swine, and does not need a copywriter to tell him about it at great length. . . .
>
> What both the scholar and the librarian do need is some indication of the author's qualifications. . . . The "argument from authority," a hangover from scholasticism, still carries much weight, and both librarians and their patrons feel warmly secure when buying and reading books whose authors can clearly be identified as Experts.

When doing copy for a "Sale" catalog, the entries can be extremely terse—the basic bibliographic details (including pub date) and perhaps a short description. A review excerpt from a reliable journal often will do a better job than the copywriter can do. Sale catalogs, for the most part, go to librarians or scholars with a special interest in the subject and the "sell" of a sharply price-reduced book is its low price.

Copy for books with interdisciplinary appeal is often enhanced by mention of the various disciplines for which the book will have appeal. However, when a book is on a single subject or discipline and the book is being promoted to that specialized audience, it is not necessary to use valuable space to tell an audience of political scientists, for example, that "this book is for political scientists."

On the other hand, the specialized scholarly book notwithstanding, a goodly number of university presses are turning toward books that make their lists more and more competitive with those of commercial publishers.

"We're in business to publish specialized scholarly works," says David Gilbert, director of the University of Nebraska Press, "but those books are hurt mainly because the libraries don't have enough money to buy them."*

Promotion copy in some university press catalogs is now being written with a view toward impressing the bookseller enough to order for stock, as well as to increase sales through direct-mail promotions to potential buyers.

FURTHER READING

Fuller, Sigfried, "Special Sale Catalogues and Library Customers," *Scholarly Publishing,* Vol. 8, No. 2, January 1977.

Schmid, Thomas M., "Why Libraries Buy—and Don't Buy Scholarly Books," *Scholarly Publishing,* Vol. 7, No. 4, July 1976.

Seltzer, Leon E., "University Presses," chapter in *What Happens in Book Publishing,* 2nd Ed., edited by Chandler B. Grannis. New York: Columbia University Press, 1967.

**13:03   Is it Catalog or Catalogue?
What Most Americans Prefer**

That the catalog is the single most frequently used promotional vehicle in scholarly publishing, as Abbot Friedland correctly states in 13:01, raises a nagging question: Is it *catalog?* Or should it be *catalogue?*

The Second College Edition of the *American Heritage Dictionary* (Houghton Mifflin, 1982) indicates the (American) preference to be for the spelling *catalogue.* It shows *catalog* as a (less preferred) secondary variant.

But numerous other references dispute this and come out strongly for *catalog* as the American preference, as do most university presses. The Library of Congress preference is for *catalog* without the *u,* and every new book published in the United States has on its copyright page the line "Library of Congress Cataloging in Publication Data."

McGraw-Hill Dictionary of Scientific and Technical Terms (1984)

---

*Quoted in *New York Times* article, "Publishing: What University Presses Are Doing," 20 April 1984.

has four entries with the word or variations, and all use *catalog*. The *Dictionary of Publishing* (by D. M. Brownstone and I. M. Franck, Van Nostrand Reinhold, 1982) also shows only *catalog*. Most American librarians prefer to spell the word without the *u*.

In a *New York Sunday Times Magazine* essay "On Language" on 22 April 1984, William Safire wrapped it up neatly when he wrote:

> ... the Library of Congress wants to be non-U ... [but] in a spirit of Atlantic amity sticks in a *u* when joining in a cooperative venture like "Anglo-American Cataloguing Rules," but to the extent that an institution (or a professional group) can be said to have a preference, our preference, as American librarians, is to spell the word without the *u*.

13:04 Harvard University Press: Annual Catalog Copy Approach

This is an annual, 8½" × 11", 128 pages with heavier-stock wrap-around cover. While it covers a full year, it is issued in mid-year and the listing of fall titles appears on the inside back cover—author's name in regular type, followed by book title in italics.

Harvard's was the only university press catalog of the many studied which used the "catalogue" spelling throughout. First right-hand page lists press name, year, and the words: "Complete Catalogue." On a separate line, above press address, is a line reading: Main Index/Classified Index/Series Index/Title Index.

On second right-hand page is start of three-page "Contents" listing. Contents are by subject, alphabetically, with page number to *left* of subject. This was the only college catalog of the many studied in which the page numbers were used this way. The catalog's four sections carry listings only, no descriptive matter. No order form is included: individuals are requested to order through booksellers and libraries are advised to order through wholesalers.

Main Index is by author (in boldface) with title and pertinent bibliographic data included. *Classified Index* has subject in boldface, all other entries in lightface: full title, period, then author. *Series Index* has series title as heading in boldface. Individually numbered entries underneath in lightface. *Title Index* is an alphabetical lightface listing of all titles, each followed by author.

13:05 University of Pennsylvania Press: Sale Catalog Copy Approach

The 8½" × 11" self-cover self-mailer is in 16 pages, two colors of ink. Cover copy in red ink, 72 point type, proclaims "THE BIG BOOK SALE!" A sub-headline in black ink half as large: "from the University of Pennsylvania Press."

About two-thirds of the outer cover under the headline is in two columns, separated by an 18-point vertical benday of black divider. Left column has sell copy, "Up to 90% discount on books in the humanities, social sciences, and sciences," followed by bulleted subject areas. Four more short selling pitches appear in the "sell" column—including a note to "Pay by MasterCard, Visa, check, money order."

Entries by subject, and contents gives not only page number but also number of titles available under that subject. Good idea. Each entry gives title, author, and a solid blurb describing the book. Nearly all descriptions are in quotes and are excerpted from reviews, academic reviewers, or from the foreword. List price in black ink, followed by sale price in red ink with percent of discount in parentheses, black ink. Where written copy is used, it is a short factual statement. Each entry is preceded by a number, and back cover order form carries corresponding order number with author name and net price. Order form is also arranged by subject.

I like the little copy touch on the front cover: "Pass along this catalog to your friends and to your library. The order form may be copied for multiple use."

13:06 Duke University Press:
Annual Catalog Copy Approach

A 26-page self-cover annual catalog is a self-mailer and carries on its cover an attractive illustration of the new home of Duke University Press. Contents by subject are on the inside front cover, accompanied by a listing of the Press staff and an invitation for book and journal proposals.

A three-column format is used throughout, with hairline rules separating the columns. Copy entries are continuous so that copy for a new title begins where the previous title ends. On featured title a jacket illustration is shown above the title. Many descriptions start with excerpts from reviews or quotes from academic reviewers. A description of each book follows, and contents are given. In some instances, the contents are the only copy given. Where contents are listed, the word "Contents:" is in boldface type and lightface type is used for the actual contents. Diagonals (/) are used to separate chapters, and this seems a useful practice since many chapter headings are compound headings with colons and commas. The diagonal serves well. Feature titles have a light benday tint background, and some series headings are in reverse-type panels. Journals are grouped on a single page with a light benday background. A full page of sales information for journals precedes the full-page journals subscription order form, and a full page of sales information for books precedes the book order form. Book order form has blank lines to be filled in. The sales information is nicely presented: prices for each category (individuals, libraries, booksellers, wholesalers), standing order plan, examination copies, textbook discount, returns policy.

13:07 **The MIT Press:**
Seasonal Catalog Approach

The 7″ × 10″ seasonal catalog contains 56 pages with a wrap-around self-mailer hard cover. Subject contents appear on inside front cover; back inside cover is blank. Pages follow a two-column format. For major books, the cover illustration occupies one column or a portion of it and the copy appears in the adjacent column. Description is about the way it would appear on jacket flap, in narrative form, and author credentials are in separate paragraph at bottom. Journals occupy a separate section and occupy a three-column format page with one journal to a column, usually with cover illustration. Order form occupies three full pages, shows list price, discount code, and page location in catalog: alphabetically by author (in boldface), followed by title (in lightface). An order envelope is bound into centerfold. It requires postage.

13:08 **Princeton University Press:**
Copy Approach for Hybrid Catalog

Like many university press catalogs, this catalog is a 16-page self-mailing self-cover, 8½″ × 11″. It covers Math and Physical Sciences for a year and features a four page "Special Sale" insert.

Cover copy features the subject matter. However, over each side of the catalog title "Math and Physical Sciences 84" is a diagonal headline: to the left "Special Sale Insert" and to the right the discounts, "Discounts up to 75% Over 70 Backlist Titles . . . 20% Off all non-sale titles."

The inside front cover has contents in a left column, Notes From the Editor in a right column, signed by the Science Editor. While the catalog starts on page 1 (first inside right hand page), the initial entry in the contents is "Special Sale Insert."

The word "New" appears over the detailed descriptive entry for each title in the regular section. About 150 to 200 words are used to describe contents of new titles. Author affiliation is at end of copy.

The Special Sale section is on four pages with a benday tint of about 30% of the dark green used for the catalog text. Listings include boldface title, author in lightface, series name, pages, Library of Congress catalog number, ISBN, sale price in boldface and regular price preceded by "Reg" in italics. Surprisingly, no publication dates are shown anywhere in the catalog, although the lead-off numbers of the Library of Congress catalog number give a clue.

Seven "Conditions of Sale" are listed on the order form. Some requirements are prepayment by individuals, purchase order by institutions and libraries, $2.75 minimum postage, 20% discount on new books, has a $20 minimum order, orders outside the United States and Canada should be placed with local bookstores. Order form requires write-in of desired books, credit card option included.

**13:09   University of Chicago Press:
Seasonal Catalog Copy Approach**

This seasonal self-mailer catalog has 64 pages, $8\frac{1}{2}''$ × 11" with a heavier-weight outside cover. The author index is on the inside front cover, referenced to the title index on the inside back cover. A guide to subjects appears on the first right-hand page (page 1) under the Contents.

Books are either two on a page or three on a page, with a one- to three-paragraph description for the book, followed by an ample description of the author, his affiliation, and credentials. Each title entry includes a listing of all the subjects covered. A printed two-page order form includes a toll-free 800 number, a regular phone number, and a telex number, and can be used by individuals, libraries, or booksellers.

14

Copywriting Techniques for Journals Promotion

14:01 **Essential Copy Ingredients for a Journal**
Promotion Flier or Prospectus: Checklist

( ) Give a clear, understandable description of the journal.

( ) State its aim and scope.

( ) List editor and members of editorial board, with affiliations.

( ) State whether subscription is by volume or by year.

( ) State frequency of publication and number of volumes per year.

( ) If a new journal, give projected contents of early issues.

( ) If an established journal, give contents of several preceding issues and what is forthcoming.

( ) Provide explicit ordering information. Will the subscription start with the next issue, or will it be by volume, or by calendar year?

( ) Give clear information on postage charges if they are additional. Can subscription begin with any volume, or only with the first one published in a given year?

( ) Describe form of production: Printed form only? Also in microfiche, microfilm, miniprint?

( ) Indicate whether journal is centrally indexed. List abstracting and indexing services in which journal is a participant.

( ) If flier or prospectus is being mailed to individuals, include as part of order form or with it a "Subscription Recommendation" on stub or card, which recipient can complete and forward to a person in his or her institution or organization who is responsible for periodical subscriptions.

( ) Mention, when applicable, that there is a special discount for multiple subscriptions to the same subscriber, or for multiple-year subscriptions.

( ) Provide ISSN number.

( ) State societal sponsorship.

( ) If a new journal, give expected date of first issue.

( ) State intended audience and level of presentation.

( ) Include publisher's name and address.

14:02   Optional Copy Ingredients for a Journal Promotion Flier or Prospectus: Checklist

( ) Offer of sample issue.

( ) Offer of sample issues to any names and addresses supplied.

( ) Discount if recipient has membership in a related association or society (provided association or society agrees to participate and will promote the offer).

( ) Toll-free 800 number for information.

( ) Credit card payment option.

( ) Discount for multi-year subscription.

( ) If there is a reduced rate for personal subscription with an institutional subscription, mention this.

( ) Instructions to contributors.

( ) Illustrations of sample pages.

14:03   Copy That Invites Readers to Suggest Ideas for New Publications

While most journal promotions concentrate on generating subscriptions for existing journals, Learned Information, Inc., places emphasis in the inside front cover of its catalog on ideas from readers for new publications. In a letter addressed to "Dear Colleague" and signed by Thomas H. Hogan, President, it states:

This catalog contains descriptions of publications currently offered . . . [in] library and information science with particular emphasis on the rapidly expanding fields of on-line database retrieval and electronic publishing.

If you, the reader of this catalog, have an idea for a new publication in an area related to [our] existing publications, we invite you to write us. . . . Alternatively you may call me at (phone number). I would be delighted to hear from you.

14:04 Copywriting for Journals Promotions: Guidelines from a Journals Promotion Manager

According to Julie Zuckman, former MIT Press Journals Promotion Manager, copywriting for journals involves all the same skills described in Chapter 1 (see entry 1:10):

1. The hunt for information.
2. Evaluating and determining characteristics and potential size of subscriber base (audience).
3. Assessing in-house goals.
4. Finding the special selling point.

The differences are:

1. A journal may not be new when a publisher acquires it, so it may arrive complete with a mailing history, copy written by others, brochures, ads, and other materials. Get your hands on these materials. Why should you write new copy if good copy already exists, or, conversely, you may want to see where others failed.

2. Journals programs are smaller and don't usually include a Marketing Manager. There may be no one to help you nail down the marketing goals, or you may report directly to the person running the entire journals program.

3. Journals should be sold more like magazines than books. You are selling a subscription and you want the buyer to renew, to establish a tie with the publication. Direct mail is emotional, but subscriptions are intensely emotional. People identify themselves by the kinds of magazines they receive.

4. The key elements of journals promotion copy:

    Recent and future contents and authors

    Editorial board

    Editorial statement

    Editors

    The selling techniques:

A. Offer (special price, premium, charter subscription, money-back guarantee, etc.)

B. Benefits (professional, personal)

C. Time element (don't miss an issue)

D. Personalization (if appealing to individuals rather than libraries)

E. Easy response method because it's cash up front

14:05   Importance of Copy in a Journal Promotion Package

"In planning a journal promotion package," says Cynthia Smith, ACS Circulation Manager, "copy is an important factor. It is essential that it accurately describe the publication while at the same time build the need for the publication in the minds of the potential subscriber. At ACS, we make a point of integrating both copy and graphics in order for the whole promotion package to match the quality of the product we are offering. The creation of the copy is a specialized art, and shouldn't necessarily be taken upon by an amateur. We use both trained internal copywriters and outside creative talent when developing copy."

14:06   Combining Copy for a Number of Related Journals on a Single Flier

If you are promoting a number of journals in a single discipline or subject area, you can make your efforts more productive and cost-effective by incorporating all of them into a single mailing piece. Aside from cost savings, it also gives the recipient several options instead of the "yes" or "no" option of a single journal offering.

One journal publisher has had success with just such a combined journals flier, produced in self-mailer format. The 8″ × 22″ flat piece folds down to 5½″ × 8″ and provides, in addition to mailing face and business reply card, four panels, each of which contains copy for one journal.

A line of copy above the BRC bears this copy: Please . . . Pass this brochure along to your colleague or library. On the opposite side, above the card, is ordering information and a toll-free 800 number.

14:07   Copy You Can Add to Journal Promotion Flier That Will Extend Its Life

If you are writing copy for the flier or prospectus of a journal with limited subscription potential and would like it to serve for two or three years without becoming obsolete, allow for ordering of current and future volumes into the next two or three years. For example, if your current volume is volume 5 (1985), show on the same order form:

( ) Vol. 5, 1985 $00.00
( ) Vol. 6, 1986 $00.00
( ) Vol. 7, 1987 $00.00

Presuming you can obtain firm prices for two or three years, the addition of the future years' subscription prices will permit use of the flier at least through the end of the last year shown.

14:08   Copy You Can Add to Journal Promotion Flier That Produces Multi-Year Subscriptions

If information is not available on subscription rates in future years, you can still make a subscription offer in your copy that will extend a subscription beyond the year of the promotion. Just follow the procedure practiced by one major publisher of international journals. This publisher, in its journals promotion fliers directed to libraries, offers a price reduction of 5% when subscriptions are placed for two years.

The procedure works, says the publisher, because "this two-year rate also protects the libraries against any increase in price resulting from inflation or increases in number of pages, or from any charges for the supply of additional volumes not previously announced."

14:09   Copy Approach for Subscription Renewal Reminder Insert

Since 1981, it has been possible for journal publishers to enclose with the mailing of a journal a subscription renewal notice which postal regulations previously required to be sent with first-class postage. Under that regulation, first-class mail that was incidental but related to the matter mailed via another class required no additional postage.

Some journal publishers enclose renewal notices with issues *prior* to the last issue, or continue to mail them separately. However, increasingly, they also enclose *with* the last issue a notice calling attention to the fact that an invoice has already been sent and urging renewal. Such an insert may be in the form of a postcard-sized insert on colored card stock or a simulated mini-letterhead with typewritten notice.

Here is a suggested copy approach for a final-issue insert, a composite of several presently used:

YOUR LAST ISSUE . . .

This is the final issue of the current volume of this journal. We hope that you will want to continue receiving future issues.

The invoice covering your subscription for the coming year has been sent earlier either directly to you or to your subscription agent. If you have not yet renewed, we hope that you will do so without delay.

**14:10   Copy Approach for a Successful
Journal Promotion Technique**

If you have a journal that appeals to a very select audience and prospect lists or names are hard to come by, here is a useful technique for sampling and prospect list development. The technique is widely used for newsletter promotions; it is easily adaptable to journals where the numbers are relatively small.

Here is what you do: With an issue of your journal, include an insert (I recommend a letter format although some journals have used bind-in cards and blow-in cards). The copy should say something like this:

WE'D LIKE TO SEND A COMPLIMENTARY COPY OF
(JOURNAL)
TO AN INTERESTED FRIEND OR COLLEAGUE

The copy theme should follow this approach:

If you have a friend or colleague who you think might be interested in seeing a copy of (Journal), just provide us with his or her name and address in the space provided and mail this letter back to me. A complimentary copy will be mailed without delay.

At the bottom, add a coupon for fill-in information. Allow space for one or more names as desired.

Please send a complimentary copy (or complimentary copies) of (Journal) to the name(s) I have listed below:

Name _____ Dept / Affil._____

Address _____

City / State / ZIP _____

(Repeat if willing to send more than one complimentary copy)

Signed _____

The complimentary journal, when sent, should include a cover letter. One possible suggested heading:

AT THE REQUEST OF A MUTUAL FRIEND, WE ARE PLEASED
TO SEND THE ENCLOSED COMPLIMENTARY COPY OF
(NAME OF YOUR JOURNAL)

Names thus received can not only provide a source for sending the complimentary copies, but also help you develop a prospect list for the journal for later promotions. This type of promotion is designed mainly for journals that appeal to individual subscribers, rather than those aimed mainly at the library market.

14:11 Innovative Copy Approach for New Journal Announcement: Case Study

Here's a refreshing copy approach used to launch a new technical journal that leads the reader through the copy almost automatically. It's an announcement flyer for the *Journal of Lightwave Technology,* and the offering was issued by the Optical Society of America.

The flyer is 8½" × 11" flat, on heavy coated stock, and folded into thirds to 3⅝" × 8½" to go out as a self-mailer.

Back panel (opposite of mailing face) copy reads: "Announcing the *Journal of Lightwave Technology,*" with the names of the joint sponsors, OSA and IEEE.

Opened flat, the inside has copy set in two columns, a left column 2 inches wide with prominent boldface questions, and a right-hand column about 4 inches in width, in which the answers are given.

Leadoff question copy reads:

Who is the editor?

To its right, the answer is supplied in lightface type.

> The editor is Thomas G. Giallorenzi. He will be assisted by an able group of associate editors (and they are listed, along with their nationalities).

Other questions follow, in vertical sequence, in boldface, followed to their right by the answers. Some of the other questions:

Where may I submit a manuscript for publication?

Will articles on lightwave technology be published in the other journals of the societies?

When will the first issue appear?

How do I subscribe?

These questions and answers are followed on the lower third panel with a subscription order form with separate U.S. and foreign rates shown.

On the mailing side, the folds create three panels—one the mailing face, adjacent to it the *announcing* panel, and at the end a third panel with two more questions in the same two-column format:

Why a new journal?

What will be published?

OPTICAL SOCIETY OF AMERICA
EXECUTIVE OFFICE
1816 Jefferson Place, N.W.
Washington, D.C. 20036

NON-PROFIT ORG.
U.S. POSTAGE
PAID
Permit No. 1639
Washington, DC

Announcing the

Journal of
**LIGHTWAVE
TECHNOLOGY**

A NEW PUBLICATION OF THE
INSTITUTE OF ELECTRICAL AND ELECTRONICS ENGINEERS
AND THE
OPTICAL SOCIETY OF AMERICA

Why a new journal?

The development of low-loss optical fibers and efficient and reliable light sources and detectors has led to an explosion in the utilization of these components in communications and sensor systems. Much of the material heretofore published has appeared in the several journals of the Institute of Electrical and Electronics Engineers (IEEE) and the Optical Society of America (OSA). The two societies have elected to direct all applicable papers to this new journal for publication in order to provide a focus for the vigorous and growing field of lightwave technology.

**What will be
published?**

The journal will publish original contributions, both theoretical and experimental, that represent advances in the science, technology, and engineering of optical guided waves. Papers on subjects such as fiber and cable technologies; active and passive guided-wave components; integrated optics and optoelectronics; and systems, subsystems, new applications, and unique field trials will be included.

Copy responding to these two questions mentions how the development of low-loss optical fibers and efficient reliable light sources has led to an explosion in the utilization of these components in communications and that the new journal will provide a focus for the publication of all applicable papers on the subject from both sponsoring societies.

This format and question-and-answer copy approach comes through as an innovative and economical format that can be readily adapted to a variety of new journal announcements.

14:12   Creative Copy Approach to Journal Space Advertising and List Rental Offering

The Transaction Periodicals Consortium consists of a network of 32 interdisciplinary social science journals that provide an unduplicated combination of 80,000 academic and professional subscribers.

The Rutgers University-based Consortium displayed a refreshing creative approach to the marketing of space advertising and list rentals for the journals under its wing with the 1983 offering shown in Figure 11.

The letter, directed to space advertising directors, list rental managers, and marketing officers, offered a combination of options that would be hard to resist. Journals were divided into separate categories, such as American Government, Black Studies, Economics, etc. Six special options were then offered.

14:13   How *Not* to Present Benefit Copy in Journal Promotions: A Case Study

The marketer had worked up a self-mailer for a leading journal on taxation and three allied publications. It carried the headline: "Find out FREE why more than 50,000 tax experts regularly turn to the Journal of Taxation publications."

It worked extremly well. Here the magic word "FREE" was matched with the support of 50,000 of the prospect's colleagues.

After using the self-mailer to various lists for two years, the marketer decided to see if he could develop a more effective alternative piece for the journal(s). He asked several tax practitioners what they looked for in new publication offers.

From his inquiries, he came up with these benefits:

- Save time
- Make more money
- Look good to the clients

In a redesigned self-mailing piece, he used these newly developed appeals without marrying them to supporting evidence that they were true.

Result: the revised mailing piece failed to score. The benefits were right but there was no supporting authority.

Lesson learned: When your headline and supporting copy offer a benefit, give the promise credibility with an attribution from a supporting authority.

TRANSACTION
PERIODICALS
CONSORTIUM Rutgers - The State University, New Brunswick, NJ 08903.

TO: _____ Space Advertising Directors

     _____ List Rental Managers

     _____ Marketing Officers

FROM: Mark Roseman *MR*
       Advertising Director

Re: TRANS-ACTION NETWORK PURCHASE OPTIONS

Transaction is one of the most prestigious publishers of linked journals in social science and public policy.

Now, these distinguished journals are available to you through the TRANS-ACTION NETWORK to provide you with extra money-savings opportunities to agressively market your titles through advertising and direct mail.

Despite austerity budget cuts and tactic changes, you can still:

   * meet your marketing objectives

   * keep within modified budget schedules

Here are your customized TRANS-ACTION NETWORK options:

   1. Buy all the journals in any catagory .... for half price.

   2. Buy any two journals and the third page is yours .... for half price.

   3. Save 1/3 on any size ad when you repeat it in the following issue.

   4. Rent a list and the ad in journal(s) rented is yours....for half price.

Not enough?

   5. Propose your own category of at least four journals - its yours for half.

Just want to test the waters?

   6. Okay, then select any two journals and save ten percent.

The TRANS-ACTION NETWORK just may be your most effective media buy this year. For more information, call me at 201-932-2280. Or send in your insertion orders for immediate attention.

A D V E R T I S I N G

MEMO

FIGURE 11 This letter creatively combines the marketing of journal space advertising and list rental.

14:14 Periodical Subscription Guarantees: Copy Approaches

A frequently used closing in direct-mail subscription offers for periodicals is the subscription-cancellation money-back guarantee. It is used with great effectiveness by numerous periodicals, and even more by newsletters. The approach is generally the same, though the copy may vary each time. Here are several copy approaches from periodical subscription offers.

ANALYTICAL CHEMISTRY

CHANGE YOUR MIND AFTER YOU SUBSCRIBE?
Of course. And no hard feelings, either. If you ever want to cancel your subscription to *Analytical Chemistry,* you may do so—at any time. And you'll receive a full, prompt refund for all issues not yet mailed.

CHEMTECH

We'll process your trial subscription order as soon as the card arrives. Then, if you decide at any time that CHEMTECH isn't bringing you the benefits you expected, just let us know.

We'll stop your subscription immediately. And we'll send you a full refund for all paid issues still due you.

It's as simple as that. No problems. No questions. Your satisfaction with CHEMTECH is literally guaranteed.

JOURNAL OF FUTURES MARKETS

Your satisfaction is guaranteed. If, after receiving your first issue, you decide not to continue your subscription, you may return it for a full refund. Or, you may keep the issue and we will refund the pro-rata balance of your subscription price. There is literally no reason why you should not see for yourself what this compelling new publication holds for you.

14:15 Aspen Systems Copy Approach in Card-Deck Journal Offerings

In its Spring 1983 nursing card deck, referred to as "Aspen Nursing Card Catalog," the journal *Topics in Emergency Medicine* is offered on a card which has cover illustration, names of editors, and subjects to be covered in the four topical volumes issued for the year (Figure 12). Sales copy is minimal:

Add an Important New Member to your Emergency Medical Team—A *critical companion* for emergency care procedures— An *important vehicle for advanced continuing education.*

Topics in Emergency Medicine is designed to be your vital information link with the latest developments in emergency medicine.

After the subscription price is the paragraph, under a heading "Money-Back Guarantee":

34

**TOPICS IN
EMERGENCY MEDICINE**

*Editors: Marc J. Bayer, M.D. and
Carmen Germaine Warner, R.N.,
P.H.N., F.A.A.N.
Consulting Editor: Knut F. Eie, Paramedic*

Add an Important New Member to Your Emergency Medical
Team—A *critical companion* for emergency care
procedures!—An *important vehicle for advanced continuing
education!*
Topics in Emergency Medicine is designed to be your vital
information link with the latest developments in emergency
medicine.
In 1983 **TEM** examines **Psychological and Behavioral
Emergencies, Diagnostic Procedures in the Emergency
Department, Internal Medicine Emergencies,** and
Radiologic Emergencies.
Annual Subscription (4 issues): $42.00

Money-Back Guarantee:

☐ Begin my one-year subscription with this understanding: If at any
time, for any reason, I am not completely satisfied with this journal, I
will notify Aspen that I wish to cancel and Aspen will send me a full
refund for issues not yet mailed.

☐ Bill me   ☐ Bill institution P.O. Number _____
☐ Payment enclosed. Maryland orders add 5% sales tax.
   (Aspen pays postage and handling)

Affiliation _____

Name _____

Title _____

Address _____

City _____

State _____ Zip _____
                                         BSIA

**Prior Issues—TOPICS IN EMERGENCY MEDICINE—
Vital Information for the emergency clinician.**
Qty.

_____ **Priorities in Multiple Trauma** (5/79) (432257)
_____ **Cardiac Arrest** (7/79) (432265)
_____ **Poisonings and Overdose** (10/79) (432273)
_____ **The Prehospital Care System** (1/80) (432281)
_____ **Respiratory Emergencies—I** (4/80) (43229X)
_____ **Respiratory Emergencies—II** (7/80) (432303)
_____ **Environmental Medical Emergencies** (10/80) (432311)
_____ **Orthopaedic Emergencies** (1/81) (43232X)
_____ **Pediatric Emergencies** (4/81) (432338)
_____ **Controversies in Emergency Medicine** (7/81) (432346)
_____ **Thermal Injuries** (10/82) (432354)
_____ **Human Violence** (1/82) (432362)
_____ **Infectious Disease Emergencies** (4/82) (432397)
_____ **Neurological Emergencies** (7/82) (432443)
_____ **Pediatric Trauma** (10/82) (437259)
_____ **Psychological and Behavioral Emergencies** (1/83) (437267)

1-3 issues—$14.00 each
Four (4) or more issues—$10.50 each.

After using these publications for 30 days, I will honor your invoice,
plus postage and handling, or return the issue(s) and the invoice with
no further obligation.
☐ Bill me   ☐ Bill institution P.O. Number _____
☐ Payment enclosed. Maryland orders add 5% sales tax.
   (Aspen pays postage and handling)

Affiliation _____

Name _____

Title _____

Address _____

City _____

State _____ Zip _____
                                         BSIA

FIGURE 12   These cards from the Aspen Systems Nursing Card Catalog
offer a subscription to the journal *Topics in Emergency Medicine* and a selection
of prior issues.

☐ Begin my one-year subscription with this understanding: If at
any time, for any reason, I am not completely satisfied with
this journal, I will notify Aspen that I wish to cancel and Aspen
will send me a full refund for issues not yet mailed.

A separate card in the same "Nursing Card Catalog" deck lists and
invites orders for 16 prior topical issues (Figure 12). Copy indicates
that issues are $14.00 each if one to three are ordered; four or more
issues cost $10.50 each.

Return privilege is offered with the prior-issue offering with this
copy:

After using these publications for 30 days, I will honor your
invoice, plus postage and handling, or return the issue(s) and
the invoice with no further obligation.

Copy adds that "Aspen pays postage and handling" on prepaid
orders.

**14:16   American Chemical Society Journal
Copy Approach in Price List**

The American Chemical Society *subscription price list* is a masterpiece
for the depth of detail in its coverage. The 22 journals and magazines

are listed vertically on the list. Then, 16 different columnar headings provide in-depth details relating to subscriptions for each of the journals listed. Columnar headings include:

- Volume number(s) [as many as three volumes in a subscription year for some]
- Number of issues for year
- Term-Years [for some publications, separate rates given for one-, two-, and three-year terms]
- Member subscription price—delivery in the United States
- Member subscription price—foreign air freight included
- Member subscription price—foreign surface mail included
- Nonmember personal—delivery in United States
- Nonmember personal—foreign air freight included
- Nonmember personal—foreign surface mail included
- Nonmember institutional—delivery in the United States
- Nonmember institutional—foreign air freight included
- Nonmember institutional—foreign surface mail included

Separate columns are also included for supplementary materials both in hard copy and in microfiche—both U.S. and foreign shipping rates for selected journals.

Individual instructions are given for Japan where Maruzen Co., Ltd. is the ACS exclusive agent. Canadian subscriptions are treated in the foreign surface mail column.

Payment is required with all subscription orders. Payment options given: U.S. currency, in U.S. currency by international postal money order, UNESCO coupons, or U.S. bank draft. Bank advice is not acceptable.

Format is a sheet $9\frac{1}{8}''$ wide $\times$ 15" long, folded twice to $9\frac{1}{8}'' \times 3\frac{3}{4}''$. It was mailed in a No. 10 white envelope, return address printed corner card. Also enclosed was a brief letter signed by the sales manager of the books and journals division.

14:17   Academic Press Journal Copy Approach in Seasonal Catalog

The last page of the seasonal is devoted exclusively to journals. The catalog index provides a separate index for journals.

Journal listings in the catalog provide this information:

- Journal title
- Editor
- Volumes for the current year

- Subscription rate (one rate for "USA and Canada," and another higher one for "Outside the USA and Canada." The higher rate is shown for three of five journals listed (12% to 18% more than U.S. prices).
- Postage: Apparently, postage is included in the subscription price.

At the bottom of the page containing the journal listings is this copy:

> Subscription orders are entered for the calendar year and are payable in advance.
>
> Sample issues of journals are available to honor individual requests.

An order card, included in the catalog, made no provision for journal subscriptions.

(See also entry 15:14, "Telephone Script for Contacting Journal Expires.")

14:18   Overseas Surface and Air Delivery Times Enhance Journal Price List

The 1984 American Chemical Society subscription price list includes three prices for most of its journals: U.S. delivery, foreign surface-mail delivery, and foreign air-freight delivery. To reinforce its foreign delivery, it includes a small copy box at the bottom of the price list with a comparison chart of days required for typical delivery to foreign countries.

The chart indicates, for example, that surface delivery to London takes 60 days, while air delivery takes 5 days. Other typical delivery times are shown for Buenos Aires, Frankfurt, Melbourne, and Tel Aviv.

Copy at bottom of box states: "See air service rates above for faster delivery of your publications."

14:19   Publisher Uses Own Name on Envelope in Circulation Promotion: Case Study

When the U.S. publisher of *Nature* (until early 1983) tried a circulation promotion in 1981, his No. 10 envelope bore only his name, Robert Ubell, on the envelope corner card. The mailing, sent to lists of U.S. scientists, offered a subscription for one year at half the usual price.

The package's enclosure consisted of an insert, printed in script on white coated card stock measuring 8½″ wide × 7½″ long, folded in half to 8½″ × 3¾″. The cover copy, printed in black ink, read:

An Invitation
from
the American Publisher of
Nature

The inside copy, a four-paragraph message, was set ragged left and right and centered, and included at the bottom an invitation to respond by using an enclosed reply envelope. The black-ink-on-white wallet-flap reply envelope had these ordering options printed on the back: (1) one year of *Nature* at half price ($86.50); (2) six months for $50; or (3) three months for $30.

A toll-free number was also printed in boldface on the business reply envelope for credit-card orders only.

The response, according to Publisher Ubell, was a little over 1%.

**14:20   Possible Pitfall in Journal Promotion:
Postage Charges**

Before you start writing copy for a journal promotion, be sure you have a clear understanding of how postage charges should be shown on the order-form copy. If you do not, your promotion may be unclear and lead to unnecessary correspondence and possible collection problems.

- If your subscription price includes postage regardless of the country of subscription's origin, state this.

- If your subscription price includes postage only for subscriptions originating in the United States (or North America), and there is an added postage charge for other parts of the world, indicate this on the order form and include amount.

15

Telemarketing Copy:
Approaches and Examples

15:01   The Telephone as a Tool of Marketing

Telemarketing simply means using the telephone as a tool of marketing. Publishers are using the telephone in two distinct ways, *inbound* and *outbound*. The inbound vehicle now used extensively by specialized and scholarly publishers is the toll-free 800 number. When prominently displayed and in bold type in a publishing promotion, it can increase response substantially. Several entries following show how the 800 number has been used with great success by a number of publishers as a copy component in both space advertising and direct mail. Most of the catalogs of major publishers studied for this volume included an 800 number.

The outbound vehicle is the telephone salesperson, working from a telemarketing script. In some houses, full-scale telemarketing staffs are employed and successfully sell the publisher's products, often to buyers of the establishment's other products. Experience has shown that telemarketing success is higher when the publisher is known to the individual being called and is highest when the person called is already a user or subscriber to one of the publisher's other products.

Guidelines for telemarketing scripts are included in this chapter along with actual scripts that have been used successfully by a number of different publishers. These samples are designed to indicate the length of a telemarketing script, the actual wording used, and the ways in which the salesperson practices his or her craft.

15:02   Use of a Toll-Free 800 Telephone Number in Your Ad Copy: Guidelines

There are many advantages (Figure 13), and a few disadvantages, to including a 800 toll-free telephone number in your advertising copy. If your publishing establishment does not have toll-free 800 lines in-house, this is usually done by utilizing the number supplied by an outside telephone-answering service.

Many answering services will establish an account on a so-much-per-call basis, so cost is not a major factor in determining whether you should use an 800 number. If you do decide to use the toll-free number, you cannot control this cost.

The inclusion of the toll-free number is likely to generate a wide range of calls that do not involve a book order. For this reason, when you include in your advertisement an 800 number supplied by an answering service, you should reach a preliminary agreement on how you want such calls handled by the service, which ones you are prepared to pay for, and on what basis.

Your use of an 800 number for direct orders should clearly state this in your copy: "For book orders only, call 800. . . ." Further, the answering services should be provided with a direct number to your publishing establishment to which they can refer callers should the call involve anything other than a direct order. Try to make advance arrangements for a separate charge on calls that do not involve an actual order, such as referrals.

Should you decide to use the 800 number through an answering service, bear in mind that the more clearly you present the 800 number in your advertising, the better your telephone response will be. You will be pleasantly surprised to find that, if you put your 800 number in 24-point boldface type with white space around it, you will get many times more results than you get with the 800 number buried somewhere in the signature of your advertisement.

If there are any restrictions on telephone ordering, you should also state this in your copy. In other words, your copy should qualify the type of telephone ordering you want so that callers know in advance what orders will be accepted. For example, do not advertise books priced over $100 in your advertising if your house policy requires a deposit on orders over that amount, unless your ad copy clearly states this.

15:03   How Scientists and Engineers View 800 Number in Advertising

Science magazine asked readers of its 9 October 1981, issue how they

New...from Wiley-Interscience

NMR OF AROMATIC COMPOUNDS
J.D. Memory and Nancy K. Wilson
A sound, comprehensive treatment of the theory of NMR applied to aromatic compounds. Covers both theoretical, research-oriented material as well as useful experimental techniques and examples of their applications.
approx. 320 pp. **Sept. 1982** (1-08899-4) In Press

ORGANIC SYNTHESIS WITH CARBON-14
Richard R. Muccino
An up-to-date survey of the preparation of compounds labelled with Carbon 14, organized by reaction and classified by functional groups. It makes Carbon-14 labelling available as a routine tool for organic chemists and biochemists.
approx. 480 pp. **August 1982** (1-05165-9) In Press

REACTIVITY IN ORGANIC CHEMISTRY
Gerhard Klumpp
Translated by Ludmila Birladeanu
Examines essential aspects of present-day organic chemistry, focusing on reactivity and reaction mechanisms. Discusses examples of synthetically important reactions and properties and behavior of reactive intermediates. Emphasis on answering practical questions such as what products are to be expected from certain starting materials and how much reaction time is needed for a given substrate.
502 pp. **1982** (1-06285-5) $49.95

THE TOTAL SYNTHESIS OF NATURAL PRODUCTS, Vol. 5
Edited by John ApSimon
Fifth volume of this continuing series. Presents the total syntheses of Sesquiterpenes published during 1970-1979. Offers an overview of current practice in synthesis.
approx 320 pp. **August 1982** (1-09808-6) In Press

CONTEMPORARY HETEROCYCLIC CHEMISTRY
Syntheses, Reactions and Applications
George R. Newkome and William W. Paudler
A comprehensive approach to heterocyclic chemistry, based on the concept of π-excessive and π-deficient ring systems. Introduces the categorical similarities and differences among the varied heterocyclic systems. Explains the logical consistency of the numerous syntheses and relative reactivities.
approx. 832 pp. **August 1982** (1-06279-0) In Press

A DICTIONARY OF SPECTROSCOPY, 2nd Ed.
Ronald C. Denney
This new revised and updated edition defines frequently-used spectroscopy terms in non-specialist language. Well-illustrated and referenced, it is designed to bridge the gap between standard scientific dictionaries and highly-technical textbooks. A valuable sourcebook for student and technician.
approx. 208 pp. **Sept. 1982** (1-87478-7) $39.95

BIOSYNTHESIS OF ISOPRENOID COMPOUNDS, Vol. 1
Edited by John W. Porter and Sandra L. Spurgeon
The first volume of this comprehensive two-volume work contains a detailed presentation of early reactions common to the biosynthesis of all isoprenoid compounds and the later reactions leading to the formation of monoterpenes, sesquiterpenes, diterpenes, and triterpenes, including sterols and other related compounds.
558 pp. **1981** (1-04807-0) $59.50

Order through your bookstore or write to Nat Bodian, Dept. 3-6650

REAGENTS FOR ORGANIC SYNTHESIS, Vol. 10
Edited by Mary Fieser
The newest volume in this quick-reference set features references to papers published from January 1980 to June 1981. Emphasizes reagents that open new vistas in organic synthesis. Includes comprehensive index of reagents according to types and author and subject indexes.
approx. 640 pp. **July 1982** (1-86636-9) $39.50
10-Volume Set **1982** (1-86634-2) $415.00

CENTRAL ANALGETICS
Edited by Daniel Lednicer
Provides up-to-date reviews of the physiology, pharmacology, and chemistry used to develop drugs to treat pain. Experts cover such areas as the physiology of pain, test systems for potential analgetic agents, and developing fields of analgetic research.
approx. 320 pp. **Sept. 1982** (1-08314-3) In Press

TECHNIQUE OF ELECTROORGANIC SYNTHESIS: Scale-Up and Engineering Aspects (Vol. 5, Pt. 3 of Techniques of Chemistry, Arnold Weissberger, Editor)
Edited by Norman L. Weinberg and B.V. Tilak
The first comprehensive treatment of the scale-up and engineering aspects of electroorganic processes. Many important processes are covered in an in-depth, "case history" manner, providing the reader with the practical aspects of the prospective process.
536 pp. **1982** (1-06359-2) $85.00

ORGANIC REACTIONS, Vol. 28
Edited by William G. Dauben
Here's the latest volume in a series of critical discussions of important organic reactions or reaction phases. Examines the Reimer-Tieman Reaction, the Friedlander Synthesis of Quinolines and the Directed Aldol Reaction.
336 pp. **July 1982** (1-86141-3) $39.50
also just published:
ORGANIC REACTIONS, Vol. 27
416 pp. **July 1982** (1-09657-1) $45.00

TOPICS IN STEREOCHEMISTRY, Volume 13
Norman Allinger, Ernest L. Eliel, and Samuel H. Wilen
CONTENTS: Stereoselective Aldol Condensations. Application of Molecular Mechanics Calculations to Organic Chemistry. Chiral Monolayers at the Air-Water Interface. NMR Chiral Solvating Agents. Chiral Organosulfur Compounds. Subject Index. Cumulative Index.
489 pp. **1982** (1-05680-4) $85.00

ELECTRONS IN CHEMICAL REACTIONS: First Principles
Lionel Salem
Written by one of the world's leading authorities in the field of reaction mechanisms, this volume brings together for the first time all the governing principles of chemical reactions. It covers methods, potential energy surfaces, electronic structure of intermediates, orbital symmetry, state symmetry, reaction paths, electron exchange, and solvent effects.
260 pp. **1982** (1-08474-3) $35.00

DIRADICALS
Edited by Weston Thatcher Borden
An up-to-date review of the chemistry of organic diradicals. Experts discuss such topics as the effects of electron repulsion in diradicals, nonconjugated diradicals as reactive intermediates, intersystem crossing in diradicals and radical pairs, and more.
approx. 416 pp. **October 1982** (1-08661-4) In Press

FOR BOOKS ORDERS ONLY:
CALL TOLL FREE (800) 526-5368
In New Jersey, call collect (201) 797-7809
Order Code # 3-6650

1807 1982
WILEY-INTERSCIENCE
a division of John Wiley & Sons, Inc.
605 Third Avenue
New York, N.Y. 10158
In Canada: 22 Worcester Road, Rexdale, Ontario M9W 1L1
Prices subject to change without notice.
092 3-6650

FIGURE 13 Addition of boldface toll-free 800 telephone number produced approximately $1,000 in traceable orders for this list-type advertisement in a scientific journal, where previous advertising without it had produced none. An identifying order code number under the 800 number helped track the responses.

would respond to an advertised product they might need in their laboratory in the next 30 days. Of those who answered, 48% said they would dial an 800 number if one were available. Only 5% said they would dial the regular telephone number.

Plant engineering and purchasing executives who received the August 1981 issue of *U.S. Industrial Directory* were asked which number they would call if two similar products were advertised in the same issue—one with a conventional phone number and one with an 800 number.* In response, 58% said they would call both, 41% said they would call only the 800 number, and 1% said they would call only the conventional number.

Because many scientists and engineers buy or order books for their perceived immediate value to work or research, these survey results carry a message for book advertising, too.

15:04 Advantages of Including a Toll-Free 800 Number in Advertising

1. Produces faster response to advertising, instant response from impulse buyers.
2. Can replace a space-consuming order coupon, or be combined with a coupon to enhance response.
3. Can reinforce limited-time offers with cutoff dates, such as a pre-publication offer or a special sale.
4. Provides an easy vehicle for the busy scientist or professional who won't be bothered writing out and mailing in an order.
5. Easily fits into a small space advertisement.

15:05 Basics of a Book Telemarketing Sales Pitch

1. Opening line of pitch should mention that caller is calling from (name of company).
2. Second line should give reason for call, followed by brief description of the product, and an offer.
3. Third part of pitch should strive for a close on the strength of product's benefits.
4. Telephone sales personnel should be encouraged to make whatever modifications are necessary to make the pitch work for them. (Although a number of different salespeople will start with the same pitch, after completion of a telephone sales project each caller will have a pitch significantly different from the others. It is worthwhile to examine the more successful pitches for clues to more effective future telemarketing scripts.)

*Cahners Advertising Research Report No. 260.1

15:06   Preparation of Telemarketing Scripts: Guidelines

The sale of books, periodicals, and subscription services by telephone is a highly specialized activity. Success often relies heavily on the audience called, the product offered and its perceived need by the person being called, the special nature of the offer, and the existence of an ongoing relationship with the person called, as in the case of a former customer or subscriber.

The telemarketing scripts presented in the entries following have been used successfully in the past. However, they are presented here for their format value. Any script, no matter how successful in the past, may perform differently when used at another time and applied to a different audience with a different product.

Each telemarketing effort requires its own special approach. If your plans involve the use of an outside telemarketing service, involve them in your script preparation plans. Often such services can provide valuable guidance and suggestions in the effective preparation of telemarketing scripts.

15:07   Successful Formula Used for Telemarketing Script Preparation

In one publishing establishment, which relies heavily on telemarketing to sell its professional subscription products, the telemarketing script writer has developed a useful format for obtaining all the essential information needed for script preparation. An 11-question questionnaire is supplied to the editor for the product being sold, and the editor's answers provide the basis for the writing of the script.

Following are the questions used in the questionnaire:

1. List features of publication and benefits the features provide that satisfy the customer's needs.
2. What items do we already publish that are an obvious cross-sell?
3. What is the primary audience for this publication?
4. What is the secondary audience?
5. If the name is company only, what job title should we ask for within the company?
6. What associations would be interested in this publication?
7. If we were to order a broad-based outside list by job title, company, or association, what would you suggest?
8. What is the competition for our title? How does our publication differ? Why is ours better? How do we compare in terms of price?
9. Is the information in this publication covered in any of our other books or periodicals? If so, how does the new publication differ and why would a subscriber want to buy it?

10. How large do you estimate the primary and secondary markets to be.

11. Please provide a one- or two-line summary statement explaining in fundamental terms what the product will do for the customer.

15:08 Telemarketing Script for Selling Textbooks to Business and Vocational Schools

A publisher of textbooks for business and vocational schools used this three-step script in a telemarketing campaign.

FIRST CALL

To department head or curriculum coordinator: "We are publishing (name of book). What is the name of the person who is giving this course, or who decides on the textbook for this course? We'd like to send that person a copy of the book."

Upon receipt of instructors' names, send complimentary copies.

SECOND CALL

To recipients of books four or five weeks after book was sent: "Recently we sent you a copy of our new book (give book title). Did you by any chance have an opportunity to look at the new chapter on (one of the featured chapters mentioned). We'd like your opinion on it."

Teacher will usually admit he or she read book and give an opinion, or say he or she has not had a chance to look at it yet. If the latter, the caller says, "Well, then, I wonder if I could call you back in a week or two." Usually the teacher will make an appointment for the return call.

THIRD CALL

Caller telephones teacher about the date mentioned in the second call, or on the specific date suggested by teacher. The salesperson will repeat the name of the book and remind the teacher that he or she recommended a return call to solicit an opinion of the book. By that time, usually, the teacher will also advise whether he or she is considering use of the book.

15:09 Loose-Leaf Offering to Subscribers of a Related Publication

This script was used a number of years ago by a loose-leaf publisher of accounting and related publications. The script produced a favorable number of responses in calls to existing subscribers of a related publication. Close to half of those agreeing to examine on a 30-day basis remitted payment. The script:

This is (name of caller) of (publisher) in (city)

I'm calling because you are a subscriber to our accounting-type publications, and because of that I want to notify you that we have a new publication called *Guide to* _____.

This is a one-volume loose-leaf book with nine individual guides covering each functional area of your accounting control system. Each is a complete program for establishing, evaluating, and monitoring your corporate accounting controls, and provides a cost–benefit analysis as well.

The book/It's prepared by (leading accounting firm) and takes their approach to complying with the proposed SEC regulations and provisions of the Foreign Corrupt Practices Act.

To sum up, why I'm calling is to see if you'd like to look at a copy on our 30-day approval basis which includes a prepaid postage return box.

(Response)

The *Guide to* _____ is $00.00. If you decide to keep it, supplements will be sent on approval.

15:10 Telemarketing Script Offering High-Priced Aviation Book

This is (name of caller), National Aeronautical Institute in (city). I am calling to let you know that the (year of publication) edition of Jane's *All the World's Aircraft* is available now for the holiday season. [The calls were made in November.]

This beautiful, hardbound book has been difficult to purchase in the past, and we are now trying to make it more available to people like you who are professionals in the field. *All the World's Aircraft* is the most authoritative source for accurate, up-to-date information on all aspects of aircraft currently in production or under development throughout the world. Its value speaks for itself and we are now making it available on a special price basis of ($00.00) reduced from ($00.00, a saving of about 30%). We're calling right now before the holidays to see if you would like to order a book for yourself or a friend. The (price) offer is good for this time only, and if you would like to buy more than one, each additional copy will be ($00.00, about 20% less than the first-copy offer). Credit cards are accepted.

15:11 Telephone Offer of New Edition of Industry Handbook

(When there is no name of an individual listed, ask for the officer in charge of _____.)

This is (caller's name) of (publisher) in (city). The reason I'm calling is that you/ your company has a copy/copies of our (name of book), (year of publication) edition.

(At this point, most of those called won't know what caller is talking about. Caller has to explain what handbook is, whom it's geared for, usefulness, etc.)

We have just come out with a new (year) revised edition of the Handbook that has been rewritten (in an easy-to-read format) and updated to reflect changes in (several examples given).

The book is designed to help officers and employees alike (benefit given) and to be in compliance with the (name of Federal act).

So, the reason for my call is to determine if I may direct a copy of this new edition to you for 30 days' free examination so you can look it over, utilize it, pass it around, and so on. If you decide to keep it, the cost is $00.00; if not, we will provide postage for its return.

(If they say "Yes," tell them that if they feel they would like to provide for more than one department, "We are offering multiple-copy discounts." Confirm name and address.)

15:12 Directory Sales to Listed Entries: Telephone Script

We are calling because your (type of organization, name of school, etc.) has been included in the new (name of directory) published this year by (publisher) and edited by (name of editor).

This book is a national register and the best single source of access to more than (mention performing arts and civic centers information when calling that type of institution; when calling schools, mention number of schools, and information about them, that provide training in the performing arts; in other words, gear the benefits to the specific interests of the organization or school being called).

For a limited time only, the publisher has a special offer for the (schools or institutions) listed in the directory—the chance to purchase this directory at (X%) off the list price. The directory sells for (give list price). Under this special offer, the price to you is only (give net price).

This directory can be of enormous personal value, saving you both time and money. It can help you to (give a list of benefits the directory offers).

Note: If the directory updates an earlier edition, which the persons or institutions being called already have, it might be well to ask if they have the earlier edition and mention the extent to which the new edition is revised and updated and that it contains approximately X% new material.

15:13 Telemarketing Script That Scored for McGraw-Hill: Case Study

Telemarketing can be extremely effective when the publisher is well known to the audience being called. It can be even more effective when it is for a new edition of a product that is highly regarded and which the prospective customer may already own.

The McGraw-Hill Professional and Reference Book Division learned this in October 1981 when it launched the Fifth Edition of its celebrated *McGraw-Hill Encyclopedia of Science and Technology* to the library market via a telemarketing campaign.

The actual script used, which follows, was extremely effective and produced a substantial volume of orders.

Some of the features which made this script a winner:

- The McGraw-Hill name
- New edition of an established, highly regarded product
- Special prepublication price
- Combination of purchase options
- Free examination, return privilege
- Use of strong quotes from major library review media

TELEMARKETING SCRIPT 10.1.81   [page 1]

May I speak to the acquisition librarian please

(If more than one, ask for Reference or Science Librarian)

(Secure name _____)

Hello (Name), this is _____ from the McGraw-Hill Book Company in New York. I'm calling to tell you about the new fifth edition of the McGraw-Hill Encyclopedia of Science and Technology which we're publishing in a few months.

I wanted to tell you about the new edition for two reasons—first, because it's a landmark edition—the most extensive revision of this 15 volume set since it was first published.

The second reason is to tell you that we are offering librarians a special prepublication price as well as a combination of purchase options that should make this reference work accessible to most library budgets.

If you order the fifth edition now, you won't pay for it until it is published next spring, but you will save ninety dollars off the institutional price—that's more than double the usual list price discount.

I'm sure you know that this science and technology encyclopedia has received high praise from the library media and is recommended for most collections.

(If challenged, see list of quotes from media reviews at end of script)

TELEMARKETING SCRIPT 10.1.81   [page 2]

There have been so many technological advances in the last few years that we've added—1,000 more pages . . . extensively revised 2,000 of the 7,700 articles and added 315 new articles . . . added 1,800 illustrations . . . and now we have 3,000 distinguished contributors including 16 Nobel Prize winners.

We feel this revision is so monumental that it may be the most important purchase your library makes this year.

The regular institutional price will be $765, but if I can take your order now, it will only cost $675—a ninety dollar saving. May I take your order:

(If No—) May I ask if price is a problem?
(If price is a problem—go to page 3)
(If price is not a problem—go to page 4)

A (If Yes) May I have your name and billing address
Name / title / institution / address / city / state / ZIP

(Read information back to customer)

I'll send you a confirming letter about this order. When you receive my confirmation, please send me a copy of your purchase order. I'll need a purchase order before we can authorize the special pre-publication price.

(If customer requests special billing, repeat terms, thank for order and end conversation.)
(If customer has not requested special billing, continue . . .)

We won't bill you in 1981, in fact you won't be billed until after you receive the set next April.

Thank you very much for your order. It has been a pleasure talking to you. Goodbye.

TELEMARKETING SCRIPT 10.1.81 [page 3]

We can spread your payments over two fiscal years if you like. We could bill you for half the pre-publication price when the set is published in April 1982, and then bill you for the balance in January 1983, or we could do the same for 1981 and 1982. If it would help, we could even bill you for the full amount in 1981 . . . it just depends on your situation.

By the way, I hope you understand that our offer includes a 30-day examination period. If you order now, we'll ship the set on publication and you can examine the 15 volumes without obligation for 30-days. That should give you the time to see that this is the kind of accurate, up-to-date, and understandable reference you want for your readers.

You can order the set now, examine it for 30-days and return it, if it doesn't meet your expectations. If you keep it, you can pay over two fiscal years—and you still get the ninety dollar discount.

Would you like me to write up the order?

(If Yes, go back to page 2)
(If No, continue . . .) I'm sorry to hear that. In any event, I'll put your name on our mailing list for further information.

Please remember that if you don't order the set by December 31, you won't be eligible for the ninety-dollar discount.

If you change your mind, please let me know, and I'll see to it that you get the pre-publication discount.

Thank you very much.

TELEMARKETING SCRIPT 10.1.81   [page 4]

(For Customers who are not interested and price is not a problem)

(Use this statement unless the library is totally inappropriate—too small or concentrating on areas not including science & technology)

I hope you understand that our offer includes a 30-day examination period. If you order now, we'll ship the set on publication and you can examine the 15 volumes without obligation for 30 days. That should give you the time to see that this is the kind of accurate, up-to-date, and understandable reference you want for your readers.

Would you be interested in examining the set on this basis?

(If no . . .)   I'm sorry to hear that. In any event, I'll put your name on our mailing list for further information.

(If Yes . . .)   Would you be interested in having your payments spread over two fiscal years. You see we can bill you half the pre-publication price in April 1982 and the balance the following January?

(If customer gives an order go to line A, page 2)

QUOTES FROM MEDIA REVIEWS   [page 5]

The Library Journal said it was:
Quote Pre-eminent in its field . . . highly recommended for school, college, and public libraries close quote

The Catholic Library World said
Quote Every school and every library definitely must have one close quote

Booklist said
Quote The standard multivolume English-language reference work for the field and is recommended for all general reference collections serving young adults and older patrons. It is also suitable for appropriate special collections close quote

And finally, American Scientist said
Quote A major breakthrough in scientific publication close quote

---

15:14   Telephone Script for Contacting Journal Expires

Increasingly, publishers of scientific, scholarly, and professional journals are turning to the telephone to try to reinstate expired subscriptions. If you are asked to prepare a telephone script for this purpose, the model script following provides useful guidelines.

Good morning / afternoon / evening Mr. / Mrs. / Ms. _____ . Please (or) May I speak to someone who receives the (name of journal)? (or, if applicable) Sorry to bother you at home, but it is the only address we had (or) May I speak to the person who has assumed his / her responsibilities (pause) This is _____ (name) calling for (name of journal) (pause) According to our records you had been a regular subscriber, but as far as we can determine your subscription has not been renewed for (subscription year or period) (pause) I'm calling to suggest you review now in order to bring your collection up to date.

(If caller receives a "Yes" answer): Very good, we'll keep that subscription coming to you at (read name and address from card as on your records). Is that address still correct? (Make all necessary changes.) (If no response): We had been sending the journal to (read name and address from card). Is that address still correct? (Make all necessary changes.) Very good, Mr. / Miss / Ms. _____ . Since we have the correct address, all I need is your approval over the phone to continue your subscription. Is that okay? Thank you. I'll arrange for a bill to be sent for (amount of subscription) to cover your one-year subscription. Thank you again. Goodbye!

(If subscriber does not wish to renew, ask): Was there any particular reason? (Write reason on card. Terminate the call.)

(If subscriber claims renewed): I'm sure your renewal has been put through. Sometimes we get a little behind in our paper work. However, did you renew directly, or through a subscription agency? (If through an agency, ask) Will you please tell me the name of the agency so we can clear the record? (Note name of agency on card. Terminate the call.)

(If you cannot reach subscriber): Are you Mr. / Mrs. / Ms. _____ 's secretary or assistant? Maybe you can help me, please. Mr. / Miss / Ms. _____ has been a regular subscriber to our journal, but as far as we can determine, his / her subscription has not been renewed. If you would just ask him / her if he / she wishes to continue, then I'll call back at a convenient time to get your answer. Will you do that for me, please? (Note date and time on card and call back when requested to do so.)

16

Publicity Writing for Specialized and Scholarly Books

Release writing is best learned by reading the publications to which you send releases, and fathoming the techniques used to write the material in those publications.

Bruce W. Marcus, Consultant in
Public Relations and Marketing.

16:01 Importance of "News" in Publicity Writing: Release Preparation Tips

When you are about to undertake a publicity-writing assignment, bear in mind that editors of periodicals and newspapers are on the lookout for *news* for their readership, and not for *publicity*.

The information in your *news release* should be newsworthy and have the potential of appealing to the readers of the publications to which it is being sent. If your release has appeal to only a few of the periodicals on the distribution list, send the release only to those. If you send publications material that is not newsworthy, they may, from force of habit, ignore your occasional release that has legitimate news value for their readers.

RELEASE DATE

If you're sending a general release to a number of publications, be sure that the same release date is used on all the releases. This ensures that all releases will appear at the same time, or not before the release date you have specified.

USE OF "SPECIAL TO"

If your release appeals to only a few periodicals—each for different reasons—do not send them the same release. Instead, slightly rewrite each release, tailored to the special interests and, preferably, style of the periodical. So long as the release has been written especially for that publication, you may feel free to head your release "Special to (Name of Publication)"; it is likely to increase the chances of your release being used.

USE OF "EXCLUSIVE TO"

If, in your opinion, your release is newsworthy to only one periodical, or if you wish to limit its distribution to that one publication and send out only that *one* release, you may safely head your release "Exclusive to (Name of Publication)." It is helpful to have the release written in the style of the publication, addressed to the editor or concerned member of the editorial staff by name, and hand delivered or sent by registered mail. But this is all the more reason that the release must be truly news.

PITFALLS OF "EXCLUSIVE TO"

Don't ever try to fool an editor by claiming something for a news release that is not so. Editors have long memories and, once fooled or high-pressured, they may never trust one of your releases—or anything else from your press—again.

There is no guarantee that your use of "Exclusive to" on a news release will ensure that the publication to which it was sent will use it. Nor does it mean that you can expect an acknowledgment from the publication to which it was sent. The truth is that publications are deluged with publicity releases and rarely, if ever, do they acknowledge any of them. If you must know whether your release has been considered—or even received—follow up with a phone call.

There is another way you can get publicity short of using "Exclusive to" on a written news release. Sometimes it may be better to skip the writing of the release altogether and telephone the publication directly. In this way, you save the trouble of writing and you will get an immediate indication of whether your news is of interest. You may also be given an opportunity to provide more information during the course of the call, or at least to learn what sort of information the publication does want from you in order to publish your story.

**16:02   Finding the News Angle That Turns Publicity
into News: Case Study**

If you want your news releases to generate requests for review copies,
a conventional factual release, directed to the book review editor,
generally will get the desired response from appropriate media.

But if you want your release to appear as editorial matter in the
publication, you must search out the news angles in the book and
feature them in your release. Building a release around *news* often
will lead to space in the news columns where a conventional release,
no matter how well structured, will go straight into the editor's
wastebasket.

Here's a study of a release for a new edition of a classic two-volume
reference written in two different formats:

- The first format shows how a typical release might be written, and
  why, usually, when addressed to anyone except the book review
  editor, it fails to score with the editor as "news."
- The second version, built around two bits of "news," provides essentially the same information in a format most editors would find
  irresistible.

RELEASE WRITTEN IN CONVENTIONAL FORMAT

A new fourth edition of *Walker's Mammals of the World* has just
been published by Johns Hopkins University Press. The definitive
guide to mammalian life, first compiled by the late Ernest P.
Walker, has been extensively revised and expanded. The revised
edition is by Ronald M. Nowak and John L. Paradiso, both mammalogists at the U.S. Department of the Interior. They have
added to the illustrations, and rewritten many of the generic
descriptions in the classic two-volume reference.

RELEASE WRITTEN WITH NEWS ANGLE

The vampire bat sometimes consumes so much blood from its
victim that it can't fly away after dinner.

The two-toed sloth eats, sleeps, mates, and gives birth upside
down.

There are more facts where those came from in the fourth
edition of *Walker's Mammals of the World,* the definitive guide
to mammalian life first compiled by the late Ernest P. Walker
and just published by the Johns Hopkins University Press.

For the new edition, Ronald M. Nowak and John L. Paradiso,
both mammalogists at the U.S. Department of the Interior, have
expanded the text of the classic two-volume reference work,
added to the illustrations, and rewritten many of the generic
descriptions.

The latter version was actually published 29 June 1983 in *The Chronicle of Higher Education.*

16:03   Information Sources for Writing the P&S News Release

In all likelihood, your publicity efforts will involve a wide range of professional and scholarly books in areas with which you have no familiarity. Your "education" in assembling the material needed for the publicity will probably come from studying the author / marketing questionnaire for the book under consideration.

Obviously, the more information the questionnaire provides, the better you will be equipped to prepare an effective news release. If, in working with author questionnaires, you find the information insufficient and you find yourself having to contact the authors for additional information, then you should ask whoever is responsible for the author questionnaire to add additional questions to the questionnaire that will provide, without added effort, the information you have been missing.

16:04   Publicity Goals of Sci-Tech, Professional, and Scholarly Books

The publicity goal for a scientific, technical, or scholarly book, or for any book aimed at a practicing professional, is peer reviews, or reviews by qualified staff members in the media peculiar to or embracing that field.

Specialized scientific, technical, and scholarly books, as a rule, are not stocked in the average bookstore. Consequently, the review is designed not for bookstore traffic, but to acquaint the reader with an awareness of the book's availability and its content. Reviews of such books also serve as an acquisition tool for library collections in related fields.

Often, reviews appearing in specialized journals will compare the book with similar works, point out strengths and weaknesses, cite its value as a text or contribution to the literature, and recommend or warn against its acquisition.

The goal of the publicist for such books, therefore, should not be to get publicity per se, but rather to entice the periodical or a reviewer to request a copy of the book for purposes of review. There are some exceptions, such as a breakthrough book in a special area of scientific research, or a book likely to create controversy in its own field because of a non-conventional approach. However, such exceptions apply to very few books.

For the sci-tech or scholarly book, it is not necessary, and generally does little good to get publicity for the author, or for the author's non-book-related activities. Some authors of scientific works who attempt to get extra publicity through the publisher do so because they may be seeking to use their book as a vehicle for consulting work or to obtain business clients.

Another category of publicity-seeking authors that sometimes asks for or expects publicity efforts that go beyond the normal limits of what the book should be given is the author or organization behind the "sponsored book." Such titles are done on behalf of or in cooperation with a research facility or large corporation which may agree in advance to purchase a large quantity. Care should be taken in such instances to ensure that such books get their fair share of publicity, but efforts should be braked when they begin to become excessive.

Publicists should be wary of all publicity requests for a particular book that go beyond normal coverage and treatment. Such extra publicity efforts usually are both time and money wasters which do the book little extra good, drain budgeted moneys that might be applied to other books, and take up valuable time better spent elsewhere.

16:05   Preparing a News Release for a Specialized or Professional Book

Your assignment is to prepare a news release for a professional or specialized book. What elements should it contain to be most effective?

The answer lies in what you want your news release to accomplish. You should want it to accomplish either or both of these two objectives: (1) It should be interesting enough to generate a request for a review copy from a publication in or related to the field of the book. (2) It should, if sent along with a review copy of the book, provide the editor or book reviewer with a brief summary of the book which will be helpful in preparing the review.

- Your news release, because it is basically information for the reviewer, should be targeted to the attention of the book reviewer, who is a professional and most likely a specialist in the field of the book.

- You should be sure that, while the release follows basic news release format, it is factual and objective and presents the benefits and features of the book in a straightforward manner.

- You should catch the reviewer's attention up front by leading off with an effective headline.

- Your ensuing copy should not only describe the book but also emphasize its principal contributions to its intended audience, its timeliness, and its level if a text.

- Your release should include a coupon at the end which makes it convenient for the editor or reviewer to complete and return if he or she wishes to receive a copy for review. You should not, however, expect core or primary journals in the field to have to ask for a review copy; it should be sent automatically with the release enclosed.

16:06 Adjectives and Clichés in Book Publicity

The following comments are those of an unnamed editor of *The Bookseller,* the British book trade weekly, commenting on publisher publicity for an upcoming special issue, in the 11 June 1983 issue.

> Books from history, literature, and other semi-academic publishers are always vivid, and full of lively detail; provide fascination or unrivaled insight; make a unique contribution to scholarship; and will form an authoritative and invaluable reference work and guide.
>
> Books for technical publishers offer refreshing accounts which give lively coverage with their stimulating texts offering arresting insights, and forming stunning intellectual contributions.
>
> There are some things I like to take for granted—that the book is readable, well researched and informative, that the illustrations are relevant to the subject and any diagrams clear, and that the author is talented.... The proliferation of such adjectives simply cannot be taken on trust about books that haven't been seen.

16:07 A "New Product Press Release" That Wasn't: Case Study

The $8\frac{1}{2}''$ × 11″ printed sheet proclaimed in 36-point type across the top "New Product Press Release," and repeated in 24-point type as a sub-heading, the words: "Press Release Press Release Press Release Press."

What followed under this heading was a three-paragraph typed announcement followed by 10 starred features for a newly published book on a computer systems study. Nearly a third of the sheet was the order form listing credit card requirements with a "Bill me—Bill my company" option.

This blatant use of a "Press Release" heading for an announcement aimed solely at buyers, and with no apparent "press" relevance, is in my view a misleading application of such a heading.

Were such a release to fall into my hands as a publication editor, it would not only turn me off on the "release" but also on the company resorting to such artificial means to attract attention.

There is no question that a News Release or Press Release format is a useful and usable format for many different types of new book announcements, but the copywriter should make it in some way resemble a legitimate news release and prepare it in a format that would be found acceptable to the press.

Adding a "Press Release" heading to advertising copy is bad usage; don't do it.

**16:08 Reference Tools for Professional
and Scholarly Book Publicists**

1. *Ulrich's International Periodicals Directory* (annual), R. R. Bowker
2. *Standard Periodical Directory* (biennial), Oxbridge Communications
3. *Bacon's Publicity Checker* (annual), Bacon Publishing Co.
4. *MLA Directory of Periodicals* (biennial), Modern Language Association
5. *Directory of Associations* (annual), Gale Research Co.
6. *SRDS Business Publication Rates and Data* (monthly), Standard Rate & Data Service, Inc.
7. *Ayer Directory of Publications* (annual), Ayer Press
8. *Ad Guide: An Advertiser's Guide to Scholarly Periodicals* (1979–1980 edition was final issue), American University Press Services

17

The Art of Excerpting and Using Reviews and Testimonials

17:01   The Value and Importance of Review Excerpts in Promotion

A review in a prestigious scientific or scholarly journal, especially one signed by an acknowledged authority or someone having a highly regarded affiliation, carries considerable weight in influencing the purchase of a professional or scholarly book by others in the field.

For this reason, favorable excerpts from reviews help improve the effectiveness of printed book promotion—whether in periodicals or by direct mail—and can be a vital aid for the copywriter.

It is important, however, that each excerpt be selected with great care for its intended audience. Too many writers of promotion copy extract a phrase from a review and use it in all media or promotions—a very poor practice.

The end use or value of the book to the potential buyer or user should always be taken into consideration in selecting (or shaping) a review excerpt for an advertisement or piece of printed promotion. A professor seeking a text for his students has a different interest in a book from, say, that of an engineer concerned with professional obsolescence, or a reference librarian seeking to enhance a subject collection.

Always keep the reader in mind when selecting material from a review for advertising or promotional purposes. Many reviews contain numerous phrases you can use in different ways for different audiences. The entries in this chapter provide specific examples.

17:02   Ways to Acquire, Store, and Use Review Excerpts: Guidelines

Review excerpts can bring an authority to the copy for a professional or scholarly book that no copywriter can match. Learn to use and rely on review quotes, especially if the copy is to launch a new edition of a previously published, well-reviewed work.

The copywriter should bear in mind that reviews do not always present material in a manner that allows it to be lifted and used verbatim. Often, quotes from reviews need some reshaping. However, properly presented, the excerpt from the prior edition can serve as *the* copy for the edition being launched.

When copies of reviews are not available because the prior edition was published many years previously, often they may be obtained from the author. There is a pitfall in using reviews from previous editions after a new edition has been in print for some time (see case study in 17:09). However, the ideal situation is to maintain the review file for all books and have the review material readily accessible when copy preparation begins.

As reviews are received on the newer edition, the older reviews should be avoided and quotes taken from reviews of the current edition only.

17:03   Professional and Technical Book Review Excerpts: How They Differ from Trade Book Excerpts

When you are using review excerpts, the creative head of one major publishing house advises, the excerpt approach for professional and technical books is entirely different from that for trade books. Here's how:

With trade books, the briefer the quote, the better. The source is what counts . . . and the superlatives.

With professional and technical books, whenever possible, let the quote do all the selling (Figure 14). Often, professional journals ferret out good benefits that may never occur to the nonspecialist copywriter.

If you have a choice between describing the book and letting a respected outside source do the job, always choose the latter.

17:04   An Important Rule in the Use of Quotes from Reviews and Testimonials

Whether you are using a quote from a review or an excerpt from a testimonial, *always* attribute the quote to a source.

Outstanding Academic Book

selections published by Greenwood Press

17 Outstanding Academic Books
selected by Choice Magazine

Political Parties of the Americas: Canada, Latin America, and the West Indies edited by Robert J. Alexander. xxviii, 1274 pages in 2 volumes. $65.00 *Alexander's academic background and long personal involvement in Latin America qualify him eminently for the general editorship of this important work. His scholarly contributors have been meticulously selected for their individual expertise.... The uniform treatment by country is an alphabetical arrangement. ...An extremely comprehensive index accompanies this highly recommended work.* —Choice

Reckoners: The Prehistory of the Digital Computer, from Relays to the Stored Program Concept, 1935-1945 by Paul E. Ceruzzi. xii, 181 pages. $29.95 *Lucid introduction and explanation, supplemented by helpful glossaries, an appendix, and historically valuable chapter-end notes and bibliography.... Highly informative, this little book is the promising first in a new series.* —Science

United States Oil Policy and Diplomacy: A Twentieth Century Overview by Edward W. Chester. xiv, 399 pages. $35.00 *An extensively researched and comprehensive study of American oil policy and diplomacy, from the beginnings of the petroleum industry up to 1973.... The exposition is balanced and scholarly.... An examination of the many twists and turns of diplomatic policies.* —Choice

The Afro-Yankees: Providence's Black Community in the Antebellum Era by Robert J. Cottrol. xviii, 200 pages. $27.50 *Cottrol ably traces the development of black family life, the formation of black churches, schools, and voluntary associations and... also analyzes the origins of the bitter antiblack prejudice.... Cottrol's work is thoroughly documented.... It is presented in a clear, straightforward style. ... Makes a major contribution to our understanding of race relations in the antebellum North. Highly recommended.* —Choice

Voting in Revolutionary America: A Study of Elections in the Original Thirteen States, 1776-1789 by Robert J. Dinkin. x, 184 pages. $27.50 *All important aspects of the electoral process are covered.... This work, a worthy successor to the author's Voting in Provincial America, should prove an indispensable source to scholars/teachers who are interested in the evolution of the American democratic electoral process. Recommended.* —Choice

History of Black Americans: From the Compromise of 1850 to the End of the Civil War by Philip S. Foner. viii, 539 pages. $39.95 (Vol. 3 of a projected 5 vol. set) *Philip Foner adds to his impressive body of work on US history with this third volume of his History of Black Americans.... He has produced the single most important decade in US history. Recommended for all academic and public libraries.* —Choice

Sports and Physical Education: A Guide to the Reference Resources compiled by Bonnie Gratch, Betty Chan, and Judith Lingenfelter. xxi, 198 pages. $29.95 *This excellent annotated bibliography ... includes English-language monographs, serials, government publications, and ERIC documents ... Recommended.... There is no other extensive annotated bibliography available on this subject. It will be a handy source.* —Choice

Political Parties of Europe edited by Vincent McHale with the assistance of Sharon Skowronski. Two volumes. $95.00 *The complete spectrum of parties, both existing and defunct, is covered for every European country. The arrangement of this information is very convenient.... A remarkable uniform style.... No other reference work offers such information in such convenient form. Recommended for all libraries.* —Choice

Play and Playthings: A Reference Guide by Bernard Mergen. xi, 281 pages. $35.00 *A guide to children's play in America.... A narrative history of play ... and ... a lengthy narrative bibliography of relevant sources.... A book that is both scholarly and accessible. Recommended.* —Library Journal

United States Employment and Training Programs: A Selected Annotated Bibliography compiled by Frederick A. Raffa, Clyde A. Haulman, and Djehane A. Hosni. xvi, 152 pages. $29.95 *This bibliography is an excellent guide to the literature produced in government and academic publications. Including a fine introduction, thorough annotations, an author index, and a superbly useful subject index.* —Choice

Three Different Worlds: Women, Men, and Children in an Industrializing Community by Frances Abrahamer Rothstein. xii, 148 pages. $27.50 *A refreshing research effort, away from the isolated social unit approach of anthropology ... some interesting parallels among many of the social sciences.... Excellent multidisciplinary bibliography and many fine and easily understood charts and graphs. Undergraduate, graduate, and faculty-level use.* —Choice

Black Slavery in the Americas: An Interdisciplinary Bibliography, 1865-1980 compiled by John David Smith. xxix, 2712 pages in two volumes. $95.00 *This massive bibliography of 15,667 citations and 5,494 cross-references will surely be the most comprehensive compilation on slavery for a long time to come ... has included material from obscure and hitherto overlooked sources as well as the better-known books.... Highly recommended.* —Choice

Louis L. Snyder's Historical Guide to World War II by Louis L. Snyder. xii, 838 pages. $39.95 *Snyder has chosen to emphasize non-military aspects, and his Historical Guide is an interpretation of the political, economic, social, and cultural thrusts of the war ... recommended as an addition to all academic and public library reference collections.* —Choice

Third World Policies of Industrialized Nations edited by Phillip Taylor and Gregory A. Raymond. xix, 282 pages. $35.00 *A superb collection of comparative economic and analyses.... The work is not only timely but essential reading for international relations and comparative politics specialists. Strongly recommended for a wide range of libraries and reading audiences.* —Choice

Women of the English Renaissance and Reformation by Retha M. Warnicke. viii, 228 pages. $29.95 *An excellent monograph dealing with an inordinately neglected topic: the education of English women during the Tudor and early Stuart eras.... Warnicke's extensively researched and documented contribution is a pioneering effort.* —Choice

The Search for Quality Integrated Education: Policy and Research on Minority Students in School and College by Meyer Weinberg. xv, 354 pages. $35.00 *A comprehensive, balanced, and detailed analysis of hundreds of studies.... The author's own conclusions are balanced.... This is an excellent, readable, and even indispensable book.... More than a review of the literature, it defines the scope and diversity of minority education studies to date.* —Choice

Radicalism and Freethought in Nineteenth-Century Britain: The Life of Richard Carlile by Joel H. Wiener. x, 285 pages. $29.95 *The first full-length study of one of the most controversial and most important working-class reformers of late Georgian and early Victorian England.... An economical, tightly written narrative that expands considerably not only our knowledge of Carlile but also his controversial relationship to 19th-century British radicalism.* —Choice

★ ★ ★ ★ ★ ★ ★
1 Outstanding Reference Book
selected by the Reference Sources Committee of the Reference and Adult Services Division of the American Library Association

Louis L. Snyder's Historical Guide to World War II by Louis L. Snyder. xii, 838 pages, $39.95 *Snyder has chosen to emphasize non-military aspects, and his Historical Guide is an interpretation of the political, economic, social, and cultural thrusts of the war ... recommended as an addition to all academic and public library reference collections.* —Choice

Catalogs describing these and other Greenwood Press books are available on request from Greenwood Press, 88 Post Road West, Box 5007, Westport CT 06881

1240 *CHOICE, May 1984*

FIGURE 14 An outstanding example of the use of review excerpts to tell the whole story is demonstrated in this advertisement from the May 1984 issue of *Choice*. The issue featured the *Choice* twentieth annual list of outstanding books, selected from over 6,000 reviewed during a preceding 12-month period. This Greenwood Press advertisement ties in with the special issue by advertising 17 of its works appearing on the outstanding list. Copy for each of the 17 titles consists of a 50- to 60-word review excerpt set in italics. Review source appears on last line flush right, preceded by a one-em dash. Fifteen of the 17 review excerpts were from *Choice* reviews.

If the quote is from a periodical or journal, give the name of the publication, not the name of the reviewer—unless he is a well-known authority in the field. If the reviewer is well known, then you might include his name thus:

—John Smith in *American Scientist*

If the quote is from an individual, give the individual's name, or at least his or her initials. With identification, whether actual or disguised, the attribution makes the quote more credible. Without an attribution, it is a hollow claim, unlikely to be believed by a scientist or scholar.

17:05   Another Kind of Testimonial That Carries a Lot of Credibility

The preceding entry talks about excerpts from reviews and quotes from individuals. There is yet another kind of testimonial that carries an equal amount of credibility and requires no quotation marks: It's a list of buyers, users, or adopters.

A brochure or folder offering a college text, for example, which lists 100 prestigious schools which have already adopted the book often carries more weight than a good mix of reviews and testimonials. When you have them, use them.

17:06   Tips on Punctuation for Review and Testimonial Quotes

If you use, or plan to use, book review excerpts either in conjunction with or as a substitute for book jacket or promotion copy, you should be familiar with these three aspects of punctuation: *quotation marks, ellipsis points,* and *brackets.*

Quotation marks are used in pairs primarily to indicate the beginning and end of a quotation in the exact phraseology of a direct citation from a text. Some basic guidelines governing the use of quotation marks, or quotes, are in the entry following.

Brackets are used for any portion of a review excerpt that is not an actual part of the quotation taken from the review, or where a word or letter has been inserted in a review quote for clarification. Parentheses are often mistakenly used in place of brackets. Here is an example of a bracket use:

ACTUAL TEXT: Over 500 pages provide broad coverage.

QUOTE USAGE: ". . . provide[s] broad coverage."

Ellipsis points are used in a review quote to indicate the omission of one or more words or as connectives between different phrases or passages from the same review. Preferred usage in review excerpts is three consecutive periods, except where two sentences are joined. Here, the three periods are joined by the period at the end of the sentence to make four periods.

> EXAMPLE: ". . . a classical work . . . recommended . . . should be in every reference library. . . . The new edition also has textbook potential."

17:07   Guidelines for Uses of Quotation Marks

- If the sentence ends with a question mark and the quote is not a question, the punctuation is outside the quotes.
- When you have a quote within a quote, use single quotation marks. If the quote within a quote contains still another quote, this should be in double quotation marks.
- When consecutive paragraphs are quoted, place a quotation mark at the beginning of each paragraph, but at the end of only the last paragraph.
- Quotation marks can be omitted if the paragraphs containing the quotation are indented and single spaced.
- Italics may be used to indicate a quotation.
- When a review quote is used as part of your copy, and it is followed by other words in the sentence, put a comma inside the quotation mark after the last word in the quote:

  > "This is an essential reference for every engineer," according to a *Science* magazine review.

- When a quotation ends the sentence, put the period inside the quotation mark at the end. This usage is for the United States; in England, periods and commas go outside.

17:08   Review Excerpts as Copy Approach in Backlist Promotion: Case Study

In its bi-monthly "New Publications" bulletin, UNIPUB incorporates an interesting approach to promotion of backlist titles. The Table of Contents carries a listing for "Recommended Books" and the last three pages of the 8½" × 11" 32-page self-cover booklet, under the "Recommended Books" heading, carries three pages of titles. The title listings and bibliographic data are in identical format to the new title listings up front. However, in place of body copy, each contains a review excerpt, approximately 100 words in length, attributable to an important review medium in its field. Books are listed alphabetically by title. Most review excerpts are for books published a year earlier, but some are for books two and three years old.

17:09 Review Excerpt Good—But from Wrong Edition:
Case Study

The publisher's advertisement listed a number of life science titles in the leading journal in the field. One was the second edition of a work published over four years earlier, whose sales had already exceeded 10,000.

The copywriter, in writing the copy for the title, had inserted a laudatory review quote from a major source and attributed it to the *first edition* of the same work.

The review quote, I think, flawed the copy. Here's why: a review of a first edition many years after the appearance of a second edition might imply to the reader of the advertisement that the second edition had not received any favorable reviews. The copywriter should have sought out a review of the current second edition or omitted the review entirely.

The lesson learned: Use review excerpts for a current edition of a scientific work when they exist. Excerpts from reviews of older editions are liable to be misinterpreted, unless the newest edition has only recently been published and it is too early for current edition reviews. Further, when good reviews are in on a new edition, eliminate the old-edition reviews from the bibliographic file or keep them separate from the new reviews.

17:10 Book Review in *Nature:*
Selected Examples of Review Excerpts

The following excerpts are from the review of *Inorganic Chemistry: A Modern Introduction* shown in Figure 15.

For a 50- to 60-word requirement for advertisement or catalog copy:

> "Moeller [has included] almost everything that nearly all inorganic chemists would agree should form the core studies of their subject . . . immensely readable, and . . . a splendid teaching text . . . A most attractive feature is the presentation of the state of our inorganic art alongside its historical development, the relationship between old and new being well-balanced and informative."—*Nature*

Short blurb for promotion to college market:

> ". . . immensely readable . . . a splendid teaching text."
> —*Nature*

Clothing the chemist

Jon McCleverty

Inorganic Chemistry: A Modern Introduction.
By Therald Moeller.
Wiley: 1982. Pp.830. £31, $46.50.

IN TEACHING inorganic chemistry one faces a dilemma — whether to deliver the subject in a factual way based on the Periodic Table, or to present it as a series of topics. Practitioners of the first approach feel that students should know facts, supported by theories. The problem is then that the facts can be overwhelming and, in any case, there just isn't time to deal satisfactorily with 105 or so elements. Many of us now take the second route, choosing our topics partly on academic grounds and partly in terms of the constraints of time and resources. One hopes that, towards the end of a such a course, the student will be able to put together, from all the various garments we have woven, an adequate if not complete suit of inorganic clothes.

In *Inorganic Chemistry: A Modern Introduction* Moeller has opted for the "topic" approach. There are plenty of facts carefully interwoven around the central threads of theories and contemporary rationalizations. A most attractive feature is the presentation of the state of our inorganic art alongside its historical development, the relationship between old and new being well-balanced and informative. The sections dealing with coordination chemistry, which are preceded by a succinct description of the applications of group theory, are particularly well-written. There are excellent discussions of various aspects of solid-state chemistry (including metals) and of physical methods for the determination of molecular structure (there are even tables of fingerprint regions in vibrational spectra!). Such material is frequently omitted from other prominent texts. Every chapter includes a very useful list of general references which have been drawn from the international literature.

For us in Britain, one difficulty with textbooks which orginate across the Atlantic is how the subject matter relates to courses based on our three-to-four year first degree. Moeller seems to have overcome this problem by including almost everything that nearly all inorganic chemists would agree should form the core studies of their subject. What is excluded (e.g. a detailed discussion of the M–C bond) is arguably inessential for a basic course.

I really like this book — it is immensely readable, and is a splendid teaching text for the early and middle years of a modern course. I am critical, however, of the hopeless inadequacy of the contents list and of the just acceptable subject index (is the author index really necessary?). While the book certainly matches almost exactly the requirements of the inorganic chemists in my own institution, I fear it will not reach the recommended list purely and simply because of its price vis-à-vis the competition. □

Jon McCleverty is Professor of Inorganic Chemistry at the University of Birmingham.

FIGURE 15 The excerpts in entry 17:10 are taken from this review which appeared in the 31 March 1983 issue of *Nature*.

Short blurb for the library market:

"present[s] the state of . . . inorganic [chemistry] alongside its historical development . . . every chapter includes a very useful list of general references . . . immensely readable."

—*Nature*

FOLLETT, Roy H. Fertilizers and soil amendments, by Roy H. Follett, Larry S. Murphy, and Roy L. Donahue. Prentice-Hall, 1981. 557p ill bibl index 80-25799. 24.95 ISBN 0-13-314336-8. CIP A well-indexed text published at a time when information on sustaining or improving yields from the land is imperative. The subject matter is specific and current. It is structured so that data are easily understandable to the student or technically oriented individual. General plant nutrition is covered in the first chapter of the book and is followed by chapters on the major fertilizers: nitrogen, phosphorus, and potassium. Later chapters cover the secondary nutrients and the micronutrients. Application of fertilizers and users of various types and forms of fertilizers are also well covered. Soil management and economic considerations are discussed in later chapters. This is a very well-written, illustrated, and documented book, truly outstanding in every regard. The authors are well versed and their volume is suitable for all libraries, from high school through university.

FIGURE 16 The excerpts in entry 17:11 are taken from this review which appeared in the September 1981 issue of *Choice.*

17:11 Book Review in *Choice:* Selected Examples of Review Excerpts

The following excerpts are from the review of *Fertilizers and Soil Amendments* shown in Figure 16.

For a 40- to 50-word requirement for advertisement or catalog copy:

". . . at a time when information on sustaining or improving yields from the land is imperative [this] well-indexed text [offers] specific and current [information] . . . structured so that data are easily understandable to the student or technically oriented individual . . . well-written, illustrated, and documented . . . truly outstanding . . . *—Choice*

General review excerpt (long):

". . . a very well-written, illustrated, and documented book, truly outstanding in every regard."*—Choice*

General review excerpt (short):

". . . truly outstanding in every regard."*—Choice*

Short blurb for promotion to the college market:

". . . specific and current . . . easily understandable to the student . . . well-indexed . . . illustrated and documented . . . outstanding"*—Choice*

Cell Interactions and Development. Molecular Mechanisms. KENNETH M. YAMADA, Ed. Wiley-Interscience, New York, 1982. xii, 288 pp., illus. $39.95.

This collection of ten reviews by well-chosen authors summarizes and evaluates current knowledge of the molecular mechanisms underlying some of the cell interactions occurring during development. It was designed for advanced undergraduate and graduate students and for scientists who are not specialists in the subject. The intent of the editor and authors to create a thoroughly readable treatment of the subject is eminently achieved, for the papers provide current, understandable, and sometimes simplified accounts of research progress.

The first paper, by Wassarman, reviews sperm-egg interactions during fertilization, with special attention to the sea urchin and to studies by the author of the mouse zona pellucida. The paper is complemented by a treatment of the mating processes of yeast and of *Chlamydomonas* by Goodenough and Thorner. This paper contains a more detailed and comprehensive treatment of a narrower subject than any of the other papers does.

Roth gives a relatively brief but insightful account of the biochemistry of cell adhesion among vertebrate cells, and Barondes adds a discussion of developmentally regulated lectins and their possible roles in both intracellular and intercellular recognition. An interesting addition on a subject too often omitted in discussions of cell interactions is a paper by Dazzo on recognition involving plant cells. He reviews the mechanisms underlying selectivity in the fertilization process and those responsible for recognition and rejection of grafts. The emphasis of the paper, however, is on recognition between plants and microbes, including both pathogenic bacterial infections and the symbiosis between nitrogen-fixing *Rhizobium* and legumes.

Four papers deal with migrating cells and their interactions with the extracellular matrix. Harris reviews cell migration and its directional guidance. He gives only a superficial account of the proteins responsible for movement but thoughtfully discusses chemotaxis and the molecular mechanisms underlying contact guidance. The composition and morphogenetic roles of the pericellular matrix are discussed by Toole and Underhill, and Yamada reviews the structure and functions of fibronectin. The information presented in these three papers is integrated into the life history of a single group of cells in Weston's account of the migration of the neural crest cells. Weston's paper also includes an enlightening discussion of the roles of environmental influences in determining the phenotypes expressed by crest cells and of the prospects for analysis of the "conversation" between crest cells and their surroundings. This theme is further explored by Kratochwil in an excellent review of embryonic induction.

The strength of this collection comes from its coherence and from the authors' success in promoting understanding. The authors are aided in this endeavor by a wealth of superior illustrations and a substantial index. The book could serve well as the basis for a seminar or as a supplemental textbook in developmental biology courses, since many of the widely used textbooks are deficient in precisely the subjects covered by the book. The sole drawback to its wide use in this role is the book's price, which, if added to the price of a classical textbook, would make for an expensive, though exciting, course.

R. B. MARCHASE
Department of Anatomy,
Duke University Medical Center,
Durham, North Carolina 27710

FIGURE 17 The excerpts in entry 17:12 are taken from this review which appeared in the 29 April 1983 issue of *Science*.

Short blurb for the library market:

> ". . . well-indexed [and] illustrated . . . specific and current . . . easily understandable to the student or technically oriented individual . . . suitable for all libraries."—*Choice*

**17:12   Book Review in *Science:*
Selected Examples of Review Excerpts**

The following excerpts are from the review of *Cell Interactions and Development* shown in Figure 17.

For a 40- to 50-word requirement for advertisement or catalog copy:

> ". . . ten reviews by well-chosen authors summarize and evaluate current knowledge of the molecular mechanisms underlying some of the cell interactions occurring during development . . . designed for advanced undergraduate and graduate students and scientists who are not specialists in the subject."
> —*Science*

Short blurb for promotion to the college market:

> ". . . summarizes and evaluates current knowledge of the [subject] . . . could serve well as a supplemental textbook in developmental biology . . . many of the widely used textbooks are deficient in the subjects covered."—*Science*

Short blurb for the library market:

> ". . . summarizes and evaluates current knowledge of the [subject] . . . a thoroughly readable treatment [with] a wealth of superior illustrations and a substantial index."—*Science*

18

Jacket Copy Writing: Techniques and Recommended Standards

18:01 Jacket Copy Writing: A Challenge and an Opportunity

The writing of jacket copy for scholarly books is both confining and challenging . . . [you] cannot con readers who are knowledgeable in the fields about which the books are written. Copy must not misrepresent an author's work, for not just sales but reputation are at stake. The challenge is to write interesting and "selling" copy while remaining within the bounds of accuracy.

Dorothy B. Sutherland, former Publicity
Manager, The University of Chicago Press.

In many publishing establishments which send books on approval, and even in those which offer full refunds if the book is not acceptable, the book jacket copy often carries the burden of selling the book after it is in the hands of the recipient. If the jacket copy indicates that the book offers all that is expected of it, the recipient will remit payment, even if he hasn't had time to read it.

This "selling" burden of jacket copy also holds for books displayed at exhibits and conventions, and those sent to libraries through *on-approval* plans.

211

Consequently, the jacket often plays a key role in helping the sale of professional and scholarly books. What goes on the jacket—both the front flap as descriptive matter and the back flap giving the author's credentials for writing the book—is a "selling" tool which can help a book to succeed. This is particularly important during the book's early life when no reviews have yet appeared and the jacket copy must carry a heavy burden in establishing the book's credibility.

This chapter provides basic guidelines for the writing of jacket copy, discusses ways to write for scientific and other highly specialized books, gives the recommended standards for book jacket copy as devised by the American National Standards Institute (ANSI) Committee, discusses how to treat author educational credentials on flap copy, outlines procedures for dealing with and clearing jacket copy with the author, and soliciting his aid with difficult copy, and explains how and why jacket flap copy must be different from other types of book advertising.

18:02 Basics of Writing Jacket Copy

PRELIMINARY

1. Remember, your readers are knowledgeable in the field about which the book is written.
2. Present the author's work accurately in your copy.
3. Present the content of the book properly.
4. Claim nothing about the book's uniqueness you cannot substantiate in the copy.
5. Avoid adjectives and hype.

FRONT FLAP

1. Tell what the book is about.
2. Tell what the author's aims were in writing the book.
3. Tell how he or she accomplished these aims.
4. Tell who will be interested in it.
5. Tell what the author's credentials were for writing the book.
6. Clear copy with both the sponsoring editor and the author for accuracy.

BACK FLAP

1. Provide detailed biographical notes if author is eminent in the field of the book.
2. Use author photo on professional and scholarly books only if a

matter of house preference, or if author is a recognizable personality or unusually photogenic and you feel it will help.

3. Give author's credentials, and other publications for technical books; avoid personal data such as hobbies or family details.

FRONT PANEL

4. Book title.

5. Volume number if part of a series.

6. Series name if part of a series.

7. Name of author or editor. (Spelling should be identical with spelling/style used on book's title page.)

BACK PANEL: COPY OPTIONS

1. Books of related interest.

2. Alphabetical list of contributors, if book has many authors.

3. Excerpts from advance reviews of book.

4. Excerpts from preface, introduction, or a part of the book.

5. Excerpts from reviews of previous edition (if a new edition).

6. Listing of other volumes in the series (if a volume in a series).

7. If part of a series, state purposes of the series, with review excerpts about the series.

8. If author credentials are lengthy and impressive, use back panel and move prepublication quotes or previous edition review quotes to back flap.

9. Listing of potential audiences: "This book is for. . . ."

10. Repeat front cover panel and design on back panel.

18:03   Jacket Copy for Multi-Author Scientific and Technical Books

Maive O'Connor, in her excellent guide for editors of books and journals, *The Scientist as Editor: Guidelines for Editors of Books and Journals* (New York: Wiley, 1979), offers these suggestions for jacket copy of multi-author scientific and technical books in a typical 200-word blurb:

1. The first couple of sentences should set the scene explaining the need for the book or the conference on which it is based.

2. The next two sentences should make the theme or purpose of the book clear.

3. Four or five sentences then summarize the contents.

4. A final sentence might name the likely readership.

If, on the other hand, the copywriter is limited to a 60-word blurb, the summarizing sentences would be left out and the others modified as necessary.

Whether the jacket blurb is 200 words long or only 60 words long, says O'Connor, "every word must count."

18:04 Recommended Standards for Jacket Copy*

In 1969, a "Standard" was produced by the ANSI (American National Standards Institute) Standards Committee† to provide guidance to publishers and distributors in the advertising and promotion of books. Its work had been based on recommendations from a joint committee of the American Book Publishers Council and the Special Libraries Association. The standard recommended the following elements for jacket copy:

1. Author(s) (and/or editor, compiler, etc.)
2. Title
3. Subtitle, if any
4. List price‡
5. Edition (number, trade versus text, hard cover versus paper, etc.)
6. Identification of publisher
7. Standard book number
8. Special physical features (such as large-size print, unbound accompanying material; pre-processed books, or special bindings, with a listing of the type of binding standard used for those books for which this is a particularly important feature)
9. Series identification (series name and number)
10. Translation information (original title and language, original copyright, translator, etc.)
11. Description of contents of book
12. Conference information (place and date of meeting, sponsors, etc.)
13. Size (if unusual), description of number and type of graphic features (if significant), index (if any)

*Standards were applicable to books for all markets including: the book trade; schools, libraries, and other institutions; educators; and the individual reader.

†Subcommittee 19 of ANSI Standards Committee Z39 on Standardization in the Field of Library Work, Documentation and Related Publishing Practices.

‡In 1968–69 when the committee was active, book pricing for professional and scholarly books was relatively stable, and printed book prices were more prevalent. In later years, with inflationary pressures, pricing was generally omitted from jackets of such books.

**18:05 Copy Options for Back Panel
on Scholarly Book Jacket**

1. Brief blurbs on titles "Of related interest"
2. A description of the book that enhances jacket flap copy
3. A bulleted listing of features of the book
4. Author biography
5. Contents listing
6. If a contributed volume, a listing of articles with authors and, space permitting, their affiliations
7. Listing of potential audiences for book: "This book is for . . . "
8. Excerpts from reviews of a previous edition or editions
9. Testimonials from prepublication reviews
10. If part of series, describe or list aims of series, or previously published volumes

**18:06 Clearing Jacket Copy with the Author:
Suggested Procedure**

When you write jacket copy, the possibility of error can be great, since the material from which you work may be a year or more old and the author may, in the meantime, have changed jobs, or the subtitle of the book may have been changed. Further, with scientific and scholarly works, the possibility of misinterpretation looms high.

So, first clear your jacket flap copy with the book's sponsoring editor. Then send it off to the author for final approval. You may wish to adapt the letter shown below. Be sure not to use *Mr.* if *Dr.* or *Professor* or some other form is more appropriate.

In the suggested letter, there appears a statement that if the author does not respond by a certain date the copy will be presumed correct. However, there are many reasons why the copy may not reach the author. Therefore, despite the notification, another attempt should be made to reach the author, or to have the sponsoring editor try to obtain some indication that the jacket copy as submitted is acceptable.

Dear (name of author with appropriate title):

Enclosed is the proposed flap copy for the dust jacket of your forthcoming book: (book title and subtitle as it appears in copy). It has been reviewed and approved by your sponsoring editor, (editor's name). However, to make certain that it is correct, would you kindly check for accuracy in the use of:

- Your name
- Your position / affiliation
- Title / subtitle of your book
- Factual data
- Spelling of technical terms
- Use of technical phrases

If you have any corrections, kindly mark them on the enclosed copy and return the marked copy to me promptly. Or contact me at (phone number) by (date) in order to avoid delays in the production of your book.

If we do not hear from you by (date), we will assume the jacket flap copy is correct as submitted and proceed with production.

Sincere thanks for your time and cooperation, and best wishes for the success of your book.

Sincerely,

Copywriter

cc: (sponsoring editor)

18:07 Before You Mail Jacket Copy to Author for Approval: A Tip

Before sending the jacket copy to the author for approval, it makes good sense to contact the sponsoring editor and verify the author's current mailing address. The author address is usually taken off the contract and, as a rule, two or more years have elapsed from contract signing until the book is ready to go into production. If the jacket copy is mismailed, it can lead to production delays.

18:08 When You Have Difficulty Writing about a Scientific Topic: Case Study

If you experience difficulty in writing about a book on a scientific topic, solicit the assistance of the author. He or she can usually provide a clear, smooth description of the book and topic in the correct number of words you need to complete the assignment.

I recall an instance early in my publishing career when I was called upon to write jacket flap copy for a book in an advanced area of mathematics by Richard Bellman, then a research scientist with the RAND Corporation in Santa Monica, California. I struggled with the copy for half a day, trying desperately to squeeze 150 meaningful words out of two typed pages of description provided by the author in his author questionnaire.

No matter which word selections I made, it all somehow seemed not to reflect what the author was saying. Finally, I dropped a note to the author: Could you please boil down your description to 150 words or less that summarizes the book for the jacket flap?

He did, and it read well. He was pleased and I was out of a desperate situation.

Robert Gunning, the authority on clear, effective writing, summed it up when he wrote in his book *The Technique of Clear Writing* (McGraw-Hill, 1968) how he had asked Sidney Self of the *Wall Street Journal* staff how he managed to write so clearly about scientific discoveries.

Self's reply: "I go to the man at the top. The head research engineer can always put the matter simply. Usually it is a waste of time to talk to the laboratory helpers. They are lost in details."

Self's reply holds true for difficult-to-describe scientific books. Go to the top; go to the author.

18:09 Jacket Flap Copy: Why and How It Must Be Different from Other Advertising

The unique qualities of jacket flap copy are summarized by the creative head at one commercial house:

> Flap copy should encapsulate, rather than describe, the book. It should intrigue the reader to open up the actual volume, at least to the table of contents. If the flap copy tells the whole story (which is sometimes very dull), a potential buyer may be lost.
>
> Whether trade, technical, or professional book, the author bio is a key element (Who is this person who is trying to teach or tell me something?).
>
> Other key elements are reviews, if available, or endorsements (I may not trust the publisher's blurb, but surely I can trust this reviewer / professor / expert).
>
> In short, jacket flap copy differs from all other advertising copy in that the book is actually in the hands of the reader. All too often this simple fact is not capitalized upon. The jacket is there primarily (a) to attract the reader, and (b) to close the sale by leading into the book itself.

18:10 The Author's Degree on Flap Copy: Is It "a M.S." or "an M.S."?

In writing the author's educational credentials on the back jacket flap, should you say "a M.S. degree" or "an M.S. degree"? The rule, according to Robert A. Day in his *How to Write and Publish a Scientific Paper,* 2nd edition (ISI Press, 1983), is to use "a" with abbreviations beginning with a consonant sound and "an" with abbreviations beginning with a vowel sound. The M.S. degree reads like "em ess" and therefore should be referred to on the jacket flap (or anywhere in copy) as "an M.S. degree."

18:11 What Do Engineers Look for on a Book Jacket?

Engineers view a jacket as a valuable component of an engineering book if it tells the prospective buyer something about the author— his or her professional affiliations, specialized experience, and writing—and indicates to the prospective buyer that the author was competent to write the book.

A group of practicing engineers expressed this viewpoint in a discussion on the motivating factors that prompt engineers to purchase books on engineering subjects. The discussion took place in April 1981 between six engineers and members of the marketing staff of the McGraw-Hill Professional and Reference Book Division.

18:12   Misstatement on Jacket Can Harm Book's Review Potential

The first sentence on the dust jacket [says] "The first book of its kind . . ." [T]hat indeed is a fuzzy statement. This is certainly not the first book on [the subject]—[the author] lists many others. . . .

Excerpt from review of book about
fuzzy techniques in *Applied Optics*,
Vol. 22, No. 10, 12 May 1983.

When writing jacket copy, avoid first-of-its kind statements, or any similar statement that will not hold up to close scrutiny. Be sure any such claims are personally approved by the author as authentic. Unjustified copy claims can dilute the effectiveness of what might otherwise be a favorable review, as in the above excerpt.

Reviewer-specialists are quick to spot misstatements, however minor, and are likely to devote valuable review space to discrediting a questionable statement at the expense of failing to praise other worthwhile features of a professional or specialized book.

19

Copy Shoptalk: A Potpourri

Copywriting is the original "art" of advertising, and especially of mail-order writing. All the historic greats of the field started as copywriters. . . .

Ed Nash in *Direct Marketing: Strategy, Planning, Execution,* 1982, McGraw-Hill.

The trouble with many copywriters is that they think their job is to write copy. . . . the job is to sell. *Selling is the end result; writing is merely the means a copywriter uses to reach that end.*

Bob Stone, quoting Don Kantor, Vice-President of Stone & Adler, in *Successful Direct Marketing Methods, Third Edition,* 1984, Crain Books.

19:01 Job of P&R Copywriter a Fast Track to Advancement: Zeldin

"Copywriting," says Dick Zeldin, publishing consultant, "is a fast track to advancement in professional and reference publishing. It is a lot different than copywriting in the elhi or college area. The primary reason is that as a copywriter, you get a lot of exposure working with editors and with marketing people."

Zeldin recalls the copywriting staff that served under him when he was general manager of the Professional and Reference Division at McGraw-Hill in 1948–49. The four writers were Herb Burrows, Harry Brown, Bob Ewing, and Gilbert Taft.

Burrows, now retired, went on to become head of direct marketing at McGraw-Hill. Brown, also now retired, became director of all the McGraw-Hill Book Clubs. Bob Ewing went on to become general manager of McGraw-Hill Professional and Reference Books, and at the time of writing was Chairman of the Board of the Van Nostrand Reinhold Company. In a revolving-door industry such as publishing, surprisingly only one of the four fell out of publishing. Gilbert Taft, after McGraw-Hill, went on to Hollywood where he had a career as a movie script writer.

Zeldin had left McGraw-Hill to become president of R. R. Bowker Company and subsequently was a publisher in the Wiley Professional Group before leaving in 1983 to become a consultant. Zeldin's first job in publishing was as copywriter in the McGraw-Hill P&R Division in 1947.

19:02   The Role of the Copywriter
at Princeton University Press

Abbot M. Friedland, former marketing director at Princeton University Press, describes what is expected of copywriters by scholarly publishers.

> Over the years, we developed a philosophy about the requirements of a copywriter. What we felt was important was that the copywriter be a person with some sensibility as an editor, but whose strength was in scholarship— a sensitivity for scholarship *and* an ability to write.
>
> In seeking a copywriter we sought a person with qualifications in scholarship, rather than in advertising or marketing. Usually, we sought applicants with at least a masters in English or history. Most, as a rule, had no understanding of the job at hand, but did come with a certain perspective—a point of view relative to scholarship.
>
> It was our feeling that when you have a person like that working as copywriter, they tend to work from a position of strength when dealing with an author or editor. We pretested all applicants and made our selection when we felt we had found the one with the right ingredients.
>
> I stress finding someone with a certain perspective relative to scholarship because when copywriters are hired with no prior copywriting background, they tend to be influenced by the kind of copy they have seen in trade advertising. That type of writing is inappropriate for the specialized books published at Princeton, primarily in the social sciences and humanities, as well as some in the sciences.
>
> How does the copywriter operate at Princeton? As soon as a manuscript is received, it first goes to the copywriter, who studies it and becomes the authority on that book within the marketing department. The copy is prepared by the copywriter at that time and is subsequently used in all forms of promotion—seasonal catalog, jacket, advertising, etc. Because the copy is prepared when the manuscript is received, the copywriter is working well in advance of when the copy is needed. This system has been used at the Press for years and works well.

SELECTION PROCEDURE FOR COPYWRITERS AT P.U.P.

How have copywriters been selected at Princeton? Because it was felt that the copywriter must have strong sensitivity for the scholarly book, job applicants were given basic information about several books and asked to write jacket copy for each. "That test has been used over the years as the criterion for hiring a copywriter," says Friedland, "and it has worked."

19:03   Loose-Leaf Publisher's Criteria
for Hiring Copywriters

I look for a person as copywriter who is mature and understands the business world. That person has to have a liberal arts background, so that they are familiar with the words, phrases and concepts of good writing. We then train the person selected in the jargon of each of the fields we cover, and in the benefits that are looked for by the prospective buyers within that field. For example, what does a tax man look for when he is buying a professional book? When the copywriter knows and understands what benefits are appropriate for each field, he can then write effective copy that is geared to these benefits and how the particular book he is writing copy for meets them.

19:04   Book Publishers and Ad Agencies:
How Some View Each Other

There is a large gap between the ways in which specialized and scholarly publishers see themselves in their relationships with ad agencies vis à vis the way some agencies view such publisher accounts as prospective clients.

From the agency viewpoint, such accounts are sometimes visualized as "very smart," a bit too demanding, and inclined to tread on the sensitivities of the agency's copywriters and creative people. Agencies with such views shy away from taking on book publishers as clients with arguments such as: they have small budgets and large expectations . . . or they are unreasonable . . . or unbusinesslike.

Specialized and scholarly book publishers, on the other hand, see themselves as dispensers of a product that appeals to the intellect and therefore one that requires much detail and precision in ad copy, especially in small-circulation specialized journals and periodicals.

There is not much profit for the independent ad agency because of the time and work necessary to create promotions for specialized and scholarly publishers. A few have overcome the problem by specializing in publishing accounts and, thereby, generating sufficient volume either to assign specially trained personnel to work on such accounts or else to hire people with publishing experience to service them.

Some larger publishing establishments have solved the client–agency problem by creating and maintaining in-house ad agencies geared solely to publisher needs and fine-tuned to the exacting requirements of specialized and scholarly books.

19:05 Working with Advertising Agency Generalists: Ways to Get Best Results

If you choose to place your advertising through a generalist consumer ad agency, here is what you will have to do to get best results:

1. Prepare in advance most of the research and background materials. Don't expect your agency to research the background of your authors, or their area of specialty. Be prepared to digest all of the facts and give them to your agency in a carefully ordered and simple fashion.

2. Do your own media research. Advertising agency generalists know less about your media than you do. So don't expect any magic solutions from the agency's media department. Expect an expert appraisal on *Library Journal?* Want an analysis on the real reader differences between *Datamation* and *Communications of the ACM?* Get them yourself, or go through a copy of Standard Rate and Data and make your own evaluations based on the blurbs there. Or check with your authors or in-house editors who are usually well informed on the key journals in their areas of specialization.

3. Don't set your copy expectations too high. You'll get copy that can be readily understood by the average reader. You'll most likely get the information you've supplied boiled down to a series of concise and effective selling features. But you won't get the attention of their better writers whose time and effort is devoted to the larger and more lucrative accounts.

4. Check ad copy approaches carefully once conceived to ensure that the copy does not contain too much hype or offend the sensibilities of the professional, specialized, or scholarly audience your books appeal to.

19:06 Copy Expectations for Small-Publisher Accounts from Ad Agency: One Point of View

If yours is a specialized or scientific or scholarly publishing house, what kind of copy can you expect from an ad agency? We put this question to a former executive of a "specialty" agency catering to publishers and got this response:

> There are agencies which specialize in medicine, in business-to-business communication, in sales promotion, in direct mail, and yes, even in publishing. Although these organizations offer some specialized knowledge, they exist to serve the primary clients in their own industries. Your account will be ranked by budget behind those other primary influences.

In the *publishing* specialty agencies your products won't receive highly skilled abilities in specific textual areas like the law or medicine or computers. These specialists serve the heavy hitters in the publishing industry—the large trade houses with major bestseller fiction and non-fiction.

The axe they grind covers the major newspapers, *Publishers Weekly,* and the major trade journals in the publishing field. Beyond that expect little in the way of expertise beyond knowing what an ISBN number is—though not necessarily what it represents.

Most specialized and scholarly publishers have found that their needs are best met by an in-house advertising or promotion department (often a single individual), knowledgeable free lancers, small independent studios, and even some small local specialty agencies to whom your budget represents important income.

The best approach in getting maximum effectiveness from your budget is to understand your markets and the best media to reach them. Then hire a professional to carry out your program, or, hire someone who knows your kind of publishing and help him or her to learn as you do.

Whatever your choice, don't begin with any rosy preconceptions of the ability to turn it all over to the experts. *You* may be the best expert you have or can afford.

19:07   Design Must Not Overwhelm Copy: Pitfalls to Avoid in Printed Promotions

A pitfall of relying on outside agencies or studios in the preparation of printed promotions is that they are often over-heavy on design. Since the successful sale of professional and scholarly books relies on the value of the information they offer to potential buyers, such promotions must be tailored to the specialized interests of their intended audiences.

By contrast, often a piece produced by an outside agency or studio turns out to be design-driven, i.e., a creation heavily dependent on color, with boxes, dropouts, reverse-type blocks of copy (and sometimes entire panels or pages in reverse), checks, squares, and distracting background designs.

When dealing with such outside suppliers, let them know up front that the message is the predominant factor, that it should not be difficult for the reader to comprehend, that it must clearly convey the purpose of the printed piece.

When checking copy and mechanicals, here are some pitfalls to watch out for:

1. Background colors behind the copy not in sharp contrast with the printed message.
2. Large blocks of reverse-type text matter.
3. Condensed sans serif typefaces in 8-point sizes or smaller that are unleaded.
4. Long sticks of copy unbroken by smaller paragraphs.

5. Long columns of copy that do not have an occasional sub-head.

6. Long lists of features in solid paragraph form. Go for bulleted features in vertical format.

19:08   Working with Free-Lance Creative Talent: Guidelines from Cynthia Smith

Many small publishers work exclusively with in-house copy personnel and have little or no experience in dealing with or understanding the role of free-lance personnel—both copywriters and artists—in addition to their own internal staff.

At the American Chemical Society, which has an active book and journal publishing program, Cynthia Smith, journals circulation manager, makes extensive use of freelancers and discusses here some of the pros and cons of dealing with them. Says Ms. Smith, a seasoned marketing pro:

> We like to use outside creative talent, copywriters and artists, for these reasons:
>
> • They bring in new ideas and techniques in promotion.
>
> • They provide fresh approaches to product.
>
> • They introduce things we may have overlooked by being too close.
>
> • They free staff time to do all important backend analysis work.
>
> We prefer to use freelancers on a per-project basis as opposed to retaining the full services of an advertising agency. Our experience has shown that developing a stable of free-lance copywriters, artists, and agencies on a per-project basis has been the most effective way for us.
>
> You may have to experiment with five or six freelancers and agencies before you come down to the two or three that you're comfortable with and who have a good feel for your product and its market. It takes educating from you, but it's worth the investment in time for future work.
>
> We also look to combine talents of freelance copywriters with freelance artists in order to get a final package that incorporates good writing and graphics that enhance rather than detract. It is not an easy job and if you are not confident in this area, perhaps an advertising agency is a better choice since they already have done the legwork of combining talent within their shop.
>
> We have found that by rotating freelancers and agency projects, it tends to stimulate competition and we get better end results.
>
> Another important factor in dealing with freelance creative talent is fees. The key word here is "Negotiate!" There is a large market of freelance writers—some good, some fair, and some poor . . . some may have free time they are trying to fill.
>
> If you're experimenting with new writers, you may want to negotiate a special try-out rate. Another new concept that some freelancers are advocating involves a percentage of final sales. Basically, they cut their up-

front fees and instead base their final bill on a smaller up-front fee plus a percentage based on the success of the package—or on gross sales.

This percentage idea gives the publisher these advantages:

- Smaller risk on testing new packages
- Encouragement to the copywriter to give you his best since there will be some back-end benefit
- Saves advancing money before sales come in
- Gives you a chance to spread costs over a longer period

Our preference for the use of freelance creative talent is not to discourage the use of advertising agencies, but rather to think in terms of actual creative services needed. For some, an advertising agency may be the best route. For us, however, we have found that retaining the services of an advertising agency was not essential. Here are some problems that could be associated with the use of a full-service ad agency:

1. As a client, you're tied into a contract for a stipulated time—usually no less than six months.

2. The set overhead fee sometimes only covers the privilege of using the agency's administrative services and expertise. Creative copy and artwork are charged separately.

3. A client may be at the mercy of the available staff, depending on how the client load is handled. If your account is small (and those of many scholarly publishers are) it could be assigned to junior-level staff, while you may be paying senior-level costs.

4. If you are dissatisfied with the agency, you are still obligated, as a rule, to fulfill your contractual obligations.

5. It is possible that agency administrative services you are paying for in the retainer may duplicate your own internal marketing department (if you have one) and thus you could be paying twice. On the other hand, if yours is a one-person marketing department, you may find the extra agency expertise helpful; it depends on the individual set-up.

19:09   Ogilvy on the Job of Advertising Copywriter

The following tips are taken from *Ogilvy on Advertising* by David Ogilvy (New York: Crown, 1983).

- At the start of your career . . . what you *learn* is more important than what you *earn*.
- Most of the advertising techniques which worked [in 1963] still work today [1983].
- You start successful advertising by doing your homework. . . . this [is] extremely tedious but there is no substitute for it.
- It's no bad thing to learn the craft of advertising by copying your elders and betters.

19:10   Adspeak: Jargon of the Advertising Copywriter

Ball is in your court: further action is up to you

Bottom line: end result

Bounce ideas off of: get someone's opinion on

Brain-picking: getting information from

Buckshot approach: aiming in all directions or at a non-selective audience

Finalize: finish

Game plan: plan of action, ad campaign, or marketing plan

Generate: create

Have a sense: have an idea or impression

Kick-off or launch ad: first ad in a campaign or series

Opposite side of the coin: opposing point of view

Optimize: improve

Overkill: too much of something, excessive

Run it up the flagpole: expose it to others for a reaction

Simplistic: simple

Target audience: primary audience

Utilize: use

Viable: acceptable

19:11   Copywriting Bibliography

American Heritage Dictionary of the English Language, 2nd ed. Boston: Houghton Mifflin, 1982.

Bodian, Nat G., *Book Marketing Handbook: Volume One, Tips and Techniques.* New York: Bowker, 1980.

Bodian, Nat G., *Book Marketing Handbook: Volume Two, Over 1,000 More Tips and Techniques.* New York: Bowker, 1983.

Brownstone, D. M., and I. M. Franck, *The Dictionary of Publishing.* New York: Van Nostrand Reinhold. 1982.

Caples, John, *How to Make Your Advertising Make Money.* Englewood Cliffs: Prentice-Hall, 1983.

The Chicago Manual of Style, Thirteenth Edition, Revised and Enlarged. Chicago: University of Chicago Press, 1982.

Day, Robert A., *How to Write and Publish a Scientific Paper,* 2nd ed. Philadelphia: ISI Press, 1983.

Fowler, H. W., rev. by Sir Ernest Gowers, *A Dictionary of Modern English Usage,* 2nd ed. New York: Oxford, 1983.

Gunning, Robert, *The Technique of Clear Writing,* rev. ed. New York: McGraw-Hill, 1968.

Metzger, George P., *Copy.* New York: Doubleday, 1926.

Nash, Edward L., *Direct Marketing.* New York: McGraw-Hill, 1982.

Ogilvy, David, *Ogilvy on Advertising.* New York: Crown Publishers, 1983.

Rodale, J. I., rev. by Laurence Urdang, *The Synonym Finder.* Emmaus, Pa.: Rodale, 1979.

Roget's II, The New Thesaurus. Boston: Houghton Mifflin, 1980.

Schwab, Victor O., *How to Write a Good Advertisement.* New York: Harper, 1962.

Strunk, W., and E. B. White, *The Elements of Style,* 3rd ed. New York: Macmillan, 1979.

Tichy, H. J., *Effective Writing for Engineers, Managers and Scientists.* New York: Wiley, 1966.

Websters Ninth New Collegiate Dictonary. Springfield, Mass.: Merriam, 1983.

Weisman, H. M., *Technical Correspondence.* New York: Wiley, 1968.

Appendix A
Copywriter's Glossary:
A Vocabulary of Advertising
and Promotion

The special language of copywriters who write advertising and promotion copy for specialized and scholarly books and journals comes from many trades and professions.

- Copywriters must work with editors and have some familiarity with the terms related to manuscripts and editing procedures.
- Copywriters must work with authors and have some familiarity with the language of the scholar, scientist, researcher, subject specialist.
- Copywriters are involved in products which involve various levels of the graphic arts. They should therefore have some familiarity with terms related to art, typography, and to the printer and the lettershop.
- Copywriters must have some familiarity with terms relevant to the advertising profession and to publicity.

This glossary takes into account all of the above areas and enumerates many of the terms the copywriter is likely to encounter in the course of work. In providing definitions, it aims not so much at the dictionary meaning as it does at the meaning the term will have for the copywriter. It will be an especially useful tool for the beginner in working with the various entries in this handbook.

Address Correction Requested   A line added to a mailing piece requesting the Postal Service to supply correct address where addressee is no longer at the address on the mailing piece. See also **Return Postage Guaranteed.**

approval copy   A book accompanied by an invoice seeking payment or return of the book within a specified period, for consideration for purchase or recommendation to students. See also **complimentary copy; desk copy.**

attention line   Job title or function, usually printed on an envelope when a mailing label has only the name of a company or institution.

author-prepared copy, author-supplied composition (reproducible camera-ready copy)   See **camera ready copy (author-prepared).**

author questionnaire, marketing questionnaire   A form that an author completes for a publisher after the manuscript has been put into production. The answers provide guidance on the book's market and aid the copywriter in the preparation of the jacket copy.

automatic shipment   A procedure in book clubs whereby, as part of the original order, the club ships each new shipment automatically until requested to stop (in contrast to negative- or positive-option book club shipments whereby the customer is informed of each shipment). Also known as "till-forbid" offer.

basic rate   See one-time rate.

basis weight   The traditional pound designation for a ream of paper in a standard size (basis size). See also **weight.**

Benday (or **Ben Day**)   A "screen" or pattern of lines or dots, applied to an area of reproduced art by the printing-platemaker, to fill in areas that would normally reproduce in a solid color or as pure white. See also **Velox.**

b.f.   Boldface type.

big ticket   A term borrowed from the merchandising field and used in publishing to indicate a book or series being offered at a high price, or at a higher price than the usual price for a comparable item. Term interchangeable with *high ticket.*

bind-in card   A detachable reply card bound into a particular issue of a periodical. If sold to an advertiser, it usually supports an accompanying advertisement. Some periodical publishers restrict bind-in cards to "in-house" promotion only. See also **blow-in cards.**

bingo card   A term commonly used among advertisers for a reader's service card (qv).

bleed   Any printed matter (most often an illustration) that extends to the full limit of the trimmed size in any print job. It "bleeds off" the edge of the paper.

blow-in cards   Single, loose cards inserted in periodicals to solicit subscriptions. The term comes from the fact that the cards are often "blown in" by machine between the periodical pages by air pressure. See also **bind-in card.**

blow-up   A photographic enlargement of any copy.

blueprint   See **blues (blueprint).**

blues (blueprint)   A same-size contact print made from a film negative or positive for final check and proofreading purposes before platemaking. Also called a *silver print* or *vandyke.*

blurb   A short sales pitch or review of a book usually printed on its jacket flaps, or in an advertisement of it.

body copy   The major portion of the text of an advertisement or peice of printed promotion. See also **text.**

body type   Type used in text matter as opposed to display type. See also **display type.**

boldface   A heavier weight of typeface. Boldface type is usually used for emphasis.

booklet   A series of printed pages, usually bound together by saddle-wire stitching and covered with the same paper as is used for the inside pages (self cover). When a heavier paper is used on the outside, it is called a covered booklet.

BPA   See Business Publications Audit of Circulation, Inc. (BPA).

BRC   Business reply card. See also **business reply envelope.**

BRE   See **business reply envelope.**

broadside   A single sheet of advertising, usually large in size and printed on one side. A useful device when a publishing project has a large story to tell, as with an encyclopedia. Often folded down several times and used as a self-mailer.

brochure   An expensively produced booklet devoted to advertising matter. Size and format may vary. A brochure may be stitched or folded.

bullet   In printed advertising and promotion, a heavy dot used to focus attention on a feature or segment of the printed matter. Also used to set off a book's features on jacket flap copy. Bullet sizes are expressed in points—4 pt., 8 pt., etc.

bulleted copy   Usually a set of features in an advertisement or printed promotion, each preceded by a black dot or bullet. Bullets are usually vertically aligned.

Business Publications Audit of Circulation, Inc. (BPA)   A not-for-profit, independent organization that provides independent verification of all paid and controlled circulations for nearly 800 business publications and professional journals.

business reply card mailing   See **card deck.**

business reply envelope   A return envelope used as a mailing enclosure, and bearing a printed insignia, special vertical-bar insignia, and permit number obliging the mailer to pay the letter rate of postage (20¢ for the first ounce as of early 1984) for its return. New Postal Service regulations, effective July 15, 1979, require a standardized design, the addition of a bar-code pattern, a Facing Identification Mark (qv), and a size no smaller than $3\frac{1}{2}''$ × 5″ and no larger than $6\frac{1}{2}''$ × $11\frac{1}{2}''$. See also **BRC; return envelope.**

buzzwords   Words or terms used by members within a specialized field for quick communication, or sometimes to impress others.

c & lc   Capitals and lowercase letters. (Also u & lc, for upper- and lowercase.)

c & sc   Capitals and small capitals.

calendar-year basis (journals)   The subscription basis for most scientific and other scholarly journals is on a calendar-year basis. Therefore, subscriptions placed between January and December will bring all back issues.

camera-ready copy   A piece of copy ready to be photographed for reproduction without further alteration.

camera-ready copy (author-prepared)   Authors' typed manuscripts, used by some book and journal publishers. Copy is photographed for offset printing, after being supplied by the author to publisher's specifications.

campaign   A promotion effort aimed at a specific objective, over a given period of time, such as launching a new edition of a best-selling reference, handbook, etc.

campaign, direct-mail   A series of mailings designed to achieve an express objective for a specific book or group of books over a stated period of time.

campaign evaluation, period of   For professional-book direct-mail promotion, various publishers use different periods. Most responses come in within 12 weeks of the date on which the mailing was completed. Allow one week less for a first-class mailing.

caps   Capital letters of a typeface. Indicated in proofreaders' marks by three lines under all letters to be capitalized.

card deck   Also expressed as direct-response advertising, business reply card mailings, co-op mailings, loose-deck packets, action postcards, postcard mailings, product information cards, product inquiry service, etc. The card deck is a collection of business reply cards mailed in a polybag or paper envelope, each containing an advertisement that the recipient can complete and mail back (usually postage-free) to an advertiser to receive a product, service, or additional information. A useful medium for selling many types of appropriate professional books.

casting off   Estimating the number of pages or amount of space that typewritten copy will occupy when it is set in a specific size and measure of a given typeface; or how much copy must be written to fill a specific area. See also **copy fitting.**

catalog   List of all of a publisher's books currently in print. Usually organized by subject area, and within subject area by author. Usually contains book description or table of contents. See also short-title catalog.

Cataloging-in-Publication (CIP) Program   A program initiated by the Library of Congress in 1971 that allows books to be cataloged while they are in publisher's proof forms. A similar program exists in the United Kingdom through the British Library.

center spread   An advertisement on facing center pages in a publication. See also **spread.**

certified mail   First-class mail of no intrinsic value sent with a receipt, which recipient must sign.

character   In printed matter, any letter, number, punctuation mark, symbol, or type decoration. In estimating type from typewritten characters, a blank space is counted as a character.

character count   A count of all letters and spaces (using line averages), to be used in determining the area that text copy will occupy when set in type. In type composition, the number of typewritten characters (letters, numbers, and punctuation marks) that, when set in a particular typeface, will measure 1 pica ($\frac{1}{6}$ inch).

characters per pica   See **character count.**

checking copy   A copy of a specific issue of a publication in which an advertisement has been inserted. See also **tear sheet.**

clean copy   A piece of copy that is relatively free from errors or alterations.

clean proof   A proof or sheet of paper containing type composition on which there are few or no typographical errors.

closed-end series   A series of books with a finite number of volumes. See also **open-end series.**

closing date   Last date on which a publication will accept an advertisement for a specific issue.

co-edition   See **co-publishing.**

cold composition   See **cold-type composition.**

cold-type composition   Composition in which no molten metal is involved. Usually created by either "strike-on" or photographic methods. See also **hot type.**

colophon   Trademark or device used in some books or on promotional matter to identify a particular publishing house or imprint. Also, a description of how the book was designed or manufactured. (Originally, printer's statement at the end of a book.) See also **logotype; signature (in advertisement).**

column inch   Advertising space equal to publication's usual column width by 1 inch of depth. Often the smallest unit of display advertising space sold by some magazines and newspapers.

combination plate   A photoengraving or offset plate made from copy combining both line and halftone.

combination rate   Special advertising rate offered by a publisher of two or more periodicals to advertisers as an incentive to contract for space in more than one publication.

comp copy   See **complimentary copy.**

compiler (mailing list) Owns and maintains one or more lists of names and addresses, extracted and compiled usually from printed sources to reach a given market or audience; does not, as a rule, work with original data or do original research.

complimentary copy For books with text potential, a book sent or given free to a course instructor for evaluation. See also **approval copy, desk copy.**

composition The setting and arrangement of original manuscript text into type in a form suitable for platemaking and printing.

compositor One who sets type or a company performing composition services.

comprehensive, comprehensive layout A layout or working drawing of all the elements of an advertisement or printed promotion, prepared in great detail so as to closely resemble the finished work. See also **layout.**

computer composition, computer-assisted composition Composition utilizing a wide range of processes in which computer programming assists in the production of camera-ready copy.

computer-printed letter A letter printed by any high-speed computer printout machine. The entire letter is produced in seconds, in upper- and lowercase, including inserted salutation and P.S., if desired. Very similar in appearance to a typed letter. See also **word-processed letter.**

condensed type. A narrower version of a typeface which has the appearance of the face but permits a greater number of characters to fit in the same space.

continuation order An order to supply, automatically on publication, each succeeding volume of a series, or each new volume of an annual. See also **on-approval plan.**

continuous tone A photograph or illustration with continuously differing black-and-white (or color) tone values. See also **screen.**

contract rate A special discounted rate given a periodical advertiser for advertising placed within a specified period, usually a year. See also **contract year; frequency discount; short rate.**

contract year A 12-month period, effective with insertion of the first advertisement, that a space advertising contract will run. See also **contract rate; frequency discount; short rate.**

controlled circulation A business publication containing at least 25% editorial matter, issued on a regular basis, and circulated free or mainly free to individuals within a particular profession, business, or industry.

cooperative advertisement Advertisement placed by bookseller over his or her own name, advertising a publisher's book or books. The publisher and bookseller share the costs of the advertisement, frequently on a 75–25 basis, the publisher paying the 75%, the dollar amount usually limited to a percentage (5%, 10%, etc.) of the bookseller's purchases from the publisher or of the publisher's books and other conditions.

cooperative mailing A mailing to a specialized market containing advertising from more than one advertiser. See also **envelope stuffer.**

co-publishing The sharing of an edition of a book between an originating publisher and one or more other publishers, each having exclusive marketing and distribution rights within a territory. The book may carry the title-page imprint of the originating publisher only, the joint imprint of the co-publishers, or the imprint only of the publisher taking the book for a specific territory. The originating publisher may arrange for the simultaneous (initial) printing of the co-edition. Subsequent printings may be done jointly or independently.

copy From Middle Latin *copiare,* "to transcribe." The textual matter of an advertisement or printed promotion; also the "manuscript" text (usually typewritten) to be converted into printed matter.

copy chief The supervisor of one or more copywriters and the coordination of their work in a department, agency, or service.

copy fitting Estimating the type size and line width necessary to fit a piece of typed copy into a prescribed space on a printed promotion; also the space a piece of copy will occupy when set in a prescribed type size and line width. See also **casting off.**

copyright Protection of an "intellectual work" reserving to the author or other owner the right of publication. A copyright protects the work as a whole, but not the concept, idea, or theme if expressed another way. Definitions and information about fees and other services are available from: Copyright Office, Library of Congress, Washington, DC 20559. Ask for Circular R4, *Copyright Fees Effective January 1, 1979.*

copywriter The writer of text matter for advertising and promotion materials.

core journal A journal in a discipline or research area in which the most significant work is published.

cover Any of the outer four pages of a paperbound periodical, book, booklet, or catalog. The outside front cover is called the first cover (or cover 1); the inside front cover is called the second cover (cover 2); the inside back cover is called the third cover (cover 3); the outside back cover is called the fourth cover (cover 4). Advertising rates on periodical covers are usually higher than regular page rates because readership is believed to be higher. Not to be confused with jacket (qv).

cover rate (advertising) Advertising rates for covers in periodicals are generally billed at a premium over the advertising rate for inside pages.

crop marks Guidelines on a piece of artwork or printed area indicating the precise area to be reproduced (placed outside the area to be reproduced).

ctr Designer instruction to compositor or platemaker to center type or illustration copy between understood limits.

cumulative index An index which combines in a single source the entries of earlier volumes of a book or periodical.

cut A printing plate, usually metal and usually for an illustration, used in letterpress printing. Sometimes loosely used to signify any illustration, copy, or reproduction.

dash, en dash A dash the width of an en space.

database publishing Creation of publications or other information-based products from information stored in a computer database.

delete To remove.

descender That part of a type character that extends below the body size (letters g, j, p, q, and y).

desk copy A book furnished free to serve as the instructor's copy when copies have been ordered for students' use in a specific course. A complimentary copy may be considered a desk copy upon the instructor's decision to use it as a required/ supplemental text. See also **approval copy; complimentary copy; examination copy.**

direct advertising Advertising in any printed form, reproduced in quantity and distributed to prospects, usually by mail.

direct-impression composition See **cold-type composition; strike-on composition.**

direct-mail advertising Advertising sent through the mails or other direct delivery service.

direct marketing The selling of books, goods, or services directly to the consumer.

direct-response advertising Advertising through any medium designed to generate a measurable response.

direct-response mailing See **card deck.**

discount from list price The traditional billing formula of most publishers used to determine the selling price to booksellers or, in some instances, to libraries and nonprofit institutions. See also **list price, net price.**

display type Usually type 14 points or larger, or not available on a text-setting machine. Used for headlines, as distinguished from body type. See also **body type.**

drop-ship To ship an order to one address (e.g., a customer) while billing it to another (e.g., a retailer).

drop shipment Order placed by bookseller with publisher whereby book is sent directly to the customer, but billed to the bookseller.

dropout halftone Halftone with no dots in the highlight areas.

dual imprint See **joint imprint.**

dummy A preliminary layout of a planned printed work showing the position of headline, text, illustrations, and other elements of the job as a guide for the artist, copywriter, printer, and others concerned with the job. See also **rough.**

dust jacket See **jacket.**

dust wrapper See **jacket.**

earned rate An advertising rate "earned" in a publication by the use of a number of insertions within a period of one year. An advertiser billed at the one-time rate would receive a rebate to the earned three-time rate by placing three insertions within a year. See also **one-time rate; preferred position.**

edition One of the different forms in which a book is published (as applied to original, revised, reprint, textbook, etc., or paperbound, deluxe, library, large-print, illustrated, etc.). See also **impression.**

800 telephone number See **Inward-WATS.**

elhi Elementary and high school educational markets.

em The square of any type size. A 10-point em measures 10 points by 10 points.

em dash A horizontal printed line the width of an em, sometimes used to indicate a rest in reading or to separate two thoughts.

em space A space the width of an em.

en A printer's unit of measurement half the width of an em.

en dash A horizontal printed line the width of one en. Used to mean "to," as in 1985–1986.

envelope stuffer Advertising or promotional material enclosed in an envelope with letters, statements, or invoices. See also **cooperative mailing.**

examination copy, exam copy Book sent to an educator for examination and consideration as a possible classroom text. Examination periods of many publishers are 30 to 60 days. Exam copy invoices for professional and graduate-level books should state terms, period of examination, and that the invoice will be canceled on adoption or return of book. See also **desk copy.**

excerpt A quoted portion extracted from a larger work. It is usually enclosed in quotation marks, but may be in smaller size type from the rest of the text without quotation marks. See also **review excerpt.**

exchange ads Advertising exchanged between periodicals in the same or related subject areas without payment. Such ads are generally aimed at attracting subscribers from the circulation of the periodical in which the advertisement appears.

Exclusive to A heading on a news release written exclusively for the publication. The sender is obliged to issue no other publicity on the subject until the "Exclusive" release has appeared, or he or she has definite word that it will not be used. See also **Special to.**

expires Former subscribers to a publication.

f and g's See folded and gathered sheets.

face Used as abbreviation of typeface. See **typeface.**

Facing Identification Mark (FIM) A series of vertical lines or bars required on all business reply mail (cards and envelopes) since July 15, 1979, under revised postal regulations.

flap copy Descriptive copy, usually about book and author, which appears on the narrow inside folds of a book jacket.

flier, flyer A small, inexpensively produced, advertising piece, usually on a single sheet of paper, which may be distributed flat, or folded for mailing in an envelope. In publishing promotion, flyers are often letterhead size, and may use a letterhead format.

flush left Type composition set so *left-hand* margin aligns vertically. Right-hand margin is allowed to terminate normally with no attempt at vertical alignment. See also **flush right; justification.**

flush paragraphs Paragraphs having no indention.

flush right Type composition set so *right-hand* margin aligns vertically and left-hand margin has an irregular alignment. See also **flush left; justification.**

folded and gathered sheets All the signatures (folded printed sheets forming the various sections of a book) assembled in the sequence in which they are to be bound into a book. Also called *f and g's,* folded and gathered sheets are often sent to reviewers, book clubs, and exhibits to meet deadlines when bound books are not yet available.

folder A sheet of paper printed on one or both sides and folded one or more times. Individual sections (panels), after folding, may be used to constitute individual pages. Folders often are designed to fit a predetermined envelope size. Examples: Fold for No. 10 envelope, or accordion-fold for No. 10 envelope, order form concealed.

font The complete assortment of type characters for one size and design or style of type, usually roman and italic caps and lowercase, small caps, figures, punctuation marks, and a few common fractions. See also **wrong font.**

free-lance copywriter One who sells services as an independent contractor, usually by the job. Charges may be on hourly rate or at pre-agreed upon price.

French fold A single sheet of paper printed on one side and so folded that the unprinted side is folded in and the printed side constitutes four pages. Most greeting cards utilize this fold.

frequency discount A discounted advertising rate in a publication for a given number of insertions stipulated by the publisher within a contract year. See also **contract rate; contract year; short rate.**

galley proof (galley) In traditional letterpress context a proof taken from type standing in a metal tray (galley) used to hold and store type. The term is still frequently used to refer to the first set of type proofs irrespective of the method of composition used.

gang run Two or more jobs "ganged up" or printed simultaneously on the same press for reasons of economy.

gatefold A page in a publication or promotional piece that is wider than the other pages and must be folded to fit. The folded portion of the page swings out like a gate. In many mail promotions, a gatefold is used for the perforated reply card, or order form.

geographic and/or demographic edition An edition of a publication in which the advertiser may advertise to a specific geographic area or segment of the total circulation, or to a demographic segment of the total circulation that will reach individual subscribers by job title or function, type of industry, instrumentation used, etc. Approximately 250 business publications offer geographic/demographic editions. Some card-deck sponsors also offer demographic options.

hairline   The narrowest or thinnest line used in printed matter.

handle   A strong, concise summary of selling features of a book used by a rep in sales calls on booksellers and subsequently by the bookseller to describe the book to a potential buyer. A handle, says one rep, "says a lot about a book in as few words as possible."

hard copy   Copy printed on paper, as opposed to electronically stored or displayed copy. See also **soft copy.**

heads (headlines)   Secondary headlines are referred to as "subheads."

high-opacity paper   Paper with little show-through of printing from the opposite side of the sheet.

hot type   Type cast from molten metal. Some forms of hot metal composition are Monotype, Linotype, Ludlow, foundry. Today almost no composition uses hot type. See also **cold-type composition.**

house ad   An advertisement for a publisher's books or journals in a publication or promotion of that publisher.

house list   A company-owned mailing list.

hype   Abbreviation for hyperbole. Exaggeration in copy not meant to be taken literally.

impression   All copies of a book printed at one time. See also **edition.**

imprint   The name of the publisher on the title page of a book. Also the name and address of an advertiser on its advertising material. Many publishers offer advertising material to booksellers with imprint omitted. The bookstore may then add its own imprint and use the material for promotion to its own customers and prospects.

in-house   Work done on the publisher's premises.

inquiry-response mailing   A mailing aimed at eliciting inquiries rather than direct orders.

insert, book   An advertising piece that accompanies an outgoing book shipment. Some publishers use insert advertisements of related books or journals in all copies of a book printing, or as a stuffer in outgoing shipments or invoices. Also a separately printed section of a book, usually illustrations, inserted in the book at the binding stage.

insert, package   An advertising piece that accompanies any outgoing shipment or product.

insertion order   An advertising order sent to a publication.

International Standard Book Number   An established international system of book numbering, providing a 10-digit identifier unique to each book title published. The ISBN system is administered in the United States by R. R. Bowker Co. See also **International Standard Serial Number.**

International Standard Serial Number   A unique number assigned to a serial publication that remains unchanged as long as the title of the serial remains unchanged. Administered by the Library of Congress, which assigns numbers. Under U.S. Postal regulations, the ISSN must appear on the outer wrapper of all periodicals. See also **International Standard Book Number.**

International System of Units (SI)   Derived from Système International d'Unites, the SI metric system is the generally preferred system of weights and measures.

Inward-WATS   The 800 number telephone system that permits customers to receive telephone calls from anyone in the service area selected. See also **Outward-WATS; Wide Area Telecommunications Service.**

IN-WATS   See **Inward-WATS.**

ISBN   See **International Standard Book Number.**

ISSN   See **International Standard Serial Number.**

ital   Italics.

jacket   Paper cover around a bound book originally used to protect a book prior to sale. The jacket now serves primarily as an advertisement, giving information about the book and its author. Text, professional, and reference books are often published without jackets.

jacket flap copy   See **flap copy.**

jobber; book jobber, library jobber   See **wholesaler.**

joint imprint   The imprint of two publishers on the title page of a book being marketed and distributed by each to a different share of the book's market.

journal   A multi-author periodical, usually containing results of research within a scientific or professional discipline, in which most of the content is submitted by the authors, rather than solicited by the editors.

justification   Type composition set so both left-hand and right-hand margins align vertically. See also **flush left** and **flush right.**

justify   Instruction to indicate that type composition is to be set flush left and right (justified on both sides).

key   An identifying device in an advertisement to indicate the source of the response. See also **keyed advertisement.**

keyed advertisement   A letter, number, code, or mark used in print or mail advertising to identify the source of the response. If different mailing lists have been used, a different key may be used for each list. The best location for a key is on the back of a business reply card, or in the upper lefthand corner on a business reply envelope.

layout   A type specification diagram showing arrangements of elements of printed matter—page, piece—for a printer to follow. A preliminary quick pencil sketch is called a *rough* layout. A more precise drawing, closely approximating a final advertisement, for example, is called a *comprehensive.* See also **dummy; rough.**

LC   Library of Congress.

lc   Lowercase; small letters.

leaders   Dots (. . .) or short strokes (- -) used in copy to direct the reader from one part of the copy to another. Usually specified in linear measurement, such as 2, 4, or 6 units per em.

lead time   The time needed from implementation of a promotion job to deadline.

leading   The extra white space between printed lines, usually expressed in points, to permit easier reading, achieve an aesthetic effect, or pad out copy space (e.g., "10-on-12" or "10/12" signifies 10-point type on a 12-point body). See also **set solid.**

leaflet   See **folder.**

letter spacing   Addition of more space between letters in type composition than would be normally allowed in setting the type.

letterpress   Printing process in which ink is transferred from metal type or plates directly onto the paper.

lettershop   A business equipped to handle the mechanical details of mailings, such as printing, collating, folding, inserting, addressing, imprinting, sorting, mailing, list maintenance, etc.

line art   See line copy.

line copy   Any copy suitable for reproduction without using a halftone screen; solid blacks or whites. Also referred to as *line art.*

list   See **mailing list.**

list ad An advertisement containing a number or list of books as opposed to an ad featuring a single book.

list price Suggested resale price. See also **discount from list price; net price; net pricing.**

logo See **logotype.**

logotype Identifying device or trademark. Abbreviation: logo. See also **colophon; signature (in advertisement).**

long discount See **trade discount.**

loose-leaf publishing Publication of information of a current nature useful to business and professional people in their everyday activities. Because it is an ongoing publication service with updates issued at stated intervals or as required, it is usually stored in a loose-leaf binder.

loose-leaf reference One or more volumes on a specific topic published in a loose-leaf binder, updated by supplements and revisions, either on a regular basis or as required.

mail-order A book order received by mail, phone, or other medium and shipped to the customer through the mail or another carrier such as United Parcel Service (UPS).

mail-order advertising A method of sales promotion in which the entire sales transaction is done through the mail.

mail-order publication A book, series, or set with broad appeal to consumers that is designed and produced primarily for sale by mail.

mailing list A collection of names and addresses derived from a common source.

mailing package See **package (direct mail).**

market, the A logical or likely group or audience for a book or journal.

marketing In professional and scholarly publishing, all activities involved in getting the book from the warehouse or distribution center into the hands of its logical or likely buyers.

marketing plan The plan by marketing management for moving its published products to their likely or logical markets. Plan may be an overall one for the line, or on a book-by-book basis.

marketing questionnaire See **author questionnaire.**

mechanical, mechanical paste-up The elements of an advertisement or other printed piece pasted into position to conform to layout or dummy, and ready to be photographed for platemaking. The finished mechanical is said to be camera ready. See also **camera-ready copy.**

monograph A treatment, usually short, of a single subject by an author or a group of authors. See also **treatise.**

Murphy's Law "If anything can go wrong, it will."

negative option The successful mail-order technique used by most book clubs whereby a book is shipped and billed to a member automatically unless the member writes in advance and asks that it not be sent. See also **positive option.**

negative-option publishing Sometimes used as another name for book clubs. See also **no-commitment book club.**

nesting An enclosure, placed within another (nested), before being inserted into a mailing envelope.

net Price to be paid; no further discount. See also **net price.**

net price The bookseller's cost for a book, usually the list or suggested resale price less discount. Shipping or transportation charges, when levied, are usually added onto the net price. See also **discount from list price; list price; net pricing.**

net pricing Publishers' billing for a book at an established net price, with no suggested retail price. Booksellers then set retail selling prices on an individual basis. See also **list price.**

new edition   An edition containing substantial changes from the previous edition and printed from new, revised plates.

nine-digit ZIP Code   See **ZIP + 4.**

no-commitment book club   A book club that requires no commitment of a minimum purchase of books as a condition of membership. See also **negative-option publishing.**

NOP   Publisher's abbreviation for "not our publication."

NYP   Abbreviation for "not yet published."

on-line   A device connected to a telecommunications system.

one-time rate   Basic advertising rate in a publication. Rate applied to advertising in a publication when the number of insertions is insufficient to earn a contract or frequency discount. See also **earned rate.**

OP   Abbreviation for "out-of-print"; publisher has no more copies for sale, no intention to reprint. See also **OS.**

opacity   The property of paper that prevents the printing on one side of the sheet from showing through to the other. See also **show-through.**

open-end series   A series with an indeterminate length. Volumes may be published irregularly or annually. See also **closed-end series.**

OS   Abbreviation for "out-of-stock"; new shipment or new printing awaited. See also **OP.**

out-of-print   See **OP.**

out of stock   See **OS.**

Outward-WATS   A telephone company service that enables customer to place calls to any telephone number in the service area on a fixed monthly charge. See also **Inward-Wats; Wide Area Telecommunications Service.**

overs   See **overrun.**

overrun   The practice of printing a larger quantity than ordered to compensate for spoilage during the press run and binding operations.

overstock   Surplus inventory of active titles from a publisher's backlist. Such overstock may be sold off through inventory-reduction sales, pulped, or remaindered. Overstock formulas vary from one publishing establishment to another.

package (direct mail)   A mailing format used for many types of publishing promotions. Consists of an envelope, letter, folder, and reply device. See also **self-mailer.**

pamphlet   See **booklet.**

Pareto's Law   A general law stating that 80% of the total results in a given situation are produced by 20% of the participants. For example, 80% of sales come from 20% of titles, or 80% of the orders are brought in by 20% of the sales reps. Also referred to as the "80–20 principle."

patch   A section of type set as an alteration to an existing job. Often an advertisement may be repeated with only one or two replacement paragraphs "patched" in.

per-inquiry deal   See **P.I. deal.**

periodical   A publication issued at regular or irregular intervals. The preferred term by librarians for both magazines and journals.

personal letter   Letter in which recipient's name is given in the heading and salutation but not mentioned elsewhere in the letter. See also **personalized letter.**

personalized letter   Letter in a mailing in which the name of the recipient has been used in both the salutation and the body of the letter. See also **personal letter.**

photocomposition   Text set by photographic means.

photocopy   A photographic copy of an existing photograph. Such a print may be enlarged, reduced, or screened.

photostat Abbreviation: stat. A fast method of making photocopies of black-and-white original copy. Photostats may be direct positive (DP) or negative-to-positive (negative made first). A photostat may be made larger, smaller, or the same size. A requested change in size is usually expressed as percent of original copy (e.g., photostat to 85% size). If used for reproduction, a glossy stat is to be specified.

P.I. deal Payment for advertising based on the number of orders or inquiries received. Payment is a fixed amount per inquiry, or a percentage of the ultimate sale.

pica A standard unit for measuring type matter, either line width or copy depth. A pica measures 12 points or ⅙ inch. See also **point.**

point A unit of type measurement equal to $\frac{1}{72}$ inch (0.0138 inch). See also **pica.**

positive option Technique of certain book clubs that send announcements of new selections, rather than books. The member must send back an order before the club will ship. See also **negative option.**

postcard mailing See **card deck.**

PR Aids A computerized system of PR Aids, Inc., for distributing news releases and announcements, as well as review copies, to critics and editors in all media.

preferred position A desired position for which an advertiser must pay a premium over the basic rate. For magazine covers a premium over the earned rate is almost always charged. See also **earned rate; run-of-paper position.**

prepub Prior to publication. A prepub order is one received prior to publication; a prepub price is a price in effect before the designated date of publication.

prepublication price A special price usually at a discount off the publisher's list price, to encourage buyers to place orders prior to publication.

professional books Books directed to a professional audience and specifically related to its work.

professional trade title Book that is intended for use by professionals but that has sufficient appeal to be stocked in stores that normally do not carry professional and scholarly books. Such titles carry a trade discount. See also **trade title.**

protected A book trade term meaning a book that may be returned to the publisher for credit if unsold. The term "fully protected," when applied to a publisher's list, means all unsold books are returnable.

PTLA See **Publishers Trade List Annual.**

pub date (publication date) The publisher's official or record date a book becomes available for sale.

publication date See **pub date.**

Publishers' Trade List Annual A compilation of catalogs and publication lists from some 1,500 publishers, arranged alphabetically and bound into six permanent clothbound volumes. A basic reference tool for many libraries and booksellers, published annually in September by R. R. Bowker Co.

pubset type (publication-set type) Type matter set by a periodical or newspaper from copy supplied by the advertiser, for an advertisement to be published at a future date. Most newspapers and larger periodicals will charge only for the space purchased, the composition being supplied free when requested by the advertiser. Most smaller-circulation and scholarly periodicals charge for composition at their cost, or at a nominal fee.

questionaire, author See **author questionnaire.**

rag rt Instruction used by artists and type specifiers to indicate composition is to be set flush left and ragged (unjustified) right.

reader's service card A business reply card on which many numbers are printed in grid formation; the card is bound into a publication, and enables the reader to request literature, information, or other services by circling a key number on the card corresponding to a number identifying a product mentioned in an advertise-

request literature, information, or other services by circling a key number on the card corresponding to a number identifying a product mentioned in an advertisement or in the editorial matter. Some periodicals also use the key numbers as a means of ordering an advertised book. Also called bingo card (qv).

repro, repro proof See **reproduction proof.**

reproduction proof Clean and sharp typeset copy suitable for photographic reproduction and platemaking.

response device The BRC (business reply card) or BRE (business reply envelope) within a package-format mailing.

response rate Percent of returns from a mail promotion.

return, on mail promotion See **response rate.**

return envelope A self-addressed envelope used as a mail enclosure, to facilitate a reply, order, or payment from the addressee. See also **business reply envelope.**

Return Postage Guaranteed A line added to pieces in a third-class bulk mailing that instructs the Postal Service to return any undeliverable mailing piece. The straight third-class postage rate is charged for the return. See also **Address Correction Requested.**

reverse, reverse plate Negative-image copy, or printing plate, in which whites come out black and vice versa.

review excerpt, book review excerpt An extract of one or more passages or a continuous portion from a book review. Copywriters can "shape" a review when the extract by itself might be inappropriate for some reason. Example: Actual excerpt reads: ". . . a classic reference in the field of engineering, science and technology." Reshaped by copywriter, it reads: ". . . a classic reference in [its] field. . . ." See also **excerpt.**

review slip An enclosure in a book sent by a publisher for review. Usually includes such information as title, author, pub date, and price; also a request that the publication send copy(ies) of the published review.

roman An upright type style, as opposed to a slanting or italic style. Normal text style.

ROP See **run-of-paper position.**

rough A dummy or layout in rough form for an advertisement or advertising piece. See also **dummy; layout.**

run-around Usually, an illustration set into the type area. Lines of type in a column are shortened at either left or right to allow space for the illustration or other featured material. The type runs around the illustration. Sometimes called *set-around.*

run-of-book See run-of-paper position.

run-of-paper position Placement of an advertisement in a publication anywhere in the edition, at the publisher's discretion. Run-of-book has the same meaning, but usually applies to magazine advertising only.

sans serif A typeface without serifs. See also **serif.**

SBN See **International Standard Book Number.**

sc Proofreader's mark for small caps (small capital letters). These are capital letters approximately the height of lowercase (small letters). See also **x height.**

screen A term used when a continuous tone photograph is converted or broken into dots. Screen number signifies the number of dots per inch. See also **continuous tone; Velox.**

screen tint See **Benday; tint.**

self-cover booklet See **booklet.**

self-mailer Any direct-mail piece without an envelope or special wrapping. See also **package (direct mail)**

There are many varieties: square serif, old-style serif, modern, etc. See also **sans serif.**

set-around   See **run-around.**

set solid   To set type without any leading, or spacing between lines. See also **leading.**

shared mailing   See **cooperative mailing.**

short discount   A discount at a relatively low scale given to booksellers and whole-salers for handling textbooks and those professional books, reference books, and other specialized works that are primarily sold directly to users. See also **trade discount.**

short rate   An advertising rate billed to an advertiser that is higher than a lower rate previously billed because the advertiser has not purchased the amount of space or met the minimum insertion requirement on which the lower rate was based. See also **contract rate; contract year; frequency discount.**

short-title catalog   A list of all of a publisher's titles giving author, title, price, publication date, and order numbers or reference codes. See also **catalog.**

show-through   The degree to which printing on one side of a sheet can be seen from the other side. See also **opacity.**

signature (in advertisement)   Name and address at the end of an advertisement usually accompanied by the publisher's colophon or device. The signature is some-times called a logotype or logo. See also **colophon; logotype.**

small caps   Small capital letters; shaped like capital letters but about the size of the lowercase (small) *x*. Indicated in copy by two lines drawn underneath. See also **sc.**

soft copy   Information displayed visually on a video terminal, from digital storage, or in microform; also unedited manuscript copy. See also **hard copy.**

solo mailing   A mailing in which only one book is offered.

special library   A library or information center maintained by an individual cor-poration, association, government agency, or any group, or a specialized depart-mental collection within a library responsible for the organization and dissemination of information on a specific subject, primarily offering service to a specialized clientele through the use of varied media and methods.

Special to   A heading used on a news release written in a nonexclusive but special way for the publication to which it is being sent. Releases to other publications can be sent simultaneously, if written in a different format. See also **Exclusive to.**

specs   Type specifications.

spinoff   A book excerpted or resulting from a previously published larger or ency-clopedic work; also a periodical article expanded to book length.

spread   An advertisement on two facing pages. See also **center spread.**

standing order   See **continuation order.**

stat   See **photostat.** Term sometimes used as a verb (e.g., stat to 85% of copy size).

stet   Proofreading term for "let it stand as it is."

STM publisher/company   One engaged in the publication of scientific, technical, and/or medical books.

strike-on composition (direct-impression composition)   Copy prepared for plate-making and printing by use of a typewriter or other keyboard device that makes a physical impression on the paper. See also **cold-type composition.**

subhead   A useful device to increase readability when text is lengthy or is in editorial format. A subhead may be used between main headline and the main body of the advertisement. It may also be used as a single-line insert every two or three paragraphs, usually in a different typeface from the text.

subtitle   An additional or secondary title of a book, often used to explain book's content or intent. When omitted from advertising copy, it can often destroy value of the ad.

tabloid A newspaper or business publication about half the size of a standard newspaper and often printed on newsprint. Magazines in tabloid format with reader service cards are said to produce faster responses than magazines in conventional format.

tagline A line added to a mailing piece to help direct it to a specific job title or function (marketing director, publicist, vice-president, etc.).

targeted copy Advertising copy tailored to the specific or specialized interests of the group or audience which the advertising will reach.

tear sheet A page torn from a specific issue of a publication containing an advertisement and sent to an advertiser or agency as proof of insertion. See also **checking copy.**

teaser An advertisement or promotion to generate curiosity for an advertisement or promotion to follow.

teaser copy Copy on an envelope to capture the attention of the recipient and to stimulate interest in the envelope's contents.

telemarketing Use of the telephone as a sales vehicle. Most often associated with the use of toll-free telephone numbers. See also **Inward-WATS, Outward-WATS.**

text A textbook. Also the body matter in an advertisement or promotion piece as differentiated from headlines and other display matter.

text edition That edition of a two-edition book intended for use in a course of study. The other edition would be a trade edition, intended for sale through bookstores and libraries and carrying a larger trade discount.

textbook Also referred to as a text. A book used for a course of study.

third-class bulk rate Special postage rate for mailings of 200 or more identical pieces and/or weighing 50 pounds or more, and meeting other special postal requirements.

third cover Inside back cover.

till-forbid offer See **automatic shipment.**

tint A pattern of dots that reproduces as a tone.

tip-in A page pasted or glued into a bound or stapled book.

tissue overlay A transparent or translucent sheet placed over artwork either as a protective covering or as a means of bearing copy to be surprinted, the laying of a Benday screen, or to indicate color separation.

trade discount A discount given by publishers to booksellers and wholesalers on general trade fiction and nonfiction of the kind ordinarily sold in bookstores. Trade discounts differ according to publisher; they are variously scaled, according to quantity, over a range of about $33\frac{1}{3}$ to 45%, or more. See also **short discount.**

trade title Popular fiction or nonfiction book sold in the average bookstore or carried in a well-stocked public library. Trade titles carry a trade discount. See also **professional trade title.**

treatise An edited volume in which each chapter is identified with its author. See also **monograph.**

trim To reduce overlong copy. Also, abbreviation for "trimmed size" of a printed piece.

trimmed size Page size, or final size of any printed job. See also **type area.**

type area The type page size or other area (within the trimmed size) that the composition and illustrative matter will occupy. See also **trimmed size.**

type page Area of the page that type will normally occupy, margins not included.

type face A style or design of type, sometimes named after its designer.

typescript See copy.

typewriter composition Composition prepared for reproduction with a typewriter or similar strike-on device. See also **camera-ready copy (author-prepared); strike-on composition.**

typo Typographical error.

typography The selection and arrangement of type for use in printed matter. Less frequently, the business of typesetting.

upper case Capital letters.

USPS U.S. Postal Service.

volume A single book, or one of the books in a set. In a very large scientific work, parts of a single volume may be bound separately—the parts comprising a single volume. In periodicals, all of the issues published during a set period, usually one year.

Velox A screened black-and-white photoprint that can be pasted on a mechanical and used as line copy. (Screens usually have less than 100 lines per inch.) See also **Benday; screen.**

weight The basis on which paper is sold; 60-lb. (or 60 substance) means a ream of paper in a certain size (usually 25" × 38") that weighs 60 pounds. See also **basis weight.**

wf Proofreader's mark for wrong font (qv).

wholesaler, wholesale bookseller (jobber) A supplier of the books of many different publishers to libraries and bookstores. Provides the convenience of a single invoice for shipments of different titles from different publishers, and often toll-free ordering service.

Wide Area Telecommunications Service (WATS) A direct-dial service which permits telephone customers to place or receive long-distance calls at established monthly hourly rates. See also **Inward-WATS, Outward WATS.**

widow A nondialog short line of type, usually less than three-fourths of a line, starting a page or column.

word-processed letter A letter prepared through a word-processing machine. Process uses two discs—one containing the addresses to be used for mailing, and the other containing the letter. Letter is produced automatically by combining text with address information. See also **computer-printed letter.**

word-processing machine A machine that prepares text by manipulating it in magnetic storage. See also **word-processed letter.**

wrong font (wf) Letter from one type size or style of type mixed with those of another. See also **font; wf.**

x height May refer to capital or lowercase *x;* the height of a small (or lowercase) letter, typically the letter *x* in a type font; also for the capital X. See also **sc.**

ZIP Code A five-digit numerical code that identifies a specific geographic area. The first ZIP digit divides the country into 10 major areas, of which zero is New England and nine is the West Coast. The first three ZIP digits identify a smaller area within a single state. The last two digits stand for either (1) a postal zone within the limits of a major city or (2) a small city or town in which all addresses have the same ZIP Code.

ZIP + 4 (nine-digit ZIP Code) An expanded ZIP Code program of the U.S. Postal Service which allows automatic sorting of first-class mail directly to a carrier. It consists of the conventional five-digit ZIP Code followed by a hyphen and four new numbers.

Appendix B
Table of Copy Essentials
for Various Book Markets

The table presented on the next four pages provides a quick source of information on the types of material the copywriter should include when writing copy for a variety of markets.

Copy element	Engineers	Scholars	Doctors	College faculty	Book Vocational/technical	Public libraries
Book title	•	•	•	•	•	•
Author or editor	•	•	•	•	•	•
Author affiliation/ credentials	•	•	•	•	•	•
ISBN number						•
Library of Congress catalog number						•
Publication date/year	•	•	•	•	•	•
Price or tentative price	•	•	•	•	•	•
Type of binding available*				•	•	•
Discount classification						
Edition	•	•	•	•	•	•
Sent for free examination	•	•	•	•	•	
Complimentary copy available				•	•	
Reading level					•	
Mathematical prerequisite	•			•	•	
Education/audience level				•	•	
Instructor's manual available†				•		
Pages/approximate pages	•	•	•	•	•	•
Shipping weight						
Series title and volume number in series	•	•	•			
Updating service available						

markets

College libraries	Special libraries	School libraries	Book sellers	Catalog accounts	College stores	Business profes- sionals	Computer scientists
•	•	•	•	•	•	•	•
•	•	•	•	•	•	•	•
•	•	•	•	•	•	•	•
•	•	•	•		•		
•	•	•					
•	•	•	•	•	•	•	•
•	•	•	•	•	•	•	•
•		•	•	•	•	•	•
			•	•	•		
•	•	•	•	•	•		
						•	•
			•	•			•
		•					•
		•	•	•			•
					•	•	
•	•	•	•	•	•	•	•
				•			
•	•	•	•	•	•		
						•	

| | | | | | Book | |
Copy element	Engi-neers	Scholars	Doctors	College faculty	Voca-tional/tech-nical	Public libraries
SI version available	•					
No. of illustrations, tables	•		•			
No. of literature references	•	•				
Slide presentation supplements				•		
Association/society sponsorship	•	•				
Student workbook available				•	•	

* *Paper* or *paperbound* to a librarian means perfect binding. If your paperbound book or manual has a spiral or non-standard binding, be sure you specify this in your copy; it can save return shipments.
† Including solutions manuals, test banks, study guides.

markets

College libraries	Special libraries	School libraries	Book sellers	Catalog accounts	College stores	Business profes- sionals	Computer scientists
					•		
	•	•		•	•	•	
	•				•	•	
•		•					
						•	

Index

Note: References are to numbered entries within chapters. Each entry number consists of a chapter number followed by the number of the entry within the chapter. Entries followed by the word *glossary* are defined in the Glossary on pages 230–245.